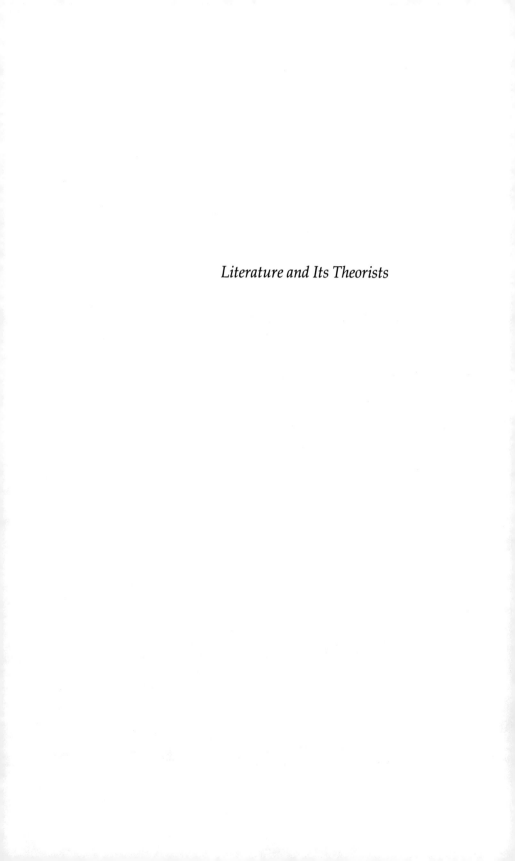

Literature and Its Theorists

Also by Tzvetan Todorov and available in English

The Fantastic: A Structural Approach to a Literary Genre
The Poetics of Prose
Encyclopedic Dictionary of the Sciences of Language
  (with Oswald Ducrot)
Theories of the Symbol
Symbolism and Interpretation
Introduction to Poetics
Mikhail Bakhtin, The Dialogical Principle
The Conquest of America

TZVETAN TODOROV

Literature and Its Theorists

A PERSONAL VIEW OF

TWENTIETH-CENTURY CRITICISM

TRANSLATED BY

CATHERINE PORTER

Cornell University Press

ITHACA, NEW YORK

Originally published in French under the title
Critique de la critique, © 1984 Editions du Seuil.

Translation copyright © 1987 by Cornell University

First published 1987 by Cornell University Press.

Library of Congress Cataloging-in-Publication Data

Todorov, Tzvetan, 1939–
   Literature and its theorists.

   Translation of: Critique de la critique.
   Bibliography: p.
   Includes index.
   1. Criticism—History—20th century. 2. Literature—History and criticism—Theory, etc. I. Title.
PN94.T613   1987   801'.95   87-47605
ISBN 0-8014-1816-X (alk. paper)

Printed in the United States of America

*The paper in this book is acid-free and meets the guidelines for permanence
and durability of the Committee on Production Guidelines for
Book Longevity of the Council on Library Resources.*

CONTENTS

TRANSLATOR'S NOTE

In the interest of keeping footnotes to a minimum, titles and page numbers of works from which Tzvetan Todorov quotes appear in the text. Complete bibliographical information will be found in the Works Cited section at the end of the volume.

For quotations from works written in Russian, German, or French, I have used a published English translation whenever one was available. These books and articles are referred to in the text by their English titles, and the page numbers given are those of the translations; the Works Cited lists these translations and, following them, the original titles, publishers, and dates. For writings never translated into English, I have worked from the quotations in French that appeared in *Critique de la critique*, occasionally consulting the original language text; the titles appear in the original language, with an English translation following in parentheses where appropriate.

C.P.

Literature and Its Theorists

1

Prefatory Explanations

Our fellow citizens do not read, we are told. And the devastating statistics that demonstrate how little in fact they do read lump all kinds of literature together: highbrow and mass-market texts, tourist guides and cookbooks. Books about books—works of literary criticism, that is—attract only a small minority of an already tiny group of readers: a few students, a handful of dedicated admirers. But criticism of criticism is an extreme case, no doubt a sign of the futility of the times: who could possibly take the slightest interest in it?

I could defend the subject of my book by arguing that criticism is not a superfluous appendage to literature, but its necessary double (a text can never *state* its whole truth), or that interpretive behavior is infinitely more common than criticism, and that it is therefore in our best interest that criticism professionalizes interpretation, so to speak, bringing out into the open what is simply unconscious practice elsewhere. But these arguments, however valid in themselves, are irrelevant here: my intention is neither to defend criticism nor to shore up its foundations. Instead, I shall focus on two interlocking subjects, pursuing a dual objective, moreover, in each case.

First, I want to examine how people have thought about literature and criticism in the twentieth century, and, *at the same time*, try to determine what shape a reasonable conception of literature and criticism might take.

Next, I want to analyze the major ideological trends of the same period as they have been manifested through reflections on literature; and, *at the same time*, try to determine which ideological position is most defensible. Within the perspective of this second subject, my choice of reflections on criticism is contingent. As it happens, I am familiar with this tradition; otherwise the history of sociology or the history of political ideas, for example, might have served equally well to provide access to more general questions. The search for an ideological position of my own comes last on the list, but that search underlies and perhaps even motivates all the rest of the inquiry.

To put it rather too succinctly, this book will deal both with the meaning of some twentieth-century critical works and with the possibility of opposing nihilism without ceasing to be an atheist.

Let me try to explain why I have felt it necessary to deal simultaneously with two subjects, each of which moreover has a dual aspect. To rule out generalizations and value judgments would have seemed naive or dishonest, would have meant breaking off the investigation midway. To rule out a detailed investigation of the subject matter in its specificity would have put me on the side of those writers who possess "the truth," and whose only problem is to figure out how to present it so they can put it across most convincingly. For my part, I am satisfied with searching for it (the undertaking seems sufficiently ambitious in itself), and I have become convinced that the most appropriate form for such a search may be a hybrid genre: a narrative, but an exemplary one—in the present case, the story of an adventure of the mind, the story of twentieth-century thinking about literature, a history that at the same time illustrates a search for truth. I am proposing—rather than imposing—this exemplary narrative in order to invite my reader to reflect on it: in other words, my aim is to launch a discussion.

My choice of authors was dictated by a number of objective and subjective criteria. The period of history in which I am interested is the mid-twentieth century, 1920–1980, roughly speaking; with one exception (Döblin), all the authors considered were born between 1890 and 1920, and thus they belong to my parents' generation.

2

Next, I have considered only texts written in French, English, German, and Russian, leaving all others aside. I have also sought variety: I have analyzed representatives of various critical currents and even of different casts of mind, looking at historians along with systematic and scientific authors, religious thinkers and political militants, essayists and creative writers.

Still, such considerations obviously do not suffice to explain why I have settled on some ten names among the hundreds of possibilities. I have of course taken reputation into account, but this factor is not sufficient, either, to explain my selection. The real explanation, finally, is this: I chose the authors who had, I felt, affected me most. I shall not be dealing with Freud, or Lukács, or Heidegger: I have perhaps made a mistake in leaving them out, but I have done so because their thinking, while noteworthy in itself, does not inspire reactions in me that I myself consider interesting. And since I am not aiming at exhaustivity but only at a certain representativeness, the criterion of private correspondence, of possible dialogue, does seem legitimate. I am closer at present to some of the authors I shall discuss than to others; there is no doubt about that. I have been stimulated by all of them, however, at one time or another, and I continue to admire them all.

Finally, I should add a more personal note. This book represents the last phase of a project begun several years ago with *Theories of the Symbol* and *Symbolism and Interpretation*: its initial design is contemporary with those texts. In the intervening years, a different theme, that of alterity, has become the focal point of my work. Not only has this delayed the completion of the earlier project, but it has also led to internal modifications. Nevertheless, the framework proposed in the first two books remains present here in the background; for that reason I should like to recall a few essential elements of those texts.

II

The fact that the writers one chooses to study are twentieth-century writers is not enough to guarantee the modernity of their thought. At every point in time, moments of the more or less distant past coexist with present and future moments. If I wish to examine the critical thought that is representative of this century, chronological objectivity is not enough; I must also make sure that the authors I choose have not been content to repeat received ideas and to corroborate tradition, but rather have expressed what is specific to their era. In order to make such a distinction, I will have to outline, at least in a general and cursory way, the heritage of the past that these critics have confronted.

Our ideas about literature and commentary do not go back to the dawn of time. The constitution of the notion of "literature" itself and all that the term currently entails is a recent phenomenon, dating from the end of the eighteenth century. Before that, people could of course identify the major genres (poetry, epic, drama) as well as the minor ones, but the whole in which they were included was something much broader than what we call literature. "Literature" was born of an opposition to utilitarian language, which finds its justification outside itself; in contrast, literature is a discourse that is sufficient unto itself. It leads on the one hand to a devaluing of the relations between works and what they designate, or express, or teach—that is, between the works themselves and everything else; on the other hand, it promotes close attention to the structure of the work itself, to the internal interweaving of its episodes, themes, images. From the Romantics to the surrealists and the *nouveau roman,* the various literary schools all lay claim to these basic principles, even though they may differ over details or terminology. When the poet Archibald MacLeish writes, in his famous programmatic poem:

> A poem should not mean
> But be,

he is only carrying this penchant for immanence to an extreme: meaning itself is perceived as excessively external.

In *On Christian Doctrine,* Saint Augustine, an author who is representative of the "classical" manner of thinking, formulated a fundamental opposition between use and enjoyment: "To enjoy something is to cling to it with love for its own sake. To use something, however, is to employ it in obtaining that which you love, provided that it is worthy of love" (I, iv, 4). This distinction has a theoretical corollary: in the final analysis, nothing but God deserves to

4

be enjoyed, to be cherished for itself. Augustine develops this idea in speaking of man's love for man:

> It is to be asked whether man is to be loved by man for his own sake or for the sake of something else. If for his own sake, we enjoy him; if for the sake of something else, we use him. But I think that man is to be loved for the sake of something else. In that which is to be loved for its own sake the blessed life resides; and if we do not have it for the present, the hope for it now consoles us. But "cursed be the man that trusteth in man." But no one ought to enjoy himself either, if you observe the matter closely, because he should not love himself on account of himself but on account of Him who is to be enjoyed. [I, xxii, 20–21]

In the case of Karl Philipp Moritz, one of the first spokesmen of the "Romantic" revolution at the end of the eighteenth century, we find that hierarchy is replaced by democracy, submission by equality; all creation can and must become the object of enjoyment. To the same question— can man become the object of enjoyment?— Moritz replies by praising man: "Man must learn to realize anew that he is there for himself—he must feel that, in every thinking being, the whole is there for each individual, just as each individual is there for the whole. Individual man must never be considered as a purely *useful* being, but also as a *noble* being, who has his own value in himself. Man's spirit is a whole, complete in itself" (*Schriften*, pp. 15–16). Thus the new society of enjoyment is launched. A few years later, Friedrich Schlegel demonstrates the continuity of aesthetics not, now, with theology but with politics: "Poetry is a republican discourse, a discourse that is its own law, an end in itself, and all its components are free citizens with the right to speak up in order to reach agreement" ("Fragments," from *Lyceum*, 65).

This *immanent* concept of literature is in harmony with the dominant ideology of the modern period (I use the term "ideology" in the sense of a system of ideas, beliefs, and values common to the members of a society, without opposing it to consciousness, or science, or truth, or anything whatsoever). Is Novalis still speaking of aesthetics when he declares: "We no longer live in the time when universally recognized forms dominated"? The replacement of the search for transcendence by the affirmation of each individual's right to be judged on his own terms has to do with ethics and politics as well as with aesthetics: the ascendancy of individualism and relativism is the hallmark of modern times. To declare that a literary work is governed solely by its own internal coherence with no reference to exterior absolutes, to assert that its meanings are infinite and not hierarchized, is also to participate in this modern ideology.

Our idea of commentary has undergone a parallel evolution. Nothing marks the break with earlier views better than Spinoza's demand, formulated in the *Tractatus theologico-politicus*, that the search for the truth of texts be abandoned in favor of concern for their meaning alone. More specifically, Spinoza, having just separated faith from reason and thus truth (even religious truth) from meaning (of the holy Scripture, in this instance), begins by denouncing the division between means and ends in the earlier Patristic strategy:

> Most interpreters posit as a basic principle (in order to understand it clearly and decipher its true meaning) that Scripture is entirely true and divine, whereas that ought to be the conclusion of a thorough examination, one which leaves no obscurity unexplained; what the study of Scripture would demonstrate much better, without the aid of any human fiction, is what they posit at the very outset as a rule for interpretation. ["Preface," p. 24]

Spinoza's critique has to do with structure, not content: he is concerned not with replacing one truth by another, but with changing the place of truth in the task of interpretation. Far from serving as the guiding principle of the interpreter's work, the new meaning will be the result of that work: one cannot look for something with the help of the thing itself. The search for a text's meaning must be carried out without reference to its truth. Nineteenth-century philology espoused Spinoza's postulate, and although the struggle had lost currency in Böckh's day, he found it necessary to include the following statements in his *Encyclopädie und Methodologie der philologischen Wissenschaften* (1886):

> It is entirely ahistorical to prescribe, in the interpretation of Holy Scripture, that everything must be explained according to the *analogia fidei et doctrinae*; here the measure that has to guide interpretation is not itself firmly established, for religious doctrine, born of the expla-

nation of Scripture, has taken on very different forms. Historical interpretation has to establish solely what works of language mean, without regard to whether this is true or false. [Pp. 120–121]

Here we can see how a barely perceptible shift has taken place.
Whereas initially we are told that prior knowledge about the truth
of a text cannot be used as a means for interpreting it, at the end
we find a declaration that any question having to do with the truth
of the text is irrelevant. By "truth," here, we are expected to understand not factual adequacy, which would be in any event impossible to establish in the case of the Bible, but general human truth,
justice, and wisdom. After Spinoza, commentators no longer need
to ask: "Does this text speak rightly?" but only "What exactly is it
saying?" Commentary, too, has become immanent: in the absence
of any common transcendence, each text becomes its own frame of
reference, and the critic's task is completed in clarification of the
text's meaning, in the description of its forms and textual func-
tioning, far removed from any value judgment. By this token, a
qualitative break is achieved between the text studied and the text
of the study. If the commentary were concerned with truth, it
would be situated at the same level as the work being commented
upon and the two would bear upon the same object. But the difference between the two is a radical one, and the text studied becomes an object (an object-language), while the commentary ac-
cedes to the category of metalanguage.

Here again, terminological diversity, like differing emphasis on
one part of the undertaking or another, helps conceal the unity of
a tradition that has dominated commentary in Europe for several
centuries. What comes to mind as a central embodiment of this
project today is structural criticism, whether it takes themes (explorations of the imaginary, conscious or unconscious obsessions) as
its object or the expressive system itself (narrative devices, figures
of speech, style). But historical and philological criticism, as it has
been practiced since the nineteenth century, is equally faithful
to the immanentist project, since the meaning of each text can be
established only with reference to its particular context, and since
the philologist's task is to make this meaning explicit without passing any judgment on it. Closer to home, criticism that is nihilist in
inspiration (and no longer positivist, like philology), criticism that
demonstrates that everything is interpretation and that the writer

is busy subverting his own ideology, still remains within the same undertaking, while making any hope of ever attaining truth more chimerical than ever.

What is at stake in this debate is perhaps clearer now. Reflection on literature and criticism is a feature of the ideological movements that have dominated intellectual life (and not only intellectual life) in Europe during what is conventionally called the modern era. Earlier, people believed in the existence of an absolute and common truth, in a universal standard (for several centuries, absolute truth happened to coincide with Christian doctrine). The breakdown of this belief, the recognition of human diversity and equality led to relativism and individualism, and finally to nihilism.

I am at last in a position to spell out the nature of the ideas I am looking for in contemporary reflections on literature. My principal interest will be directed toward whatever allows us to move beyond the dichotomy sketched out above. More specifically still, among the authors I have chosen, I shall seek doctrinal elements that question the "Romantic" aesthetic and ideology but that do so without constituting a return to the "classical" dogmas.

This use of words in quotation marks, and in particular of the term "Romantic," which I shall employ frequently, requires some explanation. In fact, there are several obvious differences between the sense in which that term is used here and the meaning it takes on when it designates the artistic movement of the nineteenth century. On the one hand, under this label I include certain phenomena and ideas that were not associated with the Romantic group, such as historicism and realism. On the other hand, I exclude certain connotations that are frequently attached to the meaning of the term, most notably a valorization of the irrational.

The discrepancy between the usual meaning of the word "Romanticism" and the meaning adopted here has a simple explanation: I am speaking of what I believe to be the ideal type of the movement rather than the historical phenomenon in itself. On the ideological level, historical Romanticism and, even more obviously, the nineteenth century as a whole are heterogeneous complexes in which disparate, even contradictory, elements coexist while forming various hierarchies. Nevertheless, I hold strongly to the term, for it was in fact in a Romantic group—the very first, the one in Jena, which brought together the Schlegel brothers, Novalis, Schelling, and a few others—that the main ideas of the modern aesthetic were formulated, with forcefulness and originality.

Each of the chapters that follows is constructed, therefore, along similar lines. First I seek to identify what the author in question owes to the Romantic ideology; next I focus on those elements of his thought that, intentionally or not, challenge the Romantic framework and go beyond it. The final chapter looks dissimilar at first glance, since I take myself as its object while attempting to pull together the findings reached in the earlier chapters. But the difference is only superficial. From a certain standpoint, those other chapters, too, relate my own personal history: I have been, I am, that "Romantic" who tries to think beyond Romanticism through the analysis of authors with whom I have identified in turn. The movement repeated in each chapter is thus combined with another, a movement of accumulation that reaches its culmination at the end—and yet this culmination is not, after all, a synthesis. To put it another way, what follows is nothing but a *Bildungsroman*, a novel of apprenticeship—and moreover one that remains unfinished.

2

Poetic Language:
The Russian Formalists

My attitude toward the Russian Formalists (I shall capitalize the word Formalist in referring to this particular group) has changed several times. This is not especially surprising, since I first became acquainted with their work over twenty years ago. My first impression was one of discovery: the Formalists showed that it was possible to speak of literature in a cheerful, irreverent, inventive manner. At the same time, their texts dealt with a topic that did not seem to interest anyone else but that had always appeared crucial to me, namely, what was rather condescendingly called "literary craft." My astonishment at these discoveries led me to seek out one text after another (not always a simple matter) and then to translate them into French. In a second phase, I thought I detected the presence of a "theoretical" project, the constitution of a poetics, in the Formalist writings. The project was not, however, consistent from one text to another (with good reason: I was reading several different authors whose writings spanned fifteen years), nor was it carried to completion: thus the task of systematizing and radicalizing the work was a necessary one. Finally, in a third phase, I began to perceive the Formalists as a historical phenomenon. The content of their ideas came to interest me less than the internal logic of these ideas and their place in the history of ideologies. This latter perspective is the one I have adopted in the current discussion. I have limited my inquiry to a small part of the Formalists' activity, namely, the definition of literature or, to use their own terms, of "poetic language." It is a small part but a complex one, for, as we shall see, the Formalists were working with more than one definition of the poetic.

I

What might be called the "standard theory" of poetic language among the Russian Formalists was stated explicitly in the movement's first collective publication, the first of the *Sborniki po teorii poèticheskogo jazyka* (Collections on the theory of poetic language, 1916) by Lev Jakubinskij. Jakubinskij was never more than a marginal participant in the Formalist group, but in 1916 he lent his authority as a linguist to the theses his friends were promoting, and his contribution was thus a major one. Within the context of a global description of the various uses of language, Jakubinskij laid the groundwork for his definition of poetic language in terms drawn by and large from linguistics:

> Linguistic phenomena should be classified from the point of view of the goal with which the speaker uses his linguistic representations in each given case. If the speaker uses them with the purely practical goal of communication, we are dealing with the system of practical language (of verbal thought), in which linguistic representations (sounds, morphological elements, etc.) do not have any independent value, but are simply a means of communication. Yet other linguistic systems are conceivable, and they exist—systems where the practical goal becomes secondary (though it may not disappear completely), and linguistic representations acquire an autonomous value. ["O zvukakh stikhotvornogo jazyka," p. 16]

Poetry is one example of these "other linguistic systems." It is indeed the prime example: an equivalence may be established between "poetic" and "having an autonomous value," as Jakubinskij showed in another text published in *Poètika* (Poetics, 1919), the third Formalist collection:

> It is necessary to distinguish human activities that have value in and of themselves from those that pursue external goals and have value as

the means for the attainment of goals. If we call activities of the first sort *poetic*. . . . ["O poèticheskom glossemosochetanii," p. 12]

So far, this is simple and straightforward enough: practical language finds its justification outside itself, in the transmission of thought or in interpersonal communication; it is a means and not an end. In scholarly terms, practical language is *heterotelic*. Poetic language, on the other hand, finds its justification (and thus its entire value) in itself; it is its own end, and no longer a means. Thus poetic language is autonomous, or *autotelic*. This formulation seems to have won over the other members of the group, since quite similar statements appeared in various texts written around the same time. For example, in an article on Potebnja (1919), Viktor Shklovskij went even further by translating poetic autotelism in terms of perception (we shall see, however, that this subtle distinction is by no means accidental):

> Poetic language differs from prose language in the palpability of its construction. We can feel the acoustic, or articulatory, or semantic aspect of the word. Sometimes it is not the structure of words that is palpable, but rather their construction, their arrangement. ["Potebnja," in *Poètika*, p. 4]

The same year, in a book on Khlebnikov (the title means "The Newest Russian Poetry"), Roman Jakobson proposed formulas that have become famous; his definitions remain entirely consonant with Jakubinskij's:

> Poetry is *an utterance with a set toward expression [vyskazyvanie s ustanovkoj na vyrazhenie].* . . . If the plastic arts involve the shaping of the autonomous material of visual representations, music the shaping of autonomous sound material, choreography of the material of autonomous gesture, then poetry is the shaping of the autonomous word, of what Khlebnikov calls the "selfsome word" [*samovitoe slovo*]. . . . This set toward expression, toward the verbal mass, which I qualify as the sole essential feature of poetry. . . . [*Novejshaja russkaja poèzija*, pp. 10–11, 41]

To say that poetry is autonomous or autotelic language is to define it by its function, by what it does rather than what it is. What linguistic forms allow this function to be fulfilled? How does one

12

recognize language that finds its end (and its value) in itself? The Formalist texts offer two answers to these questions. The first answer, a response at the level of "substance," in a sense, takes the statement literally. What is language that refers to nothing outside itself? It is language reduced to its material nature alone, sounds or letters; it is language that refuses meaning. This response does not originate in pure logical deduction. On the contrary, the fact that this response was already present within the ideological arena of the day is very probably what led the Formalists to try to find a broader justification for it and to construct a theory of poetry as autotelic language. For their theoretical speculations were closely tied to the practices of their contemporaries, the Futurists; the Formalist theories at once grew out of and laid the groundwork for Futurist practices. The most extreme aspect of these practices is known as *zaum'*, "trans-sense" or "supraconscious language," pure signifiers, a wordless poetry of sounds and letters. As we saw with Jakobson, there is no great distance between Khlebnikov's *samovitoe slovo*, "self-moving" or "selfsome word" (Khlebnikov himself rarely practiced *zaum'*) and the Formalists' *samotsennoe slovo*, the "self-valuable word" or discourse with autonomous value. In a retrospective commentary on this period, Boris Ejxenbaum thus rightly identified "trans-sense language" as the most extreme expression of the autotelic doctrine: "The Futurists' trend toward a 'transrational language' (*zaumnyj jazyk*) [is] the utmost baring of autonomous value" ("Theory of the Formal Method," p. 9).

Some ten years earlier, Shklovskij had wondered whether all poetry was not in reality trans-sense poetry, and whether poets do not resort to meaning most often only in order to find a "motivation," a camouflage or excuse:

> The poet does not decide to utter a "trans-sense word": usually the trans-sense elements are hidden behind the mask of some content, often a deceptive or illusory one that forces the poets themselves to recognize that they do not grasp the content of their own verses. . . . The facts we have adduced make us wonder whether words always have meaning in speech, not just in patently trans-sense speech but simply in poetic speech — or is this opinion just a fiction and the result of our inattentiveness? ["O poèzii i zaumnom jazyke," in *Sborniki po teorii poèticheskogo jazyka* 1, pp. 10, 13]

Jakobson takes the same point of view: "Poetic language strives, as to its limit, toward the phonetic word, or more exactly, inasmuch as the corresponding set is present, toward the euphonic word, toward trans-sense speech" (*Novejshaja*, p. 68).

Other representations of the group do not go quite that far, but they all agree on the essential value—and above all the autonomous value—of sounds in poetry. Thus Jakubinskij writes: "In *versified linguistic thought* sounds become the object of our attention, they reveal their autonomous value, they emerge in the clear field of consciousness" ("O zvukakh," pp. 18–19). And Osip Brik: "However you regard the interrelation between image and sound, one thing is undeniable: sounds and consonances are not just a euphonic adjunct, but the result of an independent poetic drive" ("Zvukovye povtory," in *Poètika*, p. 60).

But is language that denies meaning still language? Have we not obliterated the essential character of language, sound *and* meaning, simultaneous presence and absence, if we reduce it to the status of a pure physical object? And why pay such intransitive attention to mere noise? Taken to the extreme, this answer (to the question about the forms of poetic language) reveals its own absurdity. That is doubtless why the Formalists, without addressing the issue explicitly, went on to offer a second answer, one that is more abstract and less literal, more structural and less substantial. It consists in saying that poetic language fulfills its autotelic function (that is, the absence of any external function) by being more systematic than practical, everyday language. A poetic work is overstructured discourse in which everything is interdependent: that is why we perceive it in itself, rather than for the sake of something else. Thus in his famous analysis of Gogol's "Overcoat" (1918), Èjxenbaum goes out of his way to avoid any reference to external considerations, resorting instead to metaphors of construction and play, objects or activities that are characterized by their internal coherence and by their lack of external goals. "In a work of art not a single sentence can be in itself a simple 'reflection' of the author's personal feelings. It is always construction and play" ("How Gogol's 'Overcoat' Is Made," p. 131).

In a study published around the same time, on the relation between the devices used in plot construction and other stylistic devices, Shklovskij also lays claim to this structural version of autotelism. Not everything is necessarily trans-sense language in

14

poetry or (especially) in prose; but narrative prose itself obeys the laws of sound combination, the rules of construction that produce phonic "instrumentation." "The methods and devices of *syuzhet* structure [*sjuzhetoslozhenie*] are similar to, and in principle are identical with, the devices, even with acoustic instrumentation. Works of literature represent a warp [*pletenie*] of sounds, of articulatory movements and thoughts" ("The Connection between Devices of *Syuzhet* Construction and General Stylistic Devices," p. 70).

The affirmation of the systematic character of literary works thus made its entrance into the Formalist Vulgate, in widely varying formulations, from Shklovskij's—"a work of literature is a unified edifice. Everything in it is subject to the organization of the material" (*Third Factory*, p. 55)—to Juri Tynjanov's—"before this basic problem [of literary evolution] can be analyzed, it must be agreed that a literary work is a system, as is literature itself. Only after this basic agreement has been established is it possible to create a literary science" ("On Literary Evolution," p. 67).

Jakobson also fluctuated between the two answers. We have already seen the role he ascribed to trans-sense poetry. But at the time of his book on Khlebnikov, he drew upon other explanations as well. One of them, in effect an intermediate position, is formulated in the context of a discussion of Kruszewski's teaching. Kruszewski, the nineteenth-century Polish-Russian linguist, systematically described linguistic relationships in terms of the opposition between resemblance and contiguity, an opposition frequently encountered in works on general psychology at the time. Jakobson added the first inkling of a value judgment by using the terms "conservative" and "progressive," terms highly charged with political meaning in postrevolutionary Russia: "From a certain point of view, the process of language evolution appears as the eternal antagonism between progressive forces, determined by relations of similarity, and conservative forces, determined by associations of contiguity" (*Novejshaja*, p. 10). From there, Jakobson reasons as follows: the heterotelism of everyday language is well suited to relations of contiguity (arbitrary ones) between signifier and signified; the autotelism of poetic language will be favored by relations of similarity (motivation of the sign); furthermore, we have moved from "progressive" to "revolutionary," which, in the context of the times, allows each of these terms, "poetry" and "revolutionary," to cast the other in a positive light:

15

In emotive language and poetic language, verbal representations, be they phonetic or semantic, concentrate greater attention upon themselves. The connection between the sound aspect and meaning is tighter, more intimate, and consequently, language becomes more revolutionary, inasmuch as habitual associations by contiguity recede into the background. . . . The mechanical association between sound and meaning by contiguity is realized all the more rapidly as it is made from habit. Hence the conservatism of practical speech. The form of the word quickly dies out. In poetry, the role of mechanical association is reduced to a minimum. [*Novejshaja*, pp. 10, 41]

Replacing associations of contiguity with associations of similarity (a replacement that seems to coincide with the "tighter, more intimate" relation between sound and meaning) in fact reinforces the systematic character of discourse, for contiguity is simply another name for what is arbitrary, for unmotivated convention. But elsewhere in the same text, Jakobson envisaged another form of motivation, not between signifier and signified ("vertical" motivation, as it were), but between one word and another in the discursive chain ("horizontal" motivation). The latter once again points toward the autotelism that defines a poetic utterance. "We do not perceive the form of a word unless it is repeated in the given linguistic system" (ibid., p. 48). This view became Jakobson's credo forty years later, and the differences between his 1919 statement and the better-known statements of the nineteen-sixties are merely terminological. On the one hand, poetic language is defined by its autotelism: "The set (*Einstellung*) toward the *message* as such, focus on the message for its own sake, is the *poetic* function of language" ("Linguistics and Poetics" [1960], p. 25). On the other hand, this autotelism manifests itself in the particular form of overstructuring known as repetition: "The poetic function projects the principle of equivalence from the axis of selection onto the axis of combination" (ibid., p. 27). "On every level of language the essence of poetic artifice consists in recurrent returns" ("Grammatical Parallelism and Its Russian Facet" [1966], p. 98).

Such is the first Formalist conception of poetic language—not chronologically first, but first in importance. Is it really an original conception? The line of descent from the Russian Futurists has always been obvious. But that line is an immediate relationship which does more to mask than to reveal the true ideological origins of Formalist theory. At the very beginning of the nineteen-twenties, however, Zhirmunskij had pointed out, in "Zadachi poètiki" (Tasks of poetics), that the Kantian aesthetic (and also, one might add, its later elaboration during the period of German Romanticism) provided the framework for the Formalist doctrine of poetic language. The idea of autotelism as a definition of beauty and art comes straight from the aesthetic writings of Karl Philipp Moritz and Kant; even the close connection between autotelism and increased systematicity is explicitly articulated in these texts, as well as the connection between autotelism and the value of sound. In his very first text on aesthetics (in 1785), Moritz declared that, in art, an intensification of internal purpose has to compensate for the absence of external purpose:

> When an object lacks external utility or purpose, these must be sought in the object itself, if this object is to arouse pleasure in me; or else I must *find so much purpose in the separate parts of this object that I forget to ask: but what good is the whole?* To put it in different terms: seeing a beautiful object, I must feel pleasure uniquely for its own sake; to this end the absence of external purpose has to be compensated for by an internal purpose; the object must be something fully realized in itself. [*Schriften*, p. 6]

For Schelling, similarly, the loss of external function is offset by an increase in internal regularity:

> The poetic work . . . is possible only through a separation from the totality of language of the discourse by means of which the work of art expresses itself. But this separation on the one hand and this absolute character on the other are not possible if the discourse does not have in itself its own independent movement and thus its time, like the bodies of the world; thus it separates itself from all the rest, obeying an internal regularity. From an external point of view, the discourse moves freely and autonomously; it is only in itself that it is ordered and subject to regularity. [*Philosophie der Kunst* (1803), pp. 635–636]

August Wilhelm Schlegel also specifically justifies phonic repetitions (the metric constraints of verse) by the need to assert the autonomous character of poetic discourse:

> The more prosaic a discourse, the more it loses its singing stress pattern, and is simply articulated drily. Poetry has the opposite tendency. Thus, it must create its own time sequence to make clear that it

is a discourse with its own end, that it does not serve an external agency and will emerge within a time sequence established elsewhere. In this way the listener will be drawn out of reality and put into an imaginary time sequence; he will perceive a regular subdivision of sequences, a measure inherent in the discourse itself. Hence this marvelous phenomenon, the fact that in its deepest expression, when it is used as a game, language spontaneously loses its arbitrary character, which otherwise rules it firmly, and it now follows a law apparently alien to its contents. This law is measure, cadence, rhythm. [*Vorlesungen*, (1801), pp. 103–104]

One may well wonder whether the Formalists were conscious of this heritage. Yet even if they were not, it would not matter much, since they could have been steeped in Romantic ideas without having gone directly to the source; they could have received them by way of the French or Russian Symbolists. Thus we may remain skeptical of Jakobson's statements when, in 1933, he rejects comparisons that he finds excessive: "This school [Formalism], say its detractors . . . calls for an art for art's sake approach and follows in the footsteps of Kantian aesthetics. . . . Neither Tynyanov nor Mukařovský, nor Shklovsky nor I—none of us ever proclaimed the self-sufficiency of art!" ("What Is Poetry?", p. 749). But in fact Jakobson's earliest writings contain two key references, to Mallarmé and Novalis. Now Mallarmé's aesthetic is nothing but a radical version of the Romantic doctrine; as for Novalis, he is one of the principal authors of that doctrine! In a later text, Jakobson recalls the influence Novalis once had on him:

But much earlier [than 1915, the year he read Husserl], around 1912 [that is, at age sixteen], as a high school student who had resolutely chosen language and poetry as the object of my future research, I came upon the writings of Novalis, and was forever enchanted to find in him, as in Mallarmé, the indissoluble combination of a great poet and a profound theoretician of language. . . . The so-called Formalist school was still in its period of germination before World War I. The controversial notion of *self-regulation (Selbstgesetzmäßigkeit) of form*, to borrow the poet's terms, underwent its evolution in this movement, from the first mechanistic positions to a truly dialectic conception. This conception had found in Novalis's famous "Monologue" a fully synthetic starting point, one which from the very beginning had astounded and bewitched me. ["Nachwort," in *Form und Sinn* (1974), p. 77]

Inheritance is not identity, and it is certain that neither A. W. Schlegel nor Novalis—nor Baudelaire, whom Jakobson frequently invoked in his later writings—could have written the grammatical analyses that Jakobson devoted to poetry. For the ideological choice that the Formalists shared with the Romantics (the definition of poetic language) is not enough to characterize Formalist work in full; it does matter that Novalis wrote poetic fragments while Jakobson wrote articles in scholarly journals. The fact remains, nevertheless, that this conception of poetic language, particularly popular with the Formalists, is by no means theirs alone, and that in terms of this conception they remain entirely dependent upon Romantic ideology.

II

But this conception of poetic language is not the only one, nor is it even altogether the earliest, in the history of Russian Formalism. If we look at Shklovskij's first theoretical article, "The Resurrection of the Word," which appeared in 1914 and thus predates the group's formation, we discover that the doctrine presented above is blended curiously with another. Shklovskij does not appear to differentiate between them; yet in reality the second doctrine is very hard to reconcile with the first.

On the one hand, Shklovskij writes: "If we should wish to make a definition of poetic perception and 'artistic' perception in general, then doubtless we would hit upon the definition: 'artistic' perception is perception in which form is sensed (perhaps not only form, but form as an essential part)" ("The Resurrection of the Word," p. 42).

The general tone of this is quite familiar, and yet we also note a nuance that was present as well in the texts quoted earlier, one that seems indeed to be Shklovskij's personal contribution to the collective doctrine: instead of describing the work of art itself, or poetic language, Shklovskij focuses consistently on the process by which the work is perceived. What is autotelic is not language but rather its reception by reader or hearer.

On the other hand, Shklovskij proposes in passing yet another definition of art. This definition, as we shall see, is also closely linked to perception, but it rejects the notion of autotelism: "The thirst for the concrete, which constitutes the soul of art (Carlyle) requires renewal" (ibid., p. 4). Carlyle, as we know, is just another popularizer of Romantic ideas, and his conception of art is derived from Schelling's: the synthesis of the infinite and the finite, the incarnation of abstraction in concrete forms. Thus we have not departed from the Romantic tradition. But perhaps Shklovskij is referring implicitly to another *topos* of the period (especially if we bear in mind his stress on perception), namely the *topos* popularized by Impressionist aesthetics. Art rejects the representation of essences and turns toward the representation of impressions and perceptions; only individual visions of an object exist, not the object in itself. Vision constitutes the object, by renewing it. Here we come closer still to the relativist and individualist principles of that ideology.

However this may be, Shklovskij does not seem at all aware that this particular function of art (the renewal of our perception of the world) is irreconcilable with autotelism, or the absence of any external function, which is equally characteristic of art; in his later writings he continues to support both views. The lack of articulation is particularly striking in "Art as Technique" ("Iskusstvo kak priëm"), where he introduces the celebrated concept of *ostranenie*, "estrangement." For here again we find the examples of a "distant" or "strange" poetic language cited earlier in "The Resurrection of the Word" (Old Church Slavonic, Arnaut Daniel, Aristotle's glosses or *glôttai* [*Poetics*, ch. XXI]), accompanied by the following statements: "The language of poetry is, then, a difficult, roughened [*zatrudnënnyj*], impeded language. . . . In the light of these developments we can define poetry as *attenuated, tortuous* speech" ("Art as Technique," pp. 22–23).

The first conception of poetic language is indeed present here. But alongside it, sometimes even embedded within it, we find the second one as well, stressed by the author. Thus Shklovskij writes, quite inconsistently with respect to the first conception: "[Poetic] imagery [is] a means of reinforcing an impression. . . . Poetic imagery is a means of creating the strongest possible impression. As a method it is . . . neither more nor less effective than . . . all those methods which emphasize the emotional effect of an expression (including words or even articulated sounds)" (ibid., pp. 8–9). We can see how the parenthesis attempts to reconcile the two views: we return to the doctrine of artistic autotelism provided that we forget that art is different from the rest of the world! But can the "means"-image be identical with the "object"-image, the "means" with the "end"? Or again: "The purpose [of an image] is not to make us perceive meaning, but to create a special perception of the object—*it creates a 'vision' of the object instead of serving as a means for knowing it*" (ibid., p. 18).

The opposition between poetic language and practical language remains just as categorical, and just as simplistic; however, it no longer entails an opposition between autotelism and heterotelism, but instead it opposes the concrete to the abstract, the perceptible to the intelligible, the world to thought, the particular to the general. Shklovskij sometimes manages to assume both positions within a single sentence, as in the following passage, central to his essay:

> Art exists that one may recover the sensation of life; it exists to make one feel things, to make the stone *stony*. The purpose of art is to impart the sensation of things as they are perceived and not as they are known. The technique of art is to make objects "unfamiliar," to make forms difficult, to increase the difficulty and length of perception because the process of perception is an aesthetic end in itself and must be prolonged. *Art is a way of experiencing the artfulness of an object; the object is not important.* [Ibid., p. 12]

Up to the word "unfamiliar" we remain within the second Formalist conception; from there to the end of the sentence, we go back to the first one—unless art is conceived as a perceptual apparatus and not as an object of perception itself. If the process of perception becomes an end in itself (owing to "difficulty" of form), the object is less perceptible, not more; if unfamiliarity provides the definition of art, the process of perception is imperceptible, and we see the object instead, as if for the first time.

Shklovskij gives no indication that he is aware of the difficulties he has raised. To my knowledge, only one attempt to reconcile the two conceptions was made, and that appeared more than fifteen years later, in Jakobson's "What Is Poetry?" Toward the end of his study, Jakobson more or less summarizes the Formalist position, and he also takes up the definition of poetic language, or poeticity:

But how does poeticity manifest itself? Poeticity is present when the word is felt as a word and not as a mere representation of the object being named or an an outburst of emotion, when words and their composition, their meaning, their external and inner form acquire a weight and value of their own instead of referring indifferently to reality. ["What Is Poetry?", p. 750]

Up to this point Jakobson has been presenting a very pure version of the first Formalist conception, autotelism. But the following sentences require a change of perspective:

Why is all this necessary? Why is it necessary to make a special point of the fact that the sign is not identical to the object? Because besides the direct awareness of the identity between sign and object (A is A_1) we need the direct awareness of the inadequacy of that identity (A is not A_1). The reason this antinomy is essential is that without contradiction there is no mobility of concepts, no mobility of signs, and the relation between concept and sign becomes automatized. Activity comes to a halt, and the awareness of reality dies out. . . . Poetry is what protects us from automatization, from the rust threatening our formulae of love and hatred, of revolt and renunciation, of faith and negation. [Ibid., p. 31]

This reasoning could be interpreted in the spirit of general semantics *à la* Korzybski: an automatic relationship between words and things is bad for both, for it removes them from the realm of perception and grants exclusive priority to mental processes. By breaking with automatization, we benefit on both accounts: we perceive words as words, but by the same token we also perceive objects as objects, as they "really" are, beyond any act of naming. . . .[1]

The word, and the concept of, estrangement have a well-known

---

[1]We find a similar assimilation, some ten years later, in Maurice Blanchot, for whom the perception of language as object also leads to the perception of objects in themselves: "The name ceases to be the ephemeral passing of nonexistence and becomes a concrete sphere, a mass of existence. Language abandons this meaning it had tried exclusively to be, and aims for nonsense. The prime role belongs to the physical: rhythm, weight, mass, figure, and then the paper we write on, the trace of ink, the book. Yes, fortunately, language is an object: it is the written object, a piece of bark, a chip from a rock, a fragment of clay preserving the reality of this earth. The word acts not as an ideal force but as an obscure power, as an incantation that forces objects and makes them *really* present outside of themselves" (*La Part du feu*, p. 330).

history, to which we shall return. It is not clear, however, that estrangement played a particularly significant role in many of the Formalist texts themselves. To be sure, Shklovskij invokes it constantly. But in the Formalists' systematic treatises (Èjxenbaum's "Theory of the Formal Method," for example, or Tomashevskij's *Teorija literatury* [Theory of literature], both published in 1925), the device is merely mentioned in passing; in no way does it stand as the definition of art. Tomashevskij describes estrangement or defamiliarization as "a special instance of artistic motivation" ("Thematics," p. 85). What place could estrangement have occupied in the Formalists' aesthetic system? One might begin by supposing that it corresponded to the very definition of art, as Shklovskij suggested. But even if this second conception of poetic language remains Romantic in origin, the form it had assumed in the period in question put it in direct contradiction with the first conception: the first denies any external function, the second proclaims one. The relation to the external world, banished from the Romantic aesthetic as an "imitation," makes its reappearance here in a more instrumental relationship: art is to reveal the world, rather than imitate it.

A second possibility would be to retain Shklovskij's repeated emphasis on the process of perception and take this idea as the outline of a theory of reading. But in this form, too, the idea contradicts the major tendencies of Formalist practice. The object of literary study, according to the Formalists—on this point they all agree—is the work itself, not the impressions the work makes on its readers. In theory, at least, Formalists distinguish the study of a work from the study of its production or reception, and they constantly criticize their predecessors for being preoccupied with mere circumstances or with impressions. A theory of reading could be slipped into Formalist doctrine only as contraband.

Finally, there is a third possibility: estrangement could serve as the basis for a theory of literary history. This is the meaning it takes on, starting in the early nineteen-twenties, in the writings of Shklovskij, Jakobson, and Tomashevskij. Estrangement gives rise to the idea of the cycle in which the literary device is rendered automatic, then exposed ("laid bare"); it underlies the metaphor of an inheritance passed from uncle to nephew (each period canonizes texts that the previous period considered marginal). But if we take the idea of estrangement in its strict sense, we can apply it only to a limited number of cases; in order to make it more generally applicable, we would have to transform its meaning. That is what happens in the writings of Tynjanov, which thus lead to a third conception of poetic language.

III

Before we reach that point, we must recall what the Formalists' concrete activity consisted of, and then assess the extent to which this activity corresponds to some aspect of their program. Little of their writing is devoted to the elaboration of an aesthetic system, whether original or trivial, nor are they concerned with exploring the essence of art; for better or for worse, we have to admit that the Formalists were not "philosophers." On the other hand, they produced a number of works on various aspects of poetry (Brik, Jakobson, Tomashevskij, Èjxenbaum, Zhirmunskij, Tynjanov), on the organization of narrative discourse (Èjxenbaum, Tynjanov, Vinogradov), on the forms of plot construction (Shklovskij, Tomashevskij, Reformatskij, Propp), and so on.

Thus we might say, at first glance, that there is a gap between what I called the "first conception" of poetic language and the Formalists' concrete work, to the extent that it is hard to see how the studies themselves depend in any way on the initial hypothesis. If we look more closely, however, we discover that these works are made possible (without being directly inspired) by the postulate that is the Formalists' point of departure. The somewhat abstract and hollow Romantic formula according to which a work of art has to be perceived in itself, and not as a means to some other end, becomes not a doctrinal affirmation but a practical reason leading the Formalists—who are in this respect scholars rather than readers—to perceive the work itself. They discover that it has a rhythm that we must learn how to describe; that it has narrators that we must be able to differentiate; that its narrative devices are universal and yet infinitely varied. In other words, their point of departure within the Romantic aesthetic allows them to put into practice—and here they are true innovators—a new *science of discourse*. Not that, unlike other critics, they speak the truth where others were merely expressing opinions; such a view would be illusory. Still, they are renewing the link with the project initiated by Aristotle in his *Poetics* and his *Rhetoric,* that of a discipline whose object is the forms of discourse rather than individual works. Indeed, this encounter between the Aristotelian tradition and the Romantic ideology is where the originality of the Formalist movement lies, and it explains the Formalist preference for scholarly articles over poetic fragments.

Èjxenbaum turned out to be particularly aware of this distinctive feature of Formalism, and he referred to it frequently in his "Theory of the Formal Method":

> It is not the methods of studying literature but rather literature as an object of study that is of prime concern to the Formalists. . . . Neither "Formalism" as a theory of aesthetics nor "methodology" as a fully formulated scientific system is characteristic of us; what does characterize us is the endeavor to create an autonomous discipline of literary studies based on the specific properties of literary material. [Pp. 3–4]

> It became unmistakably clear, even to those outside Opoyaz [Society for the Study of Poetic Language], that the essence of our work lay, not in erecting some rigid "Formal method," but in studying the specific properties of verbal art, and that the point was not the method but the object of study. [Pp. 28–29]

Formalism is characterized not by a theory but by an object. In one sense, Èjxenbaum is right: he has no particular method at his disposal, and even terminology changes over time. But what characterizes a critical school is never a method (that notion is a convenient fiction designed to attract disciples). A critical school is characterized rather by the way it constructs the object of its studies. Historians of the previous generation had included relations with the ideological context as part of that object, and they had omitted any internal analysis of works; the Formalists did just the opposite. Now it is quite clear that, for Èjxenbaum, who illustrates the positivist attitude here, that choice remains perfectly transparent, invisible. Moreover, this explains why the Formalists never seem to offer answers to the question: "What is criticism supposed to do?" They would answer in all innocence that criticism is supposed to describe literature—as if literature existed as a natural fact.

But let us return to the object of literary studies as Èjxenbaum perceives it. This object is "literature as a specific system of facts," "the specific properties of verbal art." But just what sort of specificity is at stake? To justify the creation of a new discipline, that specificity would have to be the same in all cases recognized as belonging to literature. Yet an attentive analysis of the "works themselves"—made possible by the hypothesis of literary specificity—showed the Formalists that the specificity in question does not exist. More precisely, it exists only in historically and culturally circumscribed terms; it is not universal or eternal; by the same token to define it in terms of autotelism is untenable. Paradoxically, their Romantic presuppositions are precisely the source of the Formalists' anti-Romantic conclusions.

Tynjanov is the first to note this, in his article "Literaturnyj fakt," ("The literary fact," 1924). In the first place, he remarks: "While it is getting more and more difficult to come up with a firm definition of literature, any contemporary can point out what a *literary fact* is. . . . The older contemporary, who has lived through one or two or perhaps several literary revolutions, will observe that in his time such-and-such an event was not considered a literary fact, whereas now it has become one, and vice-versa" (p. 9). And he concludes that "the literary fact is heterogeneous, and in this sense literature is a series evolving disjunctively" (p. 29).

We readily see what degree of generalization the concept of estrangement had to undergo in order to lead to Tynjanov's new literary theory (is it by chance that his article is dedicated to Viktor Shklovskij?). Estrangement is now just one example of a broader phenomenon, the historicity of the categories we use to classify cultural facts. These facts do not exist in the absolute, like chemical substances, but depend rather upon the users' perception.

Returning to the same subject in "On Literary Evolution" (1927), Tynjanov makes his position even clearer.

> The very existence of a fact *as literary* depends on its differential quality, that is, on its interrelationship with both literary and extraliterary orders. Thus, its existence depends on its function. What in one epoch would be a literary fact would in another be a common matter of social communication, and vice versa, depending on the whole literary system in which the given fact appears. Thus the friendly letter of Deržavin is a social fact. The friendly letter of the Karamzin and Puškin epoch is a literary fact. Thus one has the literariness of memoirs and diaries in one system and their extraliterariness in another. [P. 69]

"Automatization" and "estrangement" appear here as particular examples of the process of literary transformation in general.

This thesis has devastating consequences for Formalist doctrine. In effect, it amounts to asserting that what Èjxenbaum considered the cornerstone of Formalism's identity—the object of Formalist studies, that is, the (transhistorical) specificity of literature—does not exist. Two contradictory reactions can be noted among the other members of the group. The first is Èjxenbaum's own, in *Moi vremennik* (My chronicle, 1929). He adheres completely to Tynjanov's position, accepting his conclusions as well as his examples: "Thus, for example, at times periodicals and the environment created by the activities of editing and publishing take on meaning as literary fact, while at other times the same meaning is conferred on societies, circles, salons" ("Literary Environment," p. 61). "Literary fact and literary period are complex and changing notions, inasmuch as the interrelations between the elements constituting literature and their functions are changeable" (*Moi vremennik*, p. 59). Nothing is said, on the other hand, about how this idea relates to Èjxenbaum's previous statements on the subject.

Jakobson, for his part, does not seem disturbed by these new declarations. In "What Is Poetry?", he is content to isolate an enduring kernel within the general flux; thus he somewhat limits the field in which his theses apply, but he does not modify their tenor: "As I have already pointed out, the content of the concept of *poetry* is unstable and temporally conditioned, whereas the poetic function, *poeticity*, is, as the Formalists stressed, an element *sui generis*, one that cannot be mechanically reduced to other elements" (p. 750). Jakobson's work in the nineteen-sixties continued to bear witness to his conviction that it is possible to have a linguistic (and transhistorical) definition, if not of poetry itself, then at the very least of the poetic function.

Tynjanov's thesis has radical implications. In fact, it does not allow for an autonomous knowledge of literature, but it leads toward two complementary disciplines: a science of discourse that studies stable linguistic forms but cannot account for literary specificity; and a history that makes explicit the content of the idea of literature in any given historical period, relating this idea to others at the same level. This third conception of poetic language in fact demolishes the notion itself: in its place we have the "literary fact," no longer a philosophical category but a historical one. Tynjanov takes literature down from its pedestal: he no longer sees it as in opposition to, but rather in a relation of exchange and transformation with, other discursive categories. The very structure of thought has changed: in place of everyday grayness and the poetic starburst, we discover the plurality of manners of speaking. At one stroke, the initial gap, the gap between language that refers to the world and language that expresses itself, is abolished, and the question of truth in literature can be formulated in new terms.

As far as the definition of literature itself is concerned, we can do no more than attempt to imagine what consequences the Formalists might have drawn from this spectacular reversal. One possible direction might have been a radical historicism—just as radical as their Formalism—which would have led to throwing out the entire question; thus we would not have abandoned the conceptual framework of Romanticism. Following another lead would have made it possible to seek a new definition, justified not by the authentic relationship among all the facts known as literary, but by the explanatory value of the definition itself. Yet nothing of the sort ever came about: the group fell victim to political repression toward the end of the nineteen-twenties, and all the questions it had raised became taboo, in the Soviet Union, for several decades. The only positive lesson to emerge from this brutal end to Formalist reflection is that literature and criticism apparently do not find their ends in themselves: otherwise, the State would not have bothered to bring them under control.

3

Back to the Epic:
Döblin and Brecht

A s we shift our focus from Russia to Germany, we also shift to another genre: here we shall turn away from critics to consider Alfred Döblin and Bertolt Brecht, two writers whose interest in literary criticism was sporadic. They did not concern themselves with the nature of criticism or its possibilities; they had no interest in describing literature in impartial and scientific terms. But they were deeply interested in the possibilities, even the responsibilities, of literature. In the margins, as it were, of their own literary production, they wrote theoretical justifications in defense and support of it. These writings present programs of (literary) action that are to be measured solely in terms of their effectiveness, by no means to be confused with disquisitions that aspire to reveal some truth. And yet—though I am no doubt being unfair here to current specialists in German literary theory—the line of thinking pursued in these polemical writings and manifestos is more compelling, I find, than anything in the work of the theorists. This explains my choice of texts.

If I am being unfair toward professional criticism, I run just as great a risk of being unfair toward my two authors, for I shall not attempt any comprehensive survey of their work; such an attempt would be out of place in the present context. Instead, I shall focus exclusively on the aspect of their doctrine that is evoked by the term "epic," a term Döblin and Brecht both use to designate their own productions. What interests me here is not the accuracy of such a designation ("Were the works in question truly epics?"), or, from a different point of view, its legitimacy ("Would a good literary historian have used the term in this sense?"), but only its meaning. What exactly did our authors have in mind when they referred to some play or novel as an "epic"?

I

Alfred Döblin used the word "epic" as early as 1928 in a very specific sense, in a lecture called "Schriftstellerei und Dichtung"; the title might be translated as "Scribbling and Poetry." Döblin presents this opposition as an innovation, although it will certainly be familiar to any reader who sees it in the context of the aesthetic doctrine of Romanticism. Döblin indeed contrasts the utilitarian attitude of the writer, who is oriented toward external ends, with the intransitive attitude of the poet, who is exclusively concerned with issues peculiar to art itself. Döblin begins by characterizing books that fall within the first category: "As a general rule, they have a certain practical goal: to distract, and then to achieve some ethical end, depending on what the author considers ethical; either they are designed to serve as political propaganda, or they are meant to act on society as its critics and tutors; or else they are intended only as the place where the poor author can empty out his soul, a literary hideaway for exhibitionists, a literary outhouse" (p. 93). It is clear that Döblin is stigmatizing the "impressive" or didactic function of art just as severely as its expressive function. Now here is the second term of the opposition: "Poetry is categorically opposed to rational scribbling that is subordinated to external ends. . . . Poetic works also have goals that act on life and men, but these goals, which are quite complex and quite contemporary, are specific to poetry" (p. 94).

Döblin's claim to originality notwithstanding, the opposition he makes here is an entirely traditional one. Less so, however, is the way he uses it interchangeably with another opposition between paired terms designating literary genres, namely, "novel" and "epic." This usage has its disconcerting aspects: on the one hand, "epic" becomes synonymous with "poetic," and Homer, Dante, and Cervantes—an author of epics, a poet, and a novelist—are linked as supreme representatives of epic art! On the other hand, the novel, which for the Romantics stood at the pinnacle of their new aesthetic, comes to represent the opposite extreme: for Döblin, the novel belongs with scribbling, not poetry. Epic works are thus endowed, in Döblin's eyes, with the characteristics that Friedrich Schlegel or Novalis attributed to novels; in particular, they are characterized by their intransitivity. This distinctive feature comes to light no matter what perspective the analyst adopts. Each element in a fable remains autonomous, instead of being subordinated to a single culminating point as happens in the novel (here Döblin reproduces Schiller's interpretation of the epic/dramatic opposition): "In epic works, the action advances bit by bit, by agglutination. Such is epic apposition. This contrasts with the development of a drama, which is an unfolding outward from a single point of departure. . . . In a good epic work, isolated characters or individual episodes taken out of context remain lifelike, whereas the ordinary novel may dash along with the greatest intensity, but it leaves no trace in the reader's memory. Autonomy resurfaces when the levels of organization of a work are examined rather than its parts: "Here are two essential distinctive features of the epic work: sovereignty of the imagination, and sovereignty of verbal art" (p. 94).

The most curious aspect of this passage lies in Döblin's use of the term "epic": it turns up in an unexpected spot and seems endowed with a meaning that is banal from the aesthetic standpoint, but has lexicological originality. The traditional meaning of the term, however, cannot be entirely obliterated. Some vestige of this meaning must remain present in Döblin's memory, as in his reader's, and this tension between the common use of the term and its new use requires an explanation. Döblin takes on that task in a much longer study published the following year, "Der Bau des epischen Werks" (The structure of the epic work, 1929). Here we find the core of his original intuitions.

It is not so much that he burns all the bridges leading back to the Romantic aesthetic. He remains in perfect harmony with that doctrine as he criticizes servile imitations of reality, praises the intransitivity of the separate parts of epic works and of these works in their entirety, and compares such works, by virtue of their autonomy and the internal coherence that governs them, to musical compositions. Still other characteristics posited of epics might have come straight from the pen of Friedrich Schlegel, except that Schlegel would have been referring to the novel. For example, the epic genre absorbs all other genres: "You are going to tear your hair if I advise authors to be resolutely lyrical, dramatic, even reflective in the epic endeavor. But I shall not back off" (p. 113). Unlike the other genres, the epic is in constant transformation: "The epic is not a fixed form; like drama, it requires continuous development through stubborn resistance to tradition and its representatives" (p. 113). As a genre, it emphasizes the process of production rather than finished products: "*Thus the reader participates along with the author in the process of production. All epic works have to do with becoming and acting*" (p. 123). But on the heels of these commonplace Romantic notions we find some other more surprising declarations.

Even as he criticizes servile imitations of reality, Döblin recognizes, from his own reading experience, that narratives that may in fact allude to events in the external world (the works of Homer, Dante, and Cervantes are again cited as examples) still gain the reader's total adhesion. How can this be? There is a difference, Döblin explains, both in the nature of the material represented and in the way it is represented. Whereas the "bourgeois" novel (p. 107) describes *specific* people and situations, the epic work strives for *exemplariness*, in manner as well as material. The epic author does not settle for observing and transcribing reality; he also has to "pierce through" reality (p. 107), has to go beyond it in order to locate basic, elemental situations that characterize humanity as a whole rather than individual men: "There we find formulations of powerful basic and elemental situations of human existence; there we find fundamental human attitudes making their appearance. . . . These original human situations go well beyond the everyday verities analyzed, in terms of their proximity to origins, in truth value, and in creative power" (pp. 106–107). The European novel as it has developed since the seventeenth century is indeed marked by the value it places on the particular and by its interest in the individual; the rejection of these options, characteristic of an earlier period but perhaps also of the present, thus legitimizes the reintroduction of that ancient term, "epic."

In order to understand the second characteristic of the modern period, we must take a moment to follow the process of literature's historical transformation that Döblin outlines in broad strokes. The ancient epic poet is not singlehandedly responsible for his work: his public has an equal share in it, inasmuch as the poet is in direct contact with this public; the work is thus oriented toward its hearers, and the poet is only the individual spokesman for what is first and foremost a collective voice. But writing, and later printing, placed a screen between the producers and consumers of books; these two categories had to be identified as such, and set apart. The sterility of individualism thus affects not only a work's characters but also its author. Yet how can we escape from this aporia? Who, after all, imagines that the modern poet is about to start singing on street corners and asking for handouts?

Döblin's response is interesting. In the era of the printed book, he declares, the only way to revive the epic spirit is to internalize the voice of one's potential listeners and give it expression, without in the process—and this is a crucial point—losing the individual voice of the poet. The classical epic poet was merely a medium for transmitting the voice of the collectivity, within which his own individual voice was lost. The modern individualist poet, too, allows one voice alone to be heard; this voice, however, belongs to an individual. The new epic, for its part, is the first to allow two voices to be heard simultaneously: the poet's voice and the other's, internalized. This produces an interior dialogue.

Döblin writes:

> To put it clearly at the outset: *at this point, the author is no longer all alone in his room.* . . . From this moment on, the author bears the public in himself. This observant self takes on, in our epoch, the role and the function of the people among the ancient singers. *This self becomes public, becomes a listener, and it even begins to collaborate.* . . . From this time forward, cooperation has been established; there is collaboration between the self and the poeticizing agency. [P. 120]

This allows Döblin to imagine the various relationships established between the two emanations of the person: the internalized I-listener may control everything, or he may begin to submit to the work; he may even give way before it.

Finally, there is a third area in which a distinctive feature of the new epic is manifested, namely in the author's attitude toward language. The utterances in a literary work are considered no longer exclusively in terms of the realities they designate, but also as transmitters of voices. In the production of his work, a poet often starts with a sentence from which he retains not meanings but echoes of earlier utterances. The poet does not hear the individual voice of a particular person or the unified voice of the entire collectivity; language, for him, becomes the locus of interaction between the multiple voices characteristic of a society: he hears and brings to life social, territorial, and professional affiliations, degrees of education, preferences for archaic expressions or vulgarity, some literary subtradition or other, and so on. What counts is that this multiplicity itself be maintained. "The connoisseur knows that there are a great many levels of language on which everything has to move" (p. 131), and one could render the writer no greater service than to facilitate his access to this realm. "If the philologists wished to edit a dictionary of the styles and levels of the German language, the work would be beneficial to authors and readers alike" (p. 130). The task is an essential one, for "*in every style of language there resides a productive force and a constraining factor*" (pp. 130-31). For one who knows how to listen to these voices, they can take on the task of producing the text in the author's place. "We think we are speaking and we are spoken; we believe we are writing, yet we are written. . . . With good authors, 'language' always wins" (pp. 131-32). So the victory here takes place without a loser, a victory in which the self is all the more decisively present in that he is ceding his place to others.

For the past three centuries, the novel has been in harmony with the ideology of individualism, which in turn has evolved in parallel with modern bourgeois society. But in the life around him Döblin perceives the signs of a radical mutation, in the wake of which collective agencies, as compared to individuals, are beginning to play an increasingly significant role. This, for Döblin, is the common denominator of a great number of transformations in the society he is observing, both the one close at hand and also society at large. The new ideology (which we must be careful not to call "collectivist") would be more compatible with a new literature, for which Döblin reserves the label "epic." Döblin challenges the individualist ethic on one quite specific point, its underlying idea of man. Döblin wants literature to represent exemplary situations and characters rather than unique ones because he does not believe in the uniqueness of the individual, in the irreducible difference that would separate one individual from all others. This choice is based upon his conviction that *sociality* is a basic element of human nature. We encounter the same idea when we turn from man as he is represented to the man who is doing the representing: the author cannot be viewed as an isolated individual either, but must be seen rather as one who transmits, simultaneously, a plurality of voices, his own and those of others or, more precisely, his own and the voice of his public, a kind of consensus of the era. The new epic genre must be a conscious dialogue between the individual author and this collective consensus. The equally dangerous traps of pure collectivism and pure individualism must be avoided. In today's world it is a delusion to think that, like the bard in traditional cultures, we can blend in completely with the voice of our own society, but it is just as dangerous to imagine that we exist in radical solitude. The interaction between the two points of view is what must be maintained.

II

Brecht's aesthetic differs from the Romantic one in several obvious respects. His "didactic theatre" is incompatible with the artistic intransitivity the Romantics extolled so highly, and it comes as no surprise to find the idea of art itself, consubstantial with the Romantic aesthetic, becoming marginal in the Brechtian perspective. Brecht places little value on the project of bringing together everything that finds its end in itself in a single, unified concept. When he has to explain the nature of epic theatre (in "The Messingkauf Dialogues"), he does not resort to aesthetic categories; instead, he analyzes an everyday exercise: "It is relatively easy to propose a basic model for the epic theatre. While doing practical exercises, I used to take as an example of the simplest epic theatre, the most 'natural,' as it were, an incident that might occur on any street corner: someone who witnessed a traffic accident shows the crowd that has gathered how it all happened." Of course these "simple forms" of drama differ from the "learned forms" (to borrow the terms André Jolles introduced, around the same time, in his *Einfache Formen*), but the differences are functional, not structural:

35

"art" (literature) is born of "nature" (discourse). "Between the natural epic theatre and the artificial *epic theatre* there is no difference in kind at the level of their basic elements. Our street-corner theatre is rudimentary; the pretext, the goal and the means of our spectacle 'aren't worth much.' But it cannot be denied that we have a meaningful process with a clear and social function that determines each of its elements" (*Schriften I*, pp. 557-558). Art is not the *opposite* of nature, literature is not the *opposite* of everyday discourse: the latter is *transformed* into the former. Artistic writing turns out to be caught up in the network of relations between discourses, and language, as Döblin also indicated, must be understood in its plurality. In this respect, the end point of the Formalist movement coincides with Brecht's point of departure.

But Brecht's center of interest lies elsewhere, and the juxtaposition with Döblin is even more significant than we have yet seen: what is at stake is "epic theatre," exactly contemporary with Döblin's "epic novel." Brecht took satisfaction in recognizing Döblin as one of his "illegitimate fathers," and in a letter addressed to Döblin he explains his own dramaturgical project as follows: "In fact I am only attempting to find a form that would make it possible to transpose onto the stage the element that makes the difference between your novels and Mann's" (*Schriften II*, p. 118). Even though Brecht is not always quite so lavish with his praise, it does seem that the connection, in his mind, has to do specifically with the idea of the epic, for the word appears every time he refers to Döblin. "In a discussion, the great epic author Alfred Döblin leveled a fatal accusation against drama in calling it an artistic genre absolutely incapable of giving a faithful representation of life" (*Schriften I*, p. 118). "The new dramaturgy was approaching the epic form (by leaning once again on the work of a novelist, namely Alfred Döblin)" (p. 221). But the meaning Brecht ends up giving the term "epic" is not quite the same as Döblin's.

Here we have to begin with one of the best-known aspects of Brecht's doctrine, his critique of identification (*Einfühlung*, empathy). As we know, Brecht criticizes classical nonepic theatre for inviting spectators to identify with the characters, an identification that is made easier by the prior identification of the actors with these same characters: spectator, actor, and character blend into one. Classical views of the theatre, Brecht (perhaps wrongly) maintains, conceived of no other form of reception on the spectator's part; this accounts for the staying power of the catharsis theory. In

order to achieve this effect, the dramatist seeks to keep the spectator under the illusion that he has a slice of life before his eyes, and
not a spectacle; hence the image of the stage as a room that merely
lacks a fourth wall, and the admiration professed by contemporary
specialists (the Stanislawski school) for the effects of illusion, the
"make-believe," of which the best actors are capable. To this kind
of recommendation, Brecht offers an ironic retort: "Without falling
back on the actor's art, merely with a sufficient dose of alcohol, one
can get almost everyone to see maybe not rats everywhere, but at
least white mice" (p. 351).

The new aesthetic of epic theatre can be deduced negatively on
the basis of Brecht's critique. The spectator has to remain lucid,
master of his critical faculties, and for this reason must not suc-
cumb to the temptation of identification. The dramatist and director involved in the experience of the epic theatre have the task of
assisting the spectator in this effort. The playwright, for his part,
practices a form of representation of the world that consists not in
reproducing things just as we are used to perceiving them, but
rather in making them strange and unfamiliar so as to disorient us.
Brecht first refers to this device with the word *Entfremdung*, dis-
tancing, but also alienation; however, he shifts to another term,
Verfremdung, soon afterward, apparently under the influence of
the Russian Formalists and the notion of *ostranenie*, estrangement,
that Shklovskij had introduced some twelve years earlier. Brecht
may have become familiar with this parallel (and slightly earlier)
development during his own travels to Moscow, where he spent
time with Osip Brik in particular; or alternatively, as of 1931,
through the intermediary of S. M. Tretiakov, who went to Berlin
that year and met Brecht. Tretiakov, who was friendly with Eisen-
stein and Meyerhold, but also with Shklovskij and Brik, was himself the author of several "avant-garde" plays; at the end of the
nineteen-thirties he met the same fate as those whose biographical
notice in the Soviet *Concise Literary Encyclopedia* ends with the following laconic note: "Illegally suppressed. Posthumously rehabili-
tated."[1] There seems to have been mutual admiration between the
two men: Brecht adapted one of Tretiakov's plays into German and

---

[1] On Tretiakov, one may consult Fritz Mierau, *Erfindung und Korrektur. Tretjakows
Aesthetik der Operativität* (Berlin, Akademie-Verlag, 1976), making allowances for
Mierau's particular standpoint; and S. Tretiakov, *Dans le front gauche de l'art* (Paris,
Maspéro, 1977). Brecht later dedicated a poem to Tretiakov's tragic disappearance
and never believed he was guilty.

always called him his "master," while Tretiakov became Brecht's translator into Russian. The influence of these encounters led Brecht to modify his terminology so he could use an exact translation of the Russian word: the famous *Verfremdung*, estrangement, alienation, or the *A-effect*.

Like Shklovskij, Brecht considers the device common to all the arts, and he delights in spotting it in the work of classical painters (for example, Breughel) as well as modern ones: "Painting (Cézanne) alienates [estranges] when it gives exaggerated emphasis to the hollow form of a container" (*Schriften I*, p. 364). But of course he refers most often to the theatre, and he continually insists that above all else the author must succeed in transmitting this effect of strangeness: "The A-effect consists in turning the object of which one is to be made aware, to which one's attention is to be drawn, from something ordinary, familiar, immediately accessible, into something peculiar, striking and unexpected" (p. 355; *Brecht on Theatre*, p. 143).[2] Before putting this device into practice, the author shares with his spectator a conventional attitude with regard to things, that is, he recognizes them without really perceiving them. Conscious of the habitual nature of perception, the author introduces into the text itself a different program of perception; he acts upon his text in order to act upon the spectator. Owing to the effect of estrangement, the spectator no longer identifies with the character, and two subjects appear where before there had been only one.

What textual devices produce the estrangement effect? A work of language has multiple levels and aspects; however, in every epoch, literary convention leads us to associate certain of these aspects with others in a fixed and stable way. By breaking these associations, by retaining some elements of the cliché and changing others, one prevents routine, automatic perception. For example, if a prosaic subject is evoked with the help of overrefined linguistic forms, it will be estranged; the same holds true if an "elevated" subject is treated in dialect rather than in finely honed literary language. Sometimes the same effect is achieved by a shift from the present tense to the past or vice versa, or from the first person to

---

[2]*Brecht on Theatre* is a translation of selected texts from the German volume in which all his writings about theatre are collected. I have followed it for quotations of the texts it contains, but I continue to cite the page numbers of the complete collection as well, for the convenience of readers familiar with that edition. —Trans.

the third and so on. Alongside these interventions, which have to do with the very structure of the text, the metatext may also be brought into play: for example, stage directions normally intended for the actors alone may be read aloud, in which case the audience hears two different voices in alternation. All these devices recall those of parody, which also maintains some elements of the original while modifying others, and introduces duality within the author's voice itself. In the theatre, along with these textual means for producing the estrangement effect, there are also others that arise from the staging. The spectator identifies with the character because the actor has already done so; for the purpose of destroying the spectator's identification, there will be an attack on the actor's, and a plurality of subjects will be reestablished in place of unity. Brecht writes in "The Messingkauf Dialogues": "The estrangement effect does not occur when the actor, who puts on a stranger's face, entirely obliterates his own. His task is to show the two faces superimposed" (p. 610). The actor shows the noncoincidence between himself and the character and causes two voices to be heard simultaneously; this prevents the spectator in turn from identifying with the character: "The actor has to keep on being a portrayer; he has to show the character he is portraying as a different person and not eradicate from his representation all traces of *'he* did that, *he* says this.' He must not end up *wholly transforming himself* into the character portrayed. . . . He never forgets, and never lets the spectators forget, that he is not the person he is portraying, but the portrayer" (p. 553). Or, in the striking language of an earlier text: "Each [actor] should estrange himself from himself" (p. 189).

In addition to modifying his relationship with the character he is playing, the actor may also relate differently to the spectator, by addressing him directly, in a gesture that parallels the reading of stage directions; this reminds us that the characters' dialogue is embedded in the dialogue between author and spectator. Finally, the actor may also modify his relation to himself, and put himself on display observing himself: "The Chinese actor achieves the A-effect by being seen to observe his own movements" (p. 346; *Brecht on Theatre*, p. 139). The result of all these devices is that instead of *acting out* a character's words, the actor *quotes* them: "Once the idea of total transformation is abandoned the actor speaks his part not as if he were improvising it himself but like a quotation"

(p. 344; *Brecht on Theatre*, p. 138). Now what is a quotation if not an utterance with two speaking subjects, a situation in which two voices are transmitted in a single act of speaking?

The director, too, may intervene by using extratextual media: not with the aim of making all these techniques contribute to a single effect, of bringing them into total fusion, but rather using each one of them to make the others look strange. The gesture is to be dissonant with respect to the text, with the effect of making the spectator conscious of both; the same holds true for the use of music, film, masks, even stage settings: "So let us invite all the sister arts of the drama, not in order to create an 'integrated work of art' in which they all offer themselves up and are lost, but so that together with the drama they may further the common task in their different ways; and their relations with one another consist in this: that they lead to mutual alienation" (pp. 698-699; *Brecht on Theatre*, p. 204). Brecht's ideal is not total theatre but a theatre of heterogeneity, in which plurality reigns in place of unity.

The alienation, or estrangement, effect is not the only distinguishing characteristic of epic theatre, but it is its hallmark, as it were, the quintessential feature to which all other distinctive features of that theatre can be related. Brecht also stresses the narrator's presence on stage; thus the narrator embodies one of the functions that used to belong to the actor, and materializes the existence of the author-spectator exchange. The fact that the play occurs in a "past" time while the performance takes place in the "present" must not be obscured; the two time frames must coexist overtly. Referring once again to Döblin, Brecht picks up the Schillerian idea of scenic autonomy in epic drama: the individual episodes do not contribute to a single action, do not all lead to a single culminating point; their juxtaposition (the "montage" effect) points up their heterogeneity. "As we have learned, the author chops up a play into little autonomous pieces, so that the action advances by fits and starts. He challenges the imperceptible sliding from one scene into another" (p. 605). Epic theatre itself is defined, then, by this stress on the heterogeneous and the plural.

Brecht's most frequent answer to the "why?" of epic theatre is absolute and ahistorical in nature. He postulates indeed that all comprehension and knowledge require separation, estrangement, between subject and object; consequently, epic theatre is not merely a historically appropriate form but the best way of gaining access to truth. "[It was] the alienation [*Entfremdung*] that is necessary to all understanding. When something seems 'the most obvious thing in the world' it means that any attempt to understand the world has been given up" (p. 265; *Brecht on Theatre*, p. 71). Here Brecht is perhaps unwittingly espousing the Aristotelian position: for Aristotle, astonishment is mother to knowledge. But is knowledge the ultimate object of art? It is at this point that Brecht introduces a historical consideration, declaring that we live in a "scientific age," in which art's path joins that of science. "To transform himself from general passive acceptance to a corresponding state of suspicious inquiry he would need to develop that detached eye with which the great Galileo observed a swinging chandelier" (p. 681; *Brecht on Theatre*, p. 192). For Brecht, there is no room for doubt about the status of science, reason, and truth as the highest values.

In this argument it might be possible to see an attempt to pass off as universal values what are, after all, only the values of a given era or even those of an individual: Bertolt Brecht himself. We would be dealing indeed, in that case, with a historical attitude, but of the worst sort: an unconscious and egocentric one. For it seems obvious that Brecht's explanation cannot be taken at face value: even if we acknowledge that the dimension of truth is not foreign to literature, we cannot assimilate literary "truth" to scientific truth; scientific statements, taken one at a time, are either true or false, whereas the question of truthfulness loses its meaning when we are dealing with the sentences of a novel. Why then should we believe that the discovery procedures for truth must be the same in both cases?

Alongside this first explanation, however, Brecht provides another, one whose historical nature he takes for granted: this second explanation is more compatible with his other ideas, since it establishes a relationship between literary transformations and those of society. This is the crux of his debate with Lukács in the nineteen-thirties, as we know: whereas for Lukács there is an essence of realism, manifested by the classic writers of the nineteenth century (Balzac and Tolstoy), to which we must always aspire, realism for Brecht is a notion with variable content, defined by its immediate effectiveness and its adequacy to the needs of the moment: if twentieth-century writers were to imitate the nineteenth-century realists, they would be "formalists." And in his writings of epic theatre, Brecht deliberately emphasizes the dependency that exists between art forms and the realities that these forms reckon with: "If only so as to be able to grasp the new thematic areas, we already need a new dramaturgical and theatrical form. Can we talk about money in iambic pentameter? 'The rise of the mark, yesterday it was fifty, today one hundred, tomorrow more, and so on.' Is this possible? Oil is resistant to the standard five acts" (p. 197).

Here, then, is Brecht's historical explanation: the aesthetic of identification was in harmony with the ideology of individualism during its time of triumph; at the present time the individual is in the process of losing his dominant role. "The individual viewpoint no longer allows us to understand the decisive processes of our time; individuals have no influence on them" (p. 245). In place of the individual, we find environmental elements, interpersonal situations, and collective interests playing the primary role; that is why the individual characters in epic theatre must be transformed into exemplary beings who may remind us of Döblin's heroes: "It is not the outstanding passionate individual who is the initiator and questioner in epic theatre. The questions are always raised by the situations, and the individuals respond through the characteristic behavior they adopt" (p. 193).

Like Döblin, then, Brecht stresses the differences between the role the individual played in the age of the bourgeois revolutions and the individual's role in modern times, and he ends up praising plurality to the detriment of unity. As we know, this idea of estrangement is not a new one; we see it in operation from the ancient classics up through Montesquieu's *Lettres persanes*, and theoretical formulations on the subject can be found from the Romantic period on, in Novalis, Shelley, and Hegel. But for the Romantics, as later for Shklovskij, it is simply a matter of renewing the vision of the object; Brecht, on the other hand, stresses the doubling that affects the subject of discourse.

Brecht broke with individualism, but not with relativism. Like Döblin, he valorizes the presence of more than one voice in a single subject, but unlike Döblin, he does not spell out the nature of that other voice. It is no longer the voice of the social consensus; estrangement is in full sway: for Brecht, two voices—of whatever nature—are always better than one. "Each should estrange himself from himself": the direction of the movement does not seem to matter.

The rest of Brecht's work weakens this program, however, and so casts doubt on the very possibility of carrying it out. Far from taking ludic pleasure in the multiplication of voices, Brecht makes his audience hear, in a work that often strikes but a single chord, the sound of an ideology accepted as true and incontestable, that of the Communist Party. It is as though Brecht could not conceive of any alternative to nonhierarchical plurality except adherence to a dogma. It is not my intention to analyze Brecht's work here, but I find it difficult not to see his two apparently contradictory gestures —the praise of multiplicity and the rigid practice of unity—as interdependent. Each at once facilitates and excuses the other. Alienation does not include a reference to truth; but then Brecht had his own, in advance. Conversely, the dogmatic truth he has to transmit, made "strange" or "alien," becomes more attractive. Fortunately, Brecht's "epic theatre" eludes these criticisms, it seems to me, and rises above both of its author's dogmas, the aesthetic and the political: in his theatre, Brecht succeeds in skirting the dual shoals of dogmatism and skepticism.

4

Critics as Writers:
Sartre, Blanchot, Barthes

"Critics as writers" and not "writers as critics": the criticism that some writers produce is not my topic here, but rather the criticism that becomes a form of literature in itself, or, in today's jargon, a form of "writing" (although that term has been nearly drained of meaning through overuse). In any event, we shall be dealing with criticism whose literary aspect has acquired a new relevance. To represent this form of criticism, I have chosen three authors who made their mark on French letters after the Second World War (whether or not they produced works of fiction at other times is immaterial): Jean-Paul Sartre, Maurice Blanchot, and Roland Barthes.

I

Sartre's writings span the genres, and no watertight compartments separate philosophy, criticism, and fiction in his work. In order to maintain a balance among the three authors to be discussed, I shall focus here on the major texts in which Sartre deals primarily with literature. In point of fact, Sartre does not speak about Literature-in-general, but about its two major species, poetry and prose; we need to examine his views on each separately.

Poetry is the aspect of literature that can be assimilated to the other arts: painting, sculpture, music. How is it defined? "Poets are men who refuse to *utilize* language. . . . The poet has withdrawn from language-instrument in a single movement. Once and for all he has chosen the poetic attitude which considers words as things and not as signs" (*What Is Literature?*, p. 6). This transformation in the function of language entails another in its structure: the poet's words resemble the things he is evoking. The relation of signifier to signified is motivated: signification becomes natural. . . . [The poet chooses a verbal image] for its resemblance to the willow tree or the ash tree. . . . All language is for him the mirror of the world. . . . Thus, between the word and the thing signified, there is established a double reciprocal relation of magical resemblance and signification" (ibid., pp. 7-8). *Saint Genet* (1952) adds various notations that enrich the picture but change nothing so far as the underlying schema is concerned: the opposition between *signification* and *meaning* [*signification/sens*] that Sartre uses to define poetry is modeled on the Romantic pairing of allegory and symbol. Here the Romantic doctrine appears undisguised, just as it can be found in Moritz, Novalis, or A. W. Schlegel (even if Sartre actually discovered it through Valéry, Blanchot, and Mallarmé): poetry is defined by the intransitivity of language and by the motivated relation between signifiers and signifieds, which is another form of internal coherence.

Sartre does not conceal this legacy; in *Saint Genet*, for example, he refers quite frequently to Blanchot's writings on Mallarmé. But he does have one reservation. After quoting Blanchot, he appends the following note: "Blanchot adds (p. 48): 'Perhaps this trickery is the truth of all written things.' At this point I cease to follow him. He should, from this point of view, distinguish between poetry and prose" (p. 310). So Sartre's own contribution is to be found in the area of prose; in the case of poetry he is content to remind us of what he sees as truths that may have fallen into neglect but are part of common knowledge.

Prose, for its part, is not an activity that has its end in itself. The prose writer, as Sartre says in *What Is Literature?*, "has chosen to reveal the world and particularly to reveal man to other men so that the latter may assume full responsibility before the object which has been thus laid bare" (p. 18). The very form of prose literature lies behind its role as master of responsibility and thus of liberty, for "the writer's universe will only reveal itself in all its depth to the examination, the admiration, and the indignation of the reader" (p. 56). Now though it is finally up to the reader to decide as to the meaning of my work, in my role as author I incite him to a continuous exercise of his liberty; conversely, as a reader, by the very act of reading, I recognize the writer's freedom. This is why "the art of prose is bound up with the only regime in which prose has meaning, democracy" (p. 59). The Sartrean *engagement*, or commitment, amounts to nothing so much as an awareness of this function that is inherent in literary prose, even though the term "commitment" retains a double meaning: the writer is at one and the same time "committed" in the sense that he necessarily participates in his times—he is "situated"—and in the sense that he assumes his role of guide toward liberty, and thus toward transcending the situation: "With every word I utter, I involve myself a little more in the world, and by the same token I emerge from it a little more, since I go beyond it toward the future" (pp. 16-17). Committed art—*art engagé*—is not an art subject to political objectives, but an art conscious of its own identity; it is equidistant from "pure propaganda" (with which it sometimes tends to be confused) and "pure entertainment," a limit approached by poetry. However this may be, prose (literature) is defined by a transhistorical social function, one that cannot be deduced from the individualist and relativist ideology of the Romantics, since it touches upon absolute values: "although literature is one thing and morality a quite different one, at the heart of the aesthetic imperative we discern the moral imperative" (pp. 56-57).

Saint Genet is less explicit on this point. The fact remains that in this text the prose writer, unlike the poet, is always the one for whom "language is canceled so as to further the ideas of which it has been the vehicle" (p. 553); he is on the side of transparency as opposed to the opacity of poetry. In this book, Sartre focuses on a different implication of the opposition: the fact that in poetry the game is played out between the poet and his language, the reader's role being purely passive, whereas in prose it is language that is passive, and subject to the basic situation, which is one of communication between author and reader: "Prose is based upon this reciprocity of recognition" (ibid.). Now communication is a social

act, and prose therefore has a function other than that of being itself: we still remain outside the Romantic schema.

We are about to encounter a problem, however. The reader is a
constitutive factor in literature, as Sartre reiterates:

> The literary object is a peculiar top which exists only in movement. To
> make it come into view a concrete act called reading is necessary, and
> it lasts only as long as this act can last. [*What Is Literature?*, p. 34]

> All literary work is an appeal. To write is to make an appeal to the
> reader that he lead into objective existence the revelation which I have
> undertaken by means of language. [Ibid., p. 40]

The whole structure of Sartre's book tends to confirm the importance of reading and the reader: the question that serves as title of
the first chapter, "What Is Writing?", can be answered only if one
knows "Why Write?" (title and theme of the second chapter). Yet
the "why" can be understood only in terms of a third question (and
a third chapter): "For Whom Does One Write?", the capstone of
the whole work.

Now in Sartre's judgment the reader in question is necessarily a
particular reader, situated in time and space. The identity of the literary act is thus historically determined. "Even if he has his eyes
on eternal laurels, the writer is speaking to his contemporaries and
brothers of his class and race" (p. 62). This issue would be of little
importance if the reader's role were limited: however, since the
reader's role is, on the contrary, decisive, all literature finds itself
shorn of its universal dimension. Readers (and thus also authors,
and the very meaning of literary works) are characterized by their
historicity (p. 63); and Sartre concludes with a famous comparison:
"It seems that bananas have a better taste when they have just
been picked. Works of the mind should likewise be eaten on the
spot" (p. 68). What is merely a matter of degree for bananas becomes an imperative for books: their single best meaning is given
by the readers to whom they were initially addressed. The sketch
of French literary history to which Sartre devotes the middle of his
third chapter illustrates his argument, since he picks out several
major historical periods, each characterized by a particular relationship between authors and readers: the Middle Ages, the classical period, the eighteenth century, and so on—and he stresses

how much the literature of each period owes to the author-reader relationship.

This outcome is somehow disappointing. Not because Sartre's analyses are—of necessity—incomplete and sketchy: that is unavoidable in a programmatic text. Nor is it because the facts his analyses disclose are nonexistent. Quite the contrary: literary works *are* determined by the expectations of their public, and we know that Sartre's suggestion in this area has been amply exploited in the context of the "aesthetics of reception" that has flourished during the last twenty years or so in Germany. But because, within this perspective of historical determinism, all cats are gray (or worse, one finds nothing but cats): all writers are subject to the same historical pressures, since they are writing for the same public. The immediate experience of literature causes us to perceive an enormous difference between one contemporary writer and another; yet the conceptual framework Sartre proposes does not allow us to distinguish between Flaubert and the Goncourt brothers. Sartre's initial premise is that literature is a place of interaction—between the particular situation and universal freedom. In the end, however, the image is impoverished: the universal dimension has been lost along the way. A historical conception of literature rejoins Romantic relativism, and the vast difference that was supposed to separate prose from poetry is finally reduced to very little, since in both realms immanence reigns, varying merely in kind: it is aesthetic in the one case, historical in the other.

Sartre himself senses the danger, and attempts to ward it off in the pages that follow his brief history of literature: "If one were to see in it an attempt, even superficial, at sociological explanation, it would lose all significance" (p. 144). He comes back to the dialectical requirement he began with: his goal, he says, was "to discover at the end, be it as ideal, the pure essence of the literary work —that is, of society—which it requires" (p. 146). "*Being situated* is an essential and necessary characteristic of freedom. To describe the situation is not to cast aspersion on the freedom" (pp. 144-145). That, however, is exactly what happens, and Sartre's statements do no more than beg the question. Freedom and essence have strayed along the way; we are left with the situation and society alone, and that is little indeed. Or rather, Sartre has skillfully dissimulated these agencies of the universal so as to bring them forth all over again, like a magician, and turn them into the prize for a race that is far from over: "*actual* literature can only realize its full *essence* in a classless society" (p. 150). Meanwhile, in our imperfect world, "whether he identifies himself with the Good and with divine Perfection, with the Beautiful or the True, a clerk [hence a writer, an intellectual] is always on the side of the oppressors. A watchdog or a jester: it is up to him to choose" (p. 151). A sad choice, indeed: but also a disappointing outcome for so much effort.

If literature can achieve its own essence only in a classless society, whereas in the real world it is entirely "situated," we shall have accepted a pitiful gift, though it was accompanied by a wonderful promise: here we recognize an ideological structure characteristic of societies where socialism is actually practiced. Yet literature, as we feel intuitively, brings us at every moment to experience *both* its particular historical grounding *and* its universal aspiration; it is liberty *at the same time as* determinism; and it is this intuition that we should like to be able to explain and make more explicit, instead of coddling ourselves with para-Marxist utopias.

Starting from an accurate observation about the reader's significance, how could Sartre have arrived at such a disappointing conclusion? If we compare his ideas with those of Bakhtin—a critic who turns out to be akin to Sartre in many respects, as we shall see—we may find an answer. Bakhtin too continually stresses the reader's role, seeing the reader and author as sharing equal responsibility for determining the meaning of a text: not because the reader may willfully project any meaning whatsoever—that is a kind of careless freedom that it would be wrong to set up as a rule—but because the author writes with a reader in mind, anticipating his reaction, and because he himself is a reader of his predecessors. However, alongside this particular and historical addressee, Bakhtin says, the author imagines another, a "superaddressee" whose comprehension is one hundred percent accurate; this is a reader with no limitations whatsoever:

> The author can never give himself over wholly—himself and his entire verbal production—to the total and *definitive* will of the present or proximate addressees (close descendants may also be mistaken), and he always imagines (more or less consciously) a sort of higher instance of responding comprehension. . . . This derives from the nature of discourse, which always desires to be *heard*, which always

seeks a responding comprehension, and is not satisfied with the *most immediate* comprehension but opens up a path into the farthest (limitless) distance. [*Estetika* . . . , p. 306]

Might it not be his failure to reckon with the "superaddressee" that led Sartre to the historicist conclusions of *What Is Literature?*

Sartre himself may have felt a certain dissatisfaction with his argument, for the works he devoted to literature are not servile illustrations of the original program, to say the least. We are concerned here with four books (and a certain number of articles): *Baudelaire* (1947), *Saint Genet comédien et martyr* (1952), *Les Mots* (completed in 1954, published in 1963), and *L'Idiot de la famille* (three volumes published in 1971 and 1972). The very subjects of these books are suggestive: here we have four writers (Baudelaire, Genet, Sartre himself, and Flaubert), and not four publics; the reader remains present in Sartre's analyses, but no longer as a real historical reader existing outside the book; instead, we find an imagined reader, a reader constructed by each author, thus a reader internal to the author's work. In these books, we remain resolutely on the side of the writer.

This is true to such an extent that we might hesitate to include the texts in question in the category of "criticism": we are dealing with "existential" biographies that, in two cases (Sartre's and Flaubert's), stop short of reckoning with literary creation as such. This, moreover, is Sartre's explicit intention. As the opening sentences of *The Family Idiot* state: "Its subject: what, at this point in time, can we know about a man? It seemed to me that this question could only be answered by studying a specific case. What do we know, for example, about Gustave Flaubert?" (p. ix). There is an undeniably provocative element in the phrase "for example"; but what interests Sartre is indeed the man, not the writer. Sartre's project in *Saint Genet* was the same: to "account for a person in his totality" (p. 584), and the last sentence of the book on Baudelaire asserts that "the quasi-abstract circumstances of the experiment enabled him to bear witness with unequalled éclat to this truth—the free choice which a man makes of himself is completely identified with what is called his destiny" (p. 192). Thus Baudelaire is merely the witness—a particularly eloquent one, to be sure—of a general human truth; literature does not have much of a role to play in all this.

And yet, in all four cases, we do have writers; the choice cannot have been completely fortuitous. The thesis Sartre defends in his biographies is linked with part of the problematics of *What Is Literature?*: it has to do with the relationship between freedom and determinism, and if in his programmatic work Sartre was leaning, almost reluctantly, toward determinism, here, as if to show all the more clearly that he did not mean it, he is invoking the principle of freedom. This is why the public is no longer at issue, and this is why "man's destiny" is identified with the free choice he makes. This, too, can be seen as the intention underlying *Saint Genet*: "to indicate the limit of psychoanalytical interpretation and Marxist explanation," that is, of causal analyses; "to learn the choice that a writer makes of himself," "to review in detail the history of his liberation" (p. 584).

Life is freedom, then, and not fatality. But what about texts? Sartre does not meet the question head on, but his whole undertaking bears witness to his stance. Confronted with literary works (what else can we look at, in Baudelaire's case or Flaubert's? why else would we choose these "examples," these "witnesses"?), Sartre analyzes lives, writes biographies: one can hardly help thinking that only a causal relationship between the works and the authors' lives can justify such a choice. And so we find determinism, repudiated in one place, returning full strength in another, and with it the historicist explanation of literature, and the relativism of the modern era. The refusal to attend to "atemporal messages" proclaimed in the first chapter of *What Is Literature?* was in no way feigned.

In *Saint Genet*, a long footnote (itself encumbered with two more notes) spells out Sartre's ideas about criticism. Criticism is objective rather than subjective. By this we are given to understand that, even though the critic may project his own personality onto the work studied (and thus also onto its epoch, its milieu, and so on), he submits in the end to an object that exists outside himself:

Although objectivity is, to a certain extent, distorted, it is also *revealed*. . . . No doubt the critic can "force" Mallarmé, can use him for his own purposes; that is precisely proof that he can also shed light on his objective reality. . . . In a *good* critical work, we will find a good deal of information about the author who is being criticized and some information about the critic. . . . The value of objectivity must be restored in order to dispose of the subjectivist banalities that always try to beg the question. [P. 563]

Objectivity, hence independence of the (critic's) context, hence antihistoricism. But what objectivity is at stake? The two footnotes to the footnote offer two very different examples. The first cites an instance of "historical truth": "Descartes wrote the *Discourse on Method*" (ibid.). That is an objective truth, but there is nothing absolute (Sartre says "eternal") about it: it is a factual truth, a mere preliminary to the critic's work, which begins, properly speaking, only with interpretation. The second note offers a much more interesting example of the rejection of subjectivism: "'I disapprove of the death penalty,' said Clemenceau. To which Barrès, who was fond of the guillotine, replied: 'Of course. Monsieur Clemenceau can't bear the sight of blood'" (ibid.) The condemnation of the death penalty has an objectivity of a totally different sort: it cannot be true with respect to facts, but it aspires to universal justice; and it is clearly fallacious to reduce it to the expression of a personal inclination.

But this sort of objectivity is rare in Sartre's work. In his critical thinking he is on Barrès's side rather than Clemenceau's. Otherwise, of what interest would it be to know that the artist is "always on the side of the oppressors"? Why point out, after noting that critics insist on "messages," that "the critic lives badly; his wife does not appreciate him as she ought to; his children are ungrateful; the first of the month is hard on him" (*What Is Literature?*, p. 22). Why, in order to understand Flaubert and Baudelaire, Genet and Sartre, must one write their biographies, if not because the meaning of their works, far from being objective and universal, like the rejection of the death penalty, depends—like Clemenceau's opinions, according to Barrès—upon their individual inclinations?

Let us not confuse two different meanings of the subjective/objective opposition. The one Sartre is thinking about in the Barrès anecdote is close to the opposition between the particular and the universal: reducible to circumstances, or connected with the absolute. But in another passage he identifies the subject with will (and freedom), the object with submission (and determinism); the subject is I myself, the object is the other, so long as I have not granted him a dignity equal to my own, so long as I do not let him speak. "I am a subject to myself exactly insofar as my fellow man is an object to me. . . . A leader is never [an object] to his subordinates; if he is, he loses his authority. He is rarely a subject to his superiors" (*Saint Genet*, pp. 590-591). Now in speaking of criticism, Sartre slips imperceptibly from the first meaning to the second: "Man is an object for man," he writes in an argument against critical subjectivity (p. 563).

And from this point of view, Sartre's critique is quite objective (whereas it remained subjective in the first sense of the term, since it was in conformity with the Barrès argument). Between Sartre and Genet, between Sartre and Baudelaire or Flaubert, there is no dialogue; on the one hand there is Sartre who speaks, who identifies himself with universal truth (since each particular case illustrates it: Baudelaire and Genet each chose his own life), who surveys his author and encapsulates him totally, transforms him, literally speaking, into an object. Someone pointed out to Sartre that, in the case of Genet, it is a way of assimilating the living to the dead. He protested: "Why should *I* want to bury him? He doesn't bother me" (p. 574). Genet may have felt the blow, but he survived. Yet is tolerance ("he doesn't bother me") enough? On the other hand, indeed, there are authors deprived of a voice, authors whose works are reduced to historical subjectivity and at the same time to the objective status of things. These others are deprived of their capacity to rise above the singularity of their situation; Sartre himself intervenes only as the bearer of impersonal truth. If the subject-object relation is indeed hierarchichal, by what right can the critic, this general of a defunct army, claim superiority?

But for dialogue to be possible, one would have to believe in the legitimacy of the shared search for truth. Now for Sartre, in anticipation of the classless society, either truth is an indisputable dogma (the dogma of existential philosophy, always stated in a peremptory tone, even though the content of the statements may change from one text to another), or else it is particular, relative to a context, to a biography, to a milieu. Sartre moves without transition from dogmatism to skepticism, never pausing along the way, always imprisoned within his own monologue.

It is only fair to add at this point, however, that Sartre's books cannot be reduced to the ideas that they convey. This observation itself gives us an initial way of describing the surplus of meaning: his books make the distinction between ideas and works a necessary one, when we are dealing with critical texts. It is not simply that Sartre's texts are, as it were, "well written." That much is perfectly obvious, and can be attributed not only to the facility of his discourse but also to his felicitous use of metaphor ("his sentence surrounds the object, seizes it, immobilizes it and breaks its back, changes into stone and petrifies the object as well" [*What Is Literature?*, p. 124]) and the vigor of his polemical thrusts ("there is something in common, and it is not talent, between Joseph de Maistre and M. Garaudy. . . . M. Garaudy . . . accuses me of being a gravedigger. . . . I'd rather be a gravedigger than a lackey" [pp. 251, 258]). Of course, these stylistic fireworks should not have sufficed to change the status of the ideas; however, that is exactly what has happened. Sartre's novels have been criticized for being too philosophical; fortunately, his critical writings are close to being novels. Not that novelistic writing is intrinsically superior to any other; but, perhaps unwittingly, Sartre modifies our perception of the critical genre (and, by the same token, of all knowledge of human creations). His own description of the genre as an objectivity mixed with some subjectivity is clearly somewhat insufficient; otherwise, why does he write these books in hitherto unused forms? *Baudelaire* may still qualify as an essay, and *The Words* may be almost an autobiography; but what about *Saint Genet*? Sartre is asked to write a preface: he returns with an enormous volume, in which he produces a novel along with stylistic analyses and meditations on otherness. He is taking an obvious (formal) risk here, one that would be incomprehensible if that form, or rather the impossibility of getting along without it, had no meaning. The same can be said for *The Family Idiot*, except that here Sartre has (in my view) lost his wager: the project is smothered by its own hypertrophy, and the book, though not unreadable, is not read. But losing is possible only for one who has been willing to take the risk.

I have no intention of suggesting that Sartre's sentences must be savored "for themselves," as he thought poetry ought to be enjoyed (that would be a "Romantic" vision of criticism). Rather, what I mean is this: Sartre discovered, more in practice than in theory, that in knowledge of man and his works, the "form" taken by our search is inseparable from the search itself. Sartre's metaphorical style, too, is a necessity, not an ornament. *Saint Genet* is only a book of criticism, and yet to read it is an adventure: that is the mystery. Why it is so, what this bridge thrown across the gulf between "prose" and "criticism" means, we do not yet know; but it is certain that, through the often subterranean influence exercised by Sartre's books (rather than his ideas), our entire image of criticism has been profoundly altered.

II

Blanchot's critical work is so brilliant that it ends up posing a problem. His statements, at once limpid and mysterious, exercise an undeniable attraction. Nevertheless, the ultimate effect is paralyzing: any attempt to interpret Blanchot in a language other than his own seems to be impeded by an unspoken taboo. The alternative that remains open seems to be a choice between silent admiration (stupor) or imitation (paraphrase, plagiarism). A 1966 issue of the journal *Critique* devoted to Blanchot's work provides a good illustration of the second variant (with two exceptions, the articles by Georges Poulet and Paul de Man). It is Blanchot once again who seems to write, with Michel Foucault's pen: "the invincible absence," "the emptiness that serves as its space," "law without law of the world," "real presence, absolutely remote, glittering, invisible" (pp. 526-527), or in Françoise Collin's text: "silence is speech, memory forgetfulness, truth error" (p. 562), or Jean Pfeiffer's: "nowhere is indeed in some way at the bottom of this bottomless space" (p. 577). Some admit it outright: "This commentary is, I fear, only a sort of paraphrase. . . . It is difficult to speak of Blanchot without succumbing to a strange fascination, without being captivated by the writer's own voice" (Jean Starobinski, p. 513). "All has to be said here in the mode of 'perhaps,' as Blanchot himself speaks" (Emmanuel Lévinas, p. 514). Paraphrase or silence: one or the other of these fates seems to befall all who try to comprehend Blanchot. A beautifully worded passage by Roger Laporte recommends the second attitude even as it practices the first:

After all the books are closed, if one asks oneself the question: "but what is Blanchot's work really about?", one senses that it is impossible to answer, that the question has no answer. A speech speaks, but it says nothing, it only speaks; an empty speech, but not the speech of emptiness, it shows nothing, but it designates, and thus through this very speech the unknown reveals itself and remains unknown. [Pp. 589-590]

On the heels of these implicit or explicit injunctions, it feels wrong from the start to try to break through the "strange fascination" and find out exactly what Blanchot said about literature and criticism. Language is a common good, however, its words and syntax have a meaning that is not at all individual. Poetry is said to be untranslatable, but thought is not; now in the thousands of pages of criticism published under that name, there must be something of Blanchot's thought. I am thus going to take on the thankless role of spokesman for the naive and attempt to translate into my own terms those words which say nothing.

Blanchot's reflections on literature grow out of a commentary on a few passages by Mallarmé, passages invoked throughout Blanchot's work.

Mallarmé wrote of the "dual state of speech, here raw or immediate, there essential"; and Blanchot comments:

> On the one hand, useful speech, instrument and means, the language of action, work, logic, and knowledge, language that transmits directly and that, like every good tool, disappears under the habitualness of its use. On the other hand, the speech of poems and literature, where speaking is no longer a transitory, subordinate, and customary means, but seeks to realize itself in a unique experience. [*Le Livre à venir*, 1959, p. 247]

The words of everyday language are "usual, useful"; we are "used" to them. Through them "we are in the world; [they] refer us back to the life of the world where goals speak and the concern to achieve them once and for all is the rule. . . . In this respect the essential word is exactly the opposite. It is a rule unto itself; it is imposing, but it imposes nothing" (*The Space of Literature*, 1982 [1955], p. 40). In poetry, words "are not to serve to designate anything nor to give voice to anyone, but . . . they have their ends in themselves" (ibid., p. 41).

Poetic discourse is an intransitive, nonsubservient discourse; it does not signify; it is. The essence of poetry lies in the search it conducts into its own origin. These are the commonplace Romantic ideas that Blanchot reads in Mallarmé and that preside over the doctrine he presents in *The Space of Literature* and in *Le Livre à venir*.

Blanchot's thought is modeled here on a historical schema that is Hegelian in inspiration. For two centuries art has been undergoing a double transformation: it has lost its capacity to convey the absolute, to be sovereign; but the loss of that external function is made up for, as it were, by a new internal function. Art is moving closer and closer to its own essence. Now the essence of art is, tautologically, art itself, or rather the very possibility of artistic creation, interrogation as to the place from which art arises (in this respect, the idea is still related to the Romantic doctrine that valorizes, in art, its production and its becoming). Blanchot's key words are thus those denoting origin, beginning, search. It is only in our own day that art, after having been divine and human, but being so no longer, becomes that obstinate quest for its own origin. Today,

> what art wants to affirm is art. What it seeks, what it attempts to achieve, is the essence of art. . . . This is a tendency which can be interpreted in many different ways, but it forcefully reveals a movement which, in varying degrees and along diverse paths, draws all the arts toward themselves, concentrates them upon the concern for their own essence, renders them present and essential. [*The Space of Literature*, pp. 219-220]

All genuinely modern writers, all those who make up Blanchot's pantheon, are characterized by precisely this feature. Hölderlin, Joubert, Valéry, Hofmannsthal, Rilke, Proust, Joyce, Mann, Broch, Kafka, Beckett, abruptly linked, like the contemporaries Sartre evokes, make a single claim; pathetically undifferentiated, they repeat that art is a search for the origin of art.

What is striking in this schema is not only its extreme empirical fragility, which exceeds even that of Sartre's proposed literary history, but also that other decidedly Hegelian feature, the exorbitant privilege accorded to the present. A privilege that Blanchot defends openly and unquestioningly: today, he writes, art appears "for the first time as a search in which something essential is at stake" (p. 220), and elsewhere: "Today we are manifestly facing a much more important change [than the French Revolution], in which all the earlier upheavals join together, from all historical moments, to bring about a break in history" (*L'Entretien infini*, 1969, pp. 394-395). The present moment is the culminating point of our entire history, and thus the moment in which history is abolished.

The intransivity of discourse, the literary work focused on its own origin, perhaps these are the characteristics of a specific literary production, during a given period, in Western Europe; they are characteristics of a culture to which Blanchot belongs. But why does Blanchot, fond as he is of declaring the necessity of recognizing the other, turn his gaze exclusively upon figures cast in his own image? Examples contradicting this description of literature are so abundant and ready to hand that there is hardly any need to cite them. Why does he not notice that, while he was declaring the novel "an art with no future," under other skies, or even the same ones, the novel was about to undergo new and surprising transformations, placing it far from intransitive discourse as well as from a pure quest for its own origin? We can only say that Blanchot's own work bears witness, implicitly, to the acceptance of that ideal and no other, since his work itself becomes intransitive discourse, a question tirelessly pursued but never resolved; explicitly, it declares that we (but who are "we"? Westerners? Europeans? Parisians?) are the ultimate, unsurpassable moment of history. Even supposing that Blanchot's description of our time may be faithful, why must the present be the supreme moment? Is there not an inkling here of what child psychologists call the "egocentric illusion"?

Blanchot did not rest content with practicing criticism and with discussing it casually here and there, he also devoted a brief text exclusively to its definition: "Qu'en est-il de la critique?" appeared at the beginning of his *Lautréamont et Sade* (1963, reprinted 1967). He starts from what he considers self-evident: the ideal commentary is one that makes itself invisible, sacrificing itself on the altar of the comprehension of the work. One might suppose that such an experience implies a radical discontinuity between literature and criticism—the one being assertive, the other self-effacing—and forbids the critic to assume a voice that would be his own. The experience is presumably common to Blanchot and the historical criticism of the early part of the century (Lanson: "We wish to be forgotten, we want Montaigne and Rousseau alone to be seen"), along with the "scientific" descriptions produced in our day, in which all subjectivity is purportedly eliminated once formulas have supplanted words. If there are differences among these ideals, they lie only in the elegance with which Blanchot expresses himself: he says, for example, that criticism is like the snow that sets up vibrations in bells as it falls; that it must efface itself, disappear, fade away. The critic "does nothing, nothing except allow the work's profundity to speak" (p. 10). "Critical discourse, without duration, without reality, would wish to fade away in the face of the creative affirmation: critical discourse is never speaking itself when it speaks" (p. 111).

But though he espouses the same "immanent" and "Romantic" ideal as historians or "scientists," Blanchot does not see criticism as radically distinct from literature; quite the contrary. He is not content to write books of criticism that are as fine as novels, as Sartre does; Blanchot also has a theory about the continuity between the two. If his point of departure is identical to that of the other "immanentists," whereas the outcome is totally different, this is because his idea of literature is also radically other. For the "immanentists," there is no problem: Rousseau "means" something, and that is what is to be found; or in any event *La Nouvelle Héloïse* has a structure that may be described. Now for Blanchot, as we have seen, a literary work is only a search for itself. It is not something that would reveal a plenitude of meanings, as soon as the critic effaces himself; rather, it is itself an effacing, a "movement of disappearance" (p. 12). The work's statements are illusory, its truth is the absence of all concern with truth; such concern is replaced by a quest for the work's own origin. Literature and criticism come together in this movement: like the work, "criticism is tied to the search for the possibility of the literary experience," and therefore, "by virtue of disappearing in the face of the work, it grasps itself in the work, and as one of its essential moments" (pp. 13-14).

Unless one shares Blanchot's conception of literature, it is not possible to write, as he does: "criticism—literature—seems to me . . ." (p. 15). But even without going that far, it is possible to maintain his description of the critical act as being entirely immanent to the work analyzed, and this may become the basis for another requirement addressed to literary criticism, namely, that it renounce all transcendance and thus all reference to values (a requirement that Blanchot again shares with the project of historicism and that of structuralism). With Blanchot, nonetheless, the two are closely connected: it is because the novel or the poem "seeks to declare itself apart from all values" "that it escapes from all value systems"

(p. 14); and because criticism must be like literature, it is assigned this project: it must be "associated with one of the most difficult but also most important tasks of our time . . . : the task of preserving and liberating thought from the notion of value" (p. 15).

This sentence leaves me wondering (I am supposing, of course, that Blanchot's sentences say something rather than nothing; but I see no reason to doubt that, under the circumstances). It is a fact that "the" established values have been challenged in our time. One may consider this state of affairs irreversible and give in to helplessness; or one may attempt to swim against the tide and seek new values in which it would be possible to believe. There is nothing difficult about the destruction of values: it happens every day before our very eyes. But to conceive of values as tyrants from which thought must be liberated, and to make that liberation the most important task of criticism and literature, is to set forth a most singular ideal.

Blanchot's writing itself confirms at every point this concern with liberating "thought" from all reference to values and to truth —from all thought, one might say. It has often been said of Blanchot that his "I speak" is a way of rejecting any "I think." His favorite figure of speech is the oxymoron, the simultaneous assertion of contraries. "Literature may create itself by maintaining itself in a perpetual state of lack," it is "depth and also the absence of depth," he writes here (pp. 13, 14), and elsewhere (in *Le Livre à venir*): "an empty fullness" (p. 16), "emptiness as plenitude" (p. 30), "a space without place" (p. 100), "an immense face that is seen and unseen" (p. 105), "the unaccomplished accomplishment," (p. 176), "yet the same is not the same as the same" (p. 271), and so on and on without end (as we saw, this is the easiest way to write *à la* Blanchot). But to assert simultaneously A and not-A is to call into question the assertive dimension of language and in effect to maintain a discourse beyond true and false, beyond good and evil.

For it is clear that the "values" Blanchot attacks are not aesthetic values alone; he does not simply ask criticism to give up establishing prize lists; if that were the issue, it would not be "one of the most important tasks of our time." This nihilism reveals its ideological roots even more clearly when Blanchot proposes to replace reference to truth and values with "an entirely different sort . . . of affirmation" (p. 15). There is nothing particularly new about this demand: it derives from the Nietzschean tradition, and beyond that, the Sadean one, which valorizes force at the expense of law (Sade and Nietzsche are two of Blanchot's favorite authors).

One may say anything and everything about literature, without ever shocking anyone: a poet is like a will-o'-the-wisp to whom all is permitted. But Blanchot's statements in this case transcend the framework of literature, and that is no doubt why I find them disturbing. In our era, after World War II, knowing what we know about the Nazis and the Gulag, we are discovering to our horror just how far humanity can go when it rejects universal values and sets up the assertion of force in their stead. Blanchot chooses this moment in history to declare not only that we are not to regret the destruction of values, but also that literature and criticism must be enlisted in the noble task of trampling them further into the dust.

I will be told that I am introducing political considerations where only harmless matters are at stake, such as literature. But the transition has already been made in Blanchot's work. As we know, before the war Blanchot became the spokesman for a certain anti-Semitism. He changed his mind later on, and that is not what I am reproaching him for here. But it is in the postwar epoch that he would have us commit ourselves to the struggle against values. The revelation of the Nazi horrors did not shake his conviction, even though Blanchot speaks elsewhere with strength and gravity of the extermination camps: his immediate affective reactions have no effect on his principles. Other texts show Blanchot singularly tolerant with respect to Soviet totalitarianism: conscious of the continuity between the "death of philosophy" that he cherishes and the October Revolution, he prefers to accept the latter rather than give up the former: "The October Revolution is not only the epiphany of the philosophical logos, its apotheosis or its apocalypse. It is its realization and thus its destruction. . . . For a century and a half, under its own name or Hegel's, Nietzsche's, or Heidegger's, it is philosophy itself that declares or brings about its own end" (*L'Amitié*, pp. 102-103).[1]

And in the same spirit of the renunciation of universal values Blanchot calls Jaspers to task for placing the nuclear threat and the totalitarian threat on the same plane. "Where liberal philosophers

---

[1]Once does not make a habit, so I shall allow myself to refer, on this question of the "death of philosophy" and some related issues, to a recent article by Luc Ferry and Alain Renaut, "Philosopher après la fin de la philosophie?" in *Le Débat*, 28 (1984), 137–154.

—and many others with them—speak of totalitarianism, without having examined the issue critically, others—and they too have many followers—speak about liberation and the realization of human community as a whole" (ibid., pp. 121-122). Having repudiated the "old values" (p. 122), Blanchot sends the defenders and the opponents of totalitarianism off to fight it out among themselves. In the absence of any universal standard, it boils down to a simple question of point of view: some people speak one way, some another (let us overlook the fact that for Blanchot the inhabitants of the Soviet world all speak according to the official ideology, whereas Jaspers—still according to Blanchot—must have issued his condemnations only because the examination he undertook was not truly critical!).

Such, then, is the political side of Blanchot's literary theory; accepting the latter requires us also to swallow the former. Relativist and nihilist ideology reaches a culmination of sorts in Blanchot, and his texts, far from saying nothing at all, say openly what might have remained implicit elsewhere; they are not obscure, they are obscurantist. Blanchot is indeed an example of the critic-as-writer, but of a type that, for me, already belongs to the past.

III

A personal relationship linked me with Roland Barthes while he was alive, and it did not end with his death. I cannot claim even the illusion of impartiality if I am to speak of him. Not only will I be irresistibly tempted to suppress anything in him that does not suit me and to valorize the ways in which he is close to me, but I cannot find in myself the necessary strengths that would allow me to see him as a closed entity capable of being completely circumscribed, an object, as Genet had become for Sartre. So I shall not deal with Roland Barthes in the pages that follow, but with "my" Barthes.

I do not believe that this partiality prevents me from seeing all that derives, in his writings, from the "Romantic" syndrome and thus falls outside the scope of the present inquiry. I shall refer to these areas only briefly, for the record. His definition of literature, in particular, maintains two of the characteristics that the Romantics attributed to it, intransitivity and plurality of meanings.

Barthes may have gotten the idea of intransitivity from Sartre, but he extended it to literature as a whole, instead of limiting it to poetry: "The literary act . . . is an absolutely intransitive act"; "for the author, *to write* is an intransitive verb" (*Critical Essays*, pp. 135, 145); intransitivity is the basis for the opposition between writers and scribblers (poetry/prose for Sartre, already poetry/scribbling for Döblin). Ambiguity, plurality of meanings, infinite interpretations, these are modern commonplaces whose precise itinerary is hard to follow; for Barthes, this aspect of literature establishes the oppositions between readable and writable, between work and text (the second term is always the one valorized). "The Text is plural. This does not mean only that it has several meanings but that it fulfills the very plurality of meaning: an *irreducible* (and not just acceptable) plural" ("From Work to Text," in *The Rustle of Language*, p. 59).

His view of criticism, as found for example in a short essay entitled "What Is Criticism?" (reprinted in *Critical Essays*, pp. 255-260), is likewise purely "Romantic." Spinoza wanted the question of truth to be abandoned entirely in favor of meaning. Barthes takes a step further in the same direction: the critic's task is "not the decipherment of the work's meaning but the reconstruction of the rules and constraints of that meaning's elaboration" (p. 259); "the critic is not responsible for reconstructing the work's message but only its system" (p. 260); the critical task is "purely formal" (p. 258): strange vows of poverty. As for truth, it is rejected in all senses. On the one hand, on the basis of an erroneous association of criticism and logic (erroneous since only the former has an empirical object), Barthes declares that criticism must settle for "validity" alone, internal coherence without reference to meaning. His explicit model for criticism is language; but although language taken as a whole is neither true nor false, each individual utterance may be one or the other. And so it is with criticism, for which the implicit model is not in fact language, but a game: a system of rules that lacks any meaning. On the other hand, supposing that the only truth with which literature itself has to deal is a truth of equivalence (Proust's Charlus is the Count of Montesquiou), he rejects this truth and considers it of no relevance to criticism. He is right, of course; but then literature has never aspired to this kind of truth, and Proust's novel is "true" in a completely different sense of the word (one which Spinoza may have had in mind when he speculated about the truth of the Bible). Barthes takes the current coexistence of diverse ideologies and viewpoints as a sufficient reason for criticism to give up speaking "in the name of 'true' principles" once and for all (p. 257). Thus he combines a radical historicism (there is no general truth, there are only provisional ideologies) with a lack of interest in history: he knows that, in his case, critical dialogue "is egotistically shifted toward the present" (p. 260).

Finally, though Barthes is rarely concerned with more general principles, it comes as no surprise to find him defending not only relativism but individualism, and his defense is explicit, however questionable it may be in historical terms:

> For two hundred years, we have been conditioned by philosophical and political culture to valorize collectivity in general. All philosophies are philosophies of collectivity, of society, and individualism is frowned upon. . . . One should not be intimidated by this morality of the collective superego, so widespread in our society with its values of responsibility and political engagement. One should perhaps accept the scandal of individualist positions. [*The Grain of the Voice*, p. 311]

Individualism, however, has not scandalized anyone for ages; it is even our "dominant ideology"! Just as Sade and Nietzsche, authors cherished by Barthes as well as Blanchot, have long since stopped appearing scandalous.

We may as well admit it: this whole set of ideas is indeed present in Barthes's writings. But it is not only my feeling for Barthes as a person that convinces me they must not be overemphasized. There is also the status that ideas have in Barthes's discourse. Although within a given text one might take these passages as the expression of his thought, the set of texts as a whole reveals that this cannot be, since one sees Barthes constantly changing position: it suffices that he has formulated an idea for him to lose interest in it; and it becomes obvious that his constant shifts cannot be written off to frivolity but have to be attributed to a particular attitude toward ideas. Like a writer-for-hire, Barthes is concerned with finding the best formulation for each idea, but that does not lead him to espouse it. Moreover, he described himself reliably in his *Roland Barthes*: his writing is a "theft of language" (pp. 92, 138); "in relation to the systems which surround him, what is he? Say an echo chamber: he reproduces the thoughts badly, he follows the words"

(p. 74). And he adds the following sentence, which also appears on the jacket flap of his book: "All this must be considered as if spoken by a character in a novel—or rather by several characters" (p. 119).

The word "novel" is not here by chance. In fact the status of fiction is what these unespoused ideas call to mind: the author has his characters speak without identifying personally with what they are saying. Barthes's text differs from a novel in two ways. First, at the time its statements were uttered, its characters were invisible (readers had to wait for 1975, and *Roland Barthes*, in order to have it from Barthes himself that he did not believe in them; nothing in "What Is Criticism?" indicates that he does not adhere to what he is declaring, that it was merely a question of "thefts of language"). Second, rather than making everyday statements, his characters give voice to theoretical discourse, using the language of mastery for which the dimension of truth is what matters most. Barthes can thus say of himself: "For my part, I do not see myself as a critic, but rather as a novelist, one who crafts not novels, to be sure, but the 'novelesque'" ("Réponses," p. 102); and in *Roland Barthes* he is still more specific: "Let the essay avow itself *almost* a novel: a novel without proper names" (p. 120). As utterances, the essay and the novel diverge; the one refers to the world of individuals, the other does not; but they are alike in the mode of their enunciation: in both cases there is discourse not assumed by its author—there is a fiction.

Barthes thus rejoins the other writer-critics, and he does so not only through the qualities of his style, but also because he brackets the truth value of criticism, and because he insists, on the contrary, on its fictional or poetic aspect (language ceases to be an instrument and becomes a problem). This is even, in his eyes, the distinctive feature of contemporary criticism: "If the new criticism has any reality, it lies here: . . . in the solitude of the critical act, which is henceforth declared to be an act of authentic writing, far from the alibis of science or institutions" (*Critique et vérité*, 1966, pp. 46-47). And it is certain that Barthes's books challenge the tradition of the genre through their very form: who could have predicted *S/Z*, *Roland Barthes*, or *A Lover's Discourse: Fragments*? Scandalizing some, delighting others, Barthes's texts were those of a writer drawn by the vicissitudes of destiny to pursue his career in the world of ideas and knowledge.

If he had really written novels, the entire originality of the gesture would clearly have disappeared. Toward the end of his life, Barthes was planning to write a "true" novel, with descriptions and proper names. But we have no assurance that the project could ever have been completed: Barthes explained that he was experiencing a "tenacious desire to paint those I love" (*Prétexte: Roland Barthes*, 1978, p. 368), and that he was counting on novelistic writing to serve this end; but the very last text he completed bears a melancholy title: "On échoue toujours à parler de ce qu'on aime" (One always fails at talking about what one loves). However this may be, if he had written novels, Barthes would have been one more novelist among others, just as, when he does recount his own life, in *Camera lucida*, he becomes one more autobiographer or memoir writer among others (although one of the best): there is no formal invention. Barthes's originality depends upon an *almost*, it lies entirely in the transition between the two genres.

I do not share Barthes's attitude with respect to truth: literature already has a relationship with truth, and criticism has more than one. I subscribe, however, to the idea that the result of critical activity is a *book*, and that this fact is fundamental. Observation or the formulation of general laws may be nothing more than the utterance of a state of affairs; but the work of interpretation, although it depends upon knowledge, cannot be reduced to it. Interpretation is the (re)construction of a unique whole: whether a book of history, or ethnology, or literary criticism (not to mention all the mixed genres), this construction makes up a part of the very statement one is making about the object under analysis. Readers in the social sciences and humanities may well be justified when they forget the ideas but remember the books (although this choice of target is not entirely fair).

Barthes's challenge to this discourse of mastery has had a refreshing effect in the atmosphere of arrogance and one-upmanship that characterizes the intellectual community. But beyond this prophylactic and basically negative effect, we may legitimately wonder about the meaning of this rejection of discourse that has truth as its horizon. Is it anything but adherence to generalized relativism? Barthes himself sought in particular to see in it a reflection of the internal dispersion of the individual; it is a modern variant of Montaigne's adage: "Man is nothing but scraps and patches, through and through." We have seen Brecht valorize the presence of two voices in a single subject, whatever the nature of those voices may be. Barthes, who always greatly admired Brecht, does not fail to invoke him when he is attempting to explain this plurality in his own case: "I would be so happy if these words of Brecht could be applied to me: 'He thought in the heads of others; and in his own, others than he were thinking.' That is true thought" (*The Grain of the Voice*, p. 195).

Recognizing others as oneself, recognizing the others in oneself, this is certainly a good point of departure for thought; but does it suffice? Is the other sufficiently defined by the eminently relative criterion of otherness? May I not also distinguish between the others that I approve of and those that I do not? If I think back over what I liked in Barthes, I do not find it in the statement that one heard, through his voice, the voices of others. I should be almost tempted to say the opposite: the best thing to be found in what was called "Barthes" (the life and the works) was Barthes himself. I see that he expressed a parallel idea: "Having reached this point in my life, at the end of a colloquium of which I was the pretext, I want to say that I have the impression, the feeling, and almost the certainty of having succeeded more in my friends than in my work" (*Prétexte*, p. 439). I shall be told that that has nothing to do with literary criticism. It does, though, for Barthes wrote about literature, unceasingly; thus I can say that the texts I value most today are those in which he is most present, though we have still not crossed over into the personal genre: I am speaking of *Roland Barthes*, a book that is at once intimate and public, subjective and objective (a book of criticism), the text, once again, of a transition.

Since the public and the private areas must be distinguished, let me add this: up to the publication of *Roland Barthes*, in 1975, I see Barthes as adhering fully, in his writings, to the idea of the dispersion of the subject, of the inauthenticity of being. The task of turning this dispersed subject into the object of a book led him to change, though there was nothing spectacular about the change: "I'm taking more responsibility for myself as a subject," he said (*The Grain of the Voice*, p. 337). In one of his courses, Barthes also said that one must choose between being a terrorist and being an egotist; it is this choice that accounts for the difference between the pre-1975 and post-1975 Barthes. What Barthes had been, until then, in his life and for his friends (a nonterrorist), he became also in his books; and he could write: "The playfulness of conflict, of jousting: I hate it. The French seem to love it: rugby, 'face-to-face,' round tables, bets, always stupid, etc." (*Prétexte*, p. 299). But this kind of egotism has nothing in common with the kind that had been more or less deliberately displayed in his previous criticism: instead of offering a pure discourse in his books (a type of discourse that always remains an injunction), he came to propose a being, his own. Rather than suggest how man is, he left—with uneven results, to be sure—each individual the freedom to choose his own position with regard to the proffered discourse. The risks (and the corresponding rewards) in saying "this is the way I am" are much greater than those that come from saying "others are thinking in me."

By the same token, the others—the ones that exist materially, outside Barthes's consciousness—receive their due perhaps more justly than when they were all expected to agree to a complicity that was imposed upon them. This is what Barthes himself expresses when he attempts to understand his suffering over his mother's death: "What I have lost is not a Figure (the Mother), but a being" (*Camera lucida*, p. 75). A human being is not the Other, nor the others; he or she is only himself, herself. To recognize the other's alterity (rather than continuing to say that "I" is an other or that the others are within me) is to recognize the other, period; it is to give up a little bit more of the egocentric illusion. So long as I take myself to be a pure echo chamber, the other exists only for me, undifferentiated; if "I assume myself as subject," I allow the other to do as much, thus I respect him. That is what I find, too, in the following passage in which Barthes describes his own evolution:

> Little by little, within myself, a growing desire for readability asserts itself. I want the texts I receive to be "readable," I want the texts I write to be the same. . . . I have a preposterous idea (preposterous in virtue of humanism): "No one will ever make it clear enough what love (for the other, for the reader) there is in the struggle with a sentence." [*Prétexte*, p. 301]

This preposterous humanism is something new in Barthes's writing (whereas it had always been present in his conversation), and I value it highly. In it I see, above and beyond the nihilist clichés that Barthes shared with his era, a groping for a new transcen-

dence, based not on the divine but on the social nature of humanity and the plurality of human beings. And I am moved to see that
the last words of the very last interview he gave, a few days before
his accidental death, dealt with this, even though somewhat awk-
wardly: "But despite everything, when one writes one scatters
seeds, one can imagine that one disseminates a kind of seed and
that, consequently, one returns to the general circulation of *se-
mences*" (*The Grain of the Voice*, p. 365).

5

Human and Interhuman:

Mikhail Bakhtin

Mikhail Bakhtin is one of the most fascinating and enigmatic figures in mid-twentieth-century European culture. The fascination is comprehensible enough: his work is rich and original, and the Soviets have produced nothing at all comparable in the area of the social sciences. But an element of perplexity slips in alongside this admiration, for an inevitable question arises: who is Bakhtin, and what are the distinguishing features of his thought? The truth is that his thought is so multifaceted that it is sometimes hard to believe we owe it all to one and the same person.

Bakhtin's work attracted public attention in 1963, with the appearance of a new and significantly revised edition of his 1929 work on Dostoevsky (a work that had caused a good deal of comment when it was first published). But this fascinating book, *Problems of Dostoevsky's Poetics*, is not unproblematic if one sets out to discover its unifying features. The text consists, overall, of three more or less autonomous parts. The first third is devoted to the presentation and illustration of a thesis concerning Dostoevsky's novelistic universe, expressed in philosophical and literary terms; the second explores several minor literary genres—the Socratic dialogues, the classical Menippean satire and the medieval carnival productions, all of which, for Bakhtin, constitute the generic tradition on which Dostoevsky drew; the final third of the book consists of a program of stylistic studies, illustrated by analyses of Dostoevsky's novels.

Then in 1965, Bakhtin's book on Rabelais appeared. This work could be seen as an expansion of the second part of his book on Dostoevsky (or, conversely, and more accurately, the latter could be taken as a condensed version of the former), but as such it has little relationship to the two other parts. On the one hand, Bakhtin now gives us a thematic rather than a stylistic analysis; on the other hand, we have a historical and descriptive work that leaves no room for the philosophical intuitions of *Dostoevsky*. The Rabelais book drew the attention of specialists toward phenomena such as popular culture and the *carnavalesque*.

In 1973, a thunderbolt fell: several authorized (Soviet) sources revealed that Bakhtin was the author, or at least the principal coauthor, of three books and several articles published under other names in the USSR toward the end of the nineteen-twenties. But this enrichment of the Bakhtinian bibliography inevitably increased the perplexity of his readers, who had already had difficulty grasping the relationship between his *Dostoevsky* and his *Rabelais*; the texts from the twenties spoke with yet another voice, that of a vigorous critique (sociological and Marxist in inspiration) of psychoanalysis, of linguistics (structuralist and otherwise), and of poetics as practiced by the Russian Formalists.

In 1975, the year he died, Bakhtin published a new volume entitled *The Dialogic Imagination*: the studies that compose it date for the most part from the nineteen-thirties. These studies turn out to extend the stylistic research of *Dostoevsky* and pave the way for the thematic study in *Rabelais* (the latter had actually been completed in 1940); thus they allow us to begin to orient ourselves within Bakhtin's work, as they bring to light the passage from his first major monograph to his second.

The final twist (so far): in 1979, Bakhtin's editors released another volume of previously unpublished work, under the title *Estetika slovesnogo tvorchestva* (The aesthetics of verbal creation). For the most part, it consists of Bakhtin's very *earliest* and *latest* writings: it presents a major work from his presociological period, plus notes and fragments written over the last twenty years of his life. The publication of this new collection clarifies many issues, but it also raises new ones, since to the assorted Bakhtins we already know we need to add one more, a phenomenological and perhaps "existentialist" Bakhtin. . . .

There is a problem, that much is certain: not how to impose an artificial, spurious unity on Bakhtin's thought, but how to make it intelligible, which is quite a different matter. In order to progress at all along these lines, we need to turn to history in an effort to answer the following question: how is Bakhtin to be situated with respect to the evolution of ideologies in the twentieth century?

At first glance, Bakhtin comes across as a theoretician and historian of literature. Now during the time he was making his entrance into Russian intellectual life, the center-stage position in literary investigations was held by the group of critics, linguists, and writers known as the Russian Formalists. The relations between Formalists and Marxists were uneasy, and the Formalist group was not dominant in the major institutions; however, its members had the advantage of talent, and their prestige was undeniable. In order to make a place for himself in the literary and aesthetic arguments of the day, Bakhtin thus had to take a stand vis-à-vis the Formalists. He did so twice: first, in 1924, in a lengthy article (published for the first time in *The Dialogic Imagination* in 1975), and later (1928) in the book entitled *The Formal Method in Literary Scholarship*, whose official author is Pavel N. Medvedev.

Bakhtin's first criticism of the Formalists is that they do not know what they are doing, that they fail to examine the theoretical and philosophical foundations of their own doctrine. It is not a question, here, of a chance omission: as we have seen, the Formalists, like all positivists, believe they are practicing science and seeking truth and forget they are relying upon arbitrary presuppositions. Bakhtin takes it upon himself to provide this clarification for them in order to raise the level of the discussion. The Formalist doctrine, he tells us, is an aesthetic of materiality, for it reduces the problems of poetic creation to questions of language: the reification of the notion of "poetic language" stems from this and in turn gives rise to the interest in "devices" of all sorts. This limitation leads the Formalists to neglect the other ingredients of the creative act, namely, content, or the relation with the world, and form, here understood as authorial intervention, as the choice made by a particular individual among the impersonal and general elements of language. The true central notion of aesthetic research must not be the material substance but the architectonics, or construction, or structure, of the work, understood as a meeting ground and place of interaction between material, form, and content.

Bakhtin thus criticizes not the opposition between art and non-art, between poetry and everyday language, but rather the way in which the Formalists attempt to locate this opposition. "The indices of the poetic do not belong to language and its elements, but only to poetic constructions," Medvedev writes (p. 86), and he adds, "The object of poetics must be the construction of the artistic work" (p. 103). But the poetic and the literary are defined in the same way as by the Formalists: in poetic creation, "the utterance is detached both from the object and from action. . . . The reality of the utterance itself serves no other reality" (p. 127).

Bakhtin's critique thus applies indeed to the Formalists but not to the framework of Romantic aesthetics from which their work derives. What he criticizes is not their "formalism" but their "materialism"; we might even suggest that he is more formalist than they, if we restore to the word "form" its full meaning of interaction and unity among the various elements of the work; it is that other meaning that Bakhtin is trying to revive, by introducing positively charged synonyms like "architectonics" and "construction." What he is criticizing is precisely the Formalists' non-Romantic side: the expression "aesthetics of the material" perfectly fits a program like the one Lessing develops in *Laocoön*, in which the properties of painting and poetry are deduced from their respective materials (media). Beyond Lessing, the Aristotelian tradition is evoked here, with its description of disembodied "devices" like figures and tropes, peripeteia and recognition, the parts and the elements of tragedy.

The Formalists' paradox, and their originality, as we have seen, was that they undertook to produce "classical" (Aristotelian) descriptions starting from Romantic ideological premises: Bakhtin reestablished the Romantic doctrine in all its purity. When Goethe contemplated the same sculptural group, the Laocoön, he was already putting into place notions of work, unity, and coherence as opposed to the general laws of painting and poetry dear to Lessing. We remain within the spirit of Schelling and his friends when we see the work of art as a fusion of the subjective and the objective, the singular and the universal, free will and compulsion, form and content. The Romantic aesthetic valorizes immanence, not transcendence; thus it takes very little interest in transtextual elements like metaphor, or dactylic rhyme, or devices of recognition. Bakhtin is right to criticize the Formalists for their ignorance of their own philosophy, and yet his philosophy has a very specific coloration: it is the philosophy of the Romantics. This is not, in itself, a flaw, but it does limit the originality of his position.

Let us not jump to conclusions, however. We are dealing, here, with two texts from the nineteen-twenties, and though Bakhtin never breaks his ties with the Romantic aesthetic (particularly in his theory of the novel), his thought is not limited to this aesthetic, far from it. Moreover, this very problematics of general aesthetic principles appears somewhat marginal in his work; at most it serves as a transition. Another theme, as we are only now discovering, was of central importance to Bakhtin starting in the early twenties, and he comes back to it over and over throughout his life. This theme is both more specific, for it concerns just a single aesthetic question, and more general, since it goes far beyond aesthetics as such: it is the theme of the relationship between the creator and his created beings, or, as Bakhtin puts it, between author and protagonist. This relationship is all the more worthy of study in that we discover in it—and the event is rare, in Bakhtin's long intellectual career—a spectacular reversal in his ideas on the subject.

His initial position is stated in his recently discovered early work, which is devoted specifically to that question. To summarize, it amounts to saying that a life finds its meaning, and thereby becomes a possible ingredient for aesthetic construction, only if it is seen from the outside, as a whole: it has to be entirely encompassed within someone else's horizon. For the character, that someone else is of course the author; Bakhtin refers to this position as the author's "exotopy." Aesthetic creation is thus a particularly well realized example of one type of human relationship, in which one individual completely engulfs another, thereby completing that other and endowing him with meaning. It is an asymmetrical relation of exteriority and superiority, an indispensable condition for artistic creation: the latter requires the presence of "transgredients," as Bakhtin puts it, that is, elements external to consciousness as it conceives itself from the inside, yet necessary to its constitution as a whole. With respect to this asymmetry Bakhtin unhesitatingly uses an eloquent comparison: "The artist's *divinity* lies in his assimilation to the higher exotopy" (*Estetika*, p. 166; emphasis added).

Bakhtin is not unaware that he is describing a norm here rather than a reality. Certain authors—a Dostoevsky, for example—forget that aesthetic law, that necessary superiority of the author over the character, and they give the character as much weight as the author, or, conversely, they weaken the author's position to the point where it is on the same plane as a character's; one way or another, these deviant authors put both on the same level, and the gesture has catastrophic consequences, for the author loses his claim to absolute truth on the one hand, while on the other the character loses his claim to uniqueness; there are only individual positions, there is no room for absolutes. In a 1929 text signed by Valentin Voloshinov, we learn that this sort of renunciation of absolutes is a (deplorable) characteristic of modern society; we no longer dare say anything with conviction; and, in order to hide our uncertainties, we take refuge in various degrees of citation: we no longer speak except in quotation marks.

Such a demand for a higher exotopy is perfectly "classical": God does exist and stays where he belongs; the creator is not mistaken for his creatures; the hierarchy of consciousness is unshakable; the author's transcendence allows us to assess his characters with confidence. But this requirement is not maintained. In the course of time, Bakhtin comes under the influence of his counterexample, Dostoevsky (or at least his own idea of Dostoevsky); his first book, published in 1929, is devoted to him, and it sings the praises of the path that had previously been condemned. The earlier idea, instead of being maintained in the status of a general aesthetic law, becomes the defining characteristic of a state of mind that Bakhtin stigmatizes under the label "monologism". The Dostoevskian perversion, on the contrary, is held aloft as the incarnation of "dialogism," at once a world view and a writing style for which Bakhtin thenceforth does not conceal his preference.

Whereas earlier he demanded asymmetry between character and author, with the latter necessarily superior to the former, Bakhtin now never tires of repeating: "In his [Dostoevsky's] works a hero appears whose voice is constructed exactly like the voice of the author himself in a novel of the usual type" (*Dostoevsky*, p. 7). "What the author used to do is now done by the hero" (p. 49). The author has no advantage over the protagonist, is distinguished by no semantic surplus; the two consciousnesses have perfectly equal rights. To use Buber's terms (as Bakhtin does), Dostoevsky is the first to see the author-character relationship as belonging to the "I-thou" (and not the "I-it") type.

The reference to the absolute, and thus to truth, that sustained the earlier view is now rejected. Bakhtin even writes: "The artistic representation of an idea is possible only when the idea is posed in terms beyond affirmation and repudiation, but at the same time not reduced to a simple psychical experience" (p. 80). The "mono-logic" novel has only two possibilities: either its ideas are consid-ered in terms of their content, and then they are true or false; or else they are taken as indications of the psychology of the charac-ters. The "dialogic" art has access to a third state: like the second state, but not reducible to it, this third state lies beyond truth and falsehood, beyond good and evil. Each idea belongs to someone; it is situated with respect to a voice that expresses it and to a hori-zon toward which it is directed. In place of the absolute we find a multiplicity of viewpoints, those of the characters and those of the author assimilated to them, and there are no privileged positions, no hierarchies. Dostoevsky's revolution, on the aesthetic (and eth-ical) level, is comparable to those of Copernicus and Einstein on the level of knowledge of the physical world (these images are among Bakhtin's favorites): there is no more center, and we live within a generalized relativity.

Bakhtin maintains in general that, in our contemporary world, it is impossible to assume an absolute truth, and one must be content to quote rather than to speak for oneself. He adds no condemna-tion or regret to that observation, however; irony (that is what he now calls this mode of speaking) is our wisdom, and who today would dare to proclaim truths? Rejecting irony means making the deliberate choice of "stupidity," means limiting oneself, narrowing one's horizons (see *Estetika*, p. 352); this is what Dostoevsky does in his journalistic writings. The only other possibility—but one that still does not allow us to rediscover the absolute—would be to lend an ear to being, as Heidegger recommends (p. 354).

It is striking to see to what extent Bakhtin's line of argument here parallels the one formulated more or less contemporaneously by Jean-Paul Sartre. In a 1939 article, "M. François Mauriac et la liberté" (translated in *Literary Essays*), Sartre challenges any novel-istic practice in which the author occupies a privileged position with respect to his characters; he does not use the term "mono-logic," but he is not far from identifying "novel" with "dialogism": "The novelist does not have the right to abandon the battlefield and to . . . [judge]" (p. 11). He has to be satisfied with presenting his characters; if he were to judge them, he would be identifying himself with God; now God and the novel are mutually exclusive (that is what Mauriac failed to understand): "A novel is written by a man for men. In the eyes of God, Who cuts through appearances and goes beyond them, there is no novel" (p. 23). Like Bakhtin, Sartre identifies this novelistic revolution with Dostoevsky, and like Bakhtin he compares it to Einstein's: "There is no more place for a privileged observer in a real novel than in the world of Einstein" (ibid.). Like Bakhtin, too, Sartre concludes that the absolute has disappeared: "The introduction of absolute truth" in a novel can only come from an "error of technique," for the novelist "has no right to make these absolute judgments" (p. 15).[1]

Bakhtin would not have wanted to be mistaken for a relativist, but he does not succeed in making the difference quite clear. He likes to compare Dostoevsky's pluralism, as he perceives it, to Dante's, since Dante allows us to hear, in the ideal simultaneity of eternity, the voices of the occupants of all the spheres, terrestrial and celestial (*Dostoevsky*, pp. 26-27, 30-31); but Bakhtin is content to note as a secondary phenomenon the "vertical," that is, hierarchical, character of Dante's universe, as opposed to Dostoevsky's "horizontal" world, a world of "pure . . . coexistence" (*The Dialogic Imagination*, p. 158). Now the difference is considerable, and, if it were real, it would be hard to see how Dostoevsky—and Bakhtin, who purports to be his spokesman—would escape relativism! If this were Bakhtin's last word, we would have to see him after all as representing, if not the Romantic aesthetic in its major trends, then at least the individualist and relativist ideology that dominates the modern era.

But things are not quite so simple. Even while he is illustrating

---

[1] It is rather amusing to note that when Sartre becomes acquainted with Bakhtin's book, thirty years later, he is so preoccupied with refuting "formalism" he does not recognize his own thinking: "I have just read Bakhtine on Dostoyevski, for example, and I don't see what the new formalism—semiotics—adds to the old. On the whole, what I object to in these studies is that they don't lead to anything. They do not embrace their object; the knowledge dissipates itself" ("On *The Idiot of the Family*," p. 126). The misunderstanding is complete: it is enough to make one wonder whether Sartre was already suffering at this early date from the blindness that was to strike him later on. But ideological blindness can be as decisive as the other kind.

this ideology, Bakhtin lets us hear a different voice. Only here, unlike the situation involving the early book on authors and protagonists and the later work on Dostoevsky, the conflict is no longer
overt; it does not correspond to a temporal sequence, and we may
doubt whether Bakhtin was even conscious of it. It is rather a matter of revealing inconsistencies in what Bakhtin takes to be a homogeneous affirmation; but here, perhaps, is where his most original
contribution lies.

To find this other—third—Bakhtin, we shall have to start again
with his interpretation of Dostoevsky's thought and position, since
these have a decisive influence on Bakhtin's own ideas. In the
wake of his famous speech on Pushkin, in 1880, Dostoevsky was
confronted by a contemporary writer, Konstantin Dmitrievich
Kavelin, who had an opposing view of morality: an individual is
acting morally if he is acting in perfect harmony with his own convictions. This is another version of the relativist and individualist
credo (each individual is his own judge), not basically very different from the one Bakhtin believed he had found in Dostoevsky.
Now the latter writes, in his draft of a response to Kavelin:

> It is not enough to define morality as fidelity to one's own convic-
> tions. One must continually pose oneself the question: are my convic-
> tions true? Only one verification of them exists—Christ. . . . I cannot
> recognize one who burns heretics as a moral man, because I do not ac-
> cept your thesis that morality is an agreement with internal convic-
> tions. That is merely *honesty* . . . , not morality. I have a moral model
> and an ideal, Christ. I ask: would he have burned heretics?—no. That
> means the burning of heretics is an immoral act. . . . Christ was mis-
> taken—it's been proved! A scorching feeling tells me: better remain
> with a mistake, with Christ, rather than with you. [*Literaturnoe
> nasledstvo*, vol. 83, pp. 674ff.; cited in *Dostoevsky*, p. 97]

Thus Dostoevsky does claim that a transcendence must exist; he
makes a distinction between honesty (faithfulness to one's convictions) and truth. To this he adds that human truth has to be incar-
nated rather than remaining abstract: that is the meaning of the
Christ-figure—that humanized, incarnate truth is worth even
more than the other, abstract one, and has to come first if the two
are in contradiction (Christ's "mistakes"): such is the particular nature of moral truth.

Not only does Bakhtin know and quote this text, his commentary on it is quite revealing as to his interpretation of Dostoevsky. "He prefers to remain with the mistake but with Christ," he writes (*Dostoevsky*, p. 97), or, later, "the opposition between the truth and Christ in Dostoevsky" (*Estetika*, p. 355). The one-sidedness of this interpretation makes it verge on total misrepresentation: Dostoevsky does not set up an opposition between truth and Christ, but identifies the one with the other in order to oppose them to the philosophy of "points of view" or "convictions"; and it is only at a secondary level that he opposes, within the moral world, incarnate truth to impersonal truth, preferring the former to the latter. But recognition of this would have destroyed Bakhtin's position, for in a spirit very close to Kavelin's, Bakhtin asserts that "all of Dostoevsky's major characters, as people of an idea, are absolutely unselfish, insofar as the idea has really taken control of the deepest core of their personality" (*Dostoevsky*, p. 87). Does this not amount to basing moral judgment on the faithfulness to convictions that is shared by Raskolnikov the assassin, Sonia the prostitute, Ivan the accomplice to parricide, and the "raw youth" who dreams of becoming another Rothschild?

In notes toward an abandoned novel, *The Life of a Great Sinner*, Dostoevsky writes: "But the *dominating idea* of the Life must be visible—that is, although *the entire dominating idea will not be explained in words* and will always remain a puzzle, the reader must nevertheless be aware that this idea is a devout one." Bakhtin also quotes this text (*Dostoevsky*, p. 98) in support of his argument. But Dostoevsky does not announce here that he is abandoning the distinction between impious and pious ideas; he has simply decided not to spell it out, but rather to suggest it in an indirect way. Bakhtin refers elsewhere to "the unspoken truth in Dostoevsky (Christ's kiss)" (*Estetika*, p. 353). But Christ's silence before the Grand Inquisitor does not signify any renunciation of truth; truth is simply no longer transmitted through words. Truth has to be incarnate, truth has to be indirect: but in all this one thing is quite clear, which is that for Dostoevsky, truth exists.

Let us add to this testimony of Dostoevsky's cited by Bakhtin one other, found in a 1873 entry in *The Diary of a Writer*. Discussing a play by a populist author, Dostoevsky writes:

> The author took too much liking to [his character], and not even once does he look upon Ivan from above. It would seem to us that it is in-

sufficient to set forth correctly all given qualities of a person; one has resolutely to illume him with one's own artistic vision. A genuine artist, under no circumstances, should remain on one level with the person portrayed by him, confining himself to mere realistic truth; the impression will carry no truth. [*The Diary of a Writer*, pp. 108-109]

But it is true that these sentences appear in one of Dostoevsky's "stupid" journalistic texts.

The equality between protagonist and author that Bakhtin imputes to Dostoevsky is not only in contradiction with the latter's intentions, it is in fact in its very essence impossible. Bakhtin nearly says so himself: the function of the "dominating idea" that was at issue in the passage from Dostoevsky cited above is reduced by Bakhtin to almost nothing: "It must exercise leadership only in the choice and the arrangement of the material" (*Dostoevsky*, p. 98); but the "almost" is crucial. With Dostoevsky, he says in another text, "the author is only a participant in the dialogue (and its organizer)" (*Estetika*, p. 322): but the parenthesis completely wipes out the radical nature of the preceding statement. The organizer of the dialogue is *not* just a simple participant.

Bakhtin seems to be confusing two different things. One is that the author may present his own ideas, within a novel, as just as open to question as those of other thinkers. The other is that the author may be on the same plane as his characters. Now nothing justifies this confusion, since it is still the author who is presenting both his own ideas and those of the characters. Bakhtin's assertion could be accurate only if Dostoevsky were mistaken for, let us say, Alyosha Karamazov; at that point, one might say that Alyosha's voice is on the same plane as Ivan's. But it is Dostoevsky alone who writes *The Brothers Karamazov*, and who represents Alyosha as well as Ivan. Dostoevsky is not just one voice among others within his novel, he is the unique creator, privileged and radically different from all his characters, since each of them after all has a single voice, whereas Dostoevsky is the creator of this plurality.

The confusion is all the more surprising in that, in his later writings, Bakhtin himself combats it on several occasions, in particular with regard to the notion, which he considers fallacious, of the "image of the author" (see *The Dialogic Imagination*, p. 256, and *Estetika*, p. 353). There is always, Bakhtin says, a radical difference between the author on the one hand and his characters on the other, including that particular character who is the "author's image" (or the "implicit author"): "The author can never become one of the constituent elements of his work, can never become an image or be part of the object. He is neither a *natura creata* nor a *natura naturata et creans*, but a pure *natura creans et non creata*" (*Estetika*, p. 288). It is striking to note that the scholastic definition Bakhtin uses to identify the author was applied, in its original context (for example by John Scotus Erigena), to God, and to him alone.

Bakhtin has thus indeed discovered a special feature of Dostoevsky's work, but he is mistaken about its proper designation. Dostoevsky is exceptional in that he represents several consciousnesses simultaneously and on the same level, each one as convincing as the next; but as novelist he nonetheless maintains a faith in *the* truth as the ultimate horizon. Without being embodied in a character (men are not Christ), the absolute may still serve as the governing idea for the quest in which all mankind shares. That is what Bakhtin seems to recognize, quite indirectly, when he admits that the plurality of consciousnesses and the plurality of truths are not necessarily interdependent: "It should be pointed out that the single and unified consciousness is by no means an inevitable consequence of the concept of a unified truth. It is quite possible to imagine and postulate a unified truth that requires a plurality of consciousnesses" (*Dostoevsky*, p. 81).

But then is it not also possible to recognize that the plurality of consciousnesses does not require giving up the idea of a single truth?

Bakhtin quotes and comments at length upon a passage in which Dostoevsky defines himself not as a "psychologist" but as a "realist in the higher sense." This means that Dostoevsky is not satisfied to express an inner truth, but that he describes human beings who exist outside himself, and that these individuals cannot be reduced to a single consciousness (his own): human beings are different, which implies that they are necessarily several; human multiplicity is the truth of the very being of humanity. This is the underlying cause of Dostoevsky's attraction for Bakhtin. If we now attempt to grasp in a single glance the whole of Bakhtin's intellectual itinerary, we note that its unity is achieved in the conviction, which we find in him before the Dostoevsky book and follow right up through his very last fragments, according to which *the interhuman is constitutive of the human*. This would be in effect the most general expression of a thought that can by no means be reduced to the individualist ideology, and for which Bakhtin never stopped seeking what may now appear to us to be something like different languages intended to express a single thought. From this viewpoint we might distinguish four major periods (four vocabularies), according to the nature of the field in which he is observing the action of that thought: phenomenological, sociological, linguistic, and historico-literary. In the course of a fifth period (the final years), Bakhtin attempted to synthesize these four different languages.

The phenomenological period is illustrated by Bakhtin's very first book, which focuses on the relation between author and protagonist. He considers it to be a special case of the relation between two human beings, and he thus turns toward the analysis of this latter relationship. But he notices then that such a relationship cannot be considered contingent, that is, capable of not existing; on the contrary, the relationship is indispensable, if the human being is to be constituted as a whole, for completeness can come only from outside, through the eyes of the other (this is another theme familiar to readers of Sartre). Bakhtin's demonstration focuses on two aspects of the human person. The first, or spatial, aspect is that of the body: my body becomes a whole only if it is seen from outside, or in a mirror (whereas without the slightest difficulty I see the bodies of others as completed wholes). The second is temporal, and it has to do with the "soul": only my birth and my death constitute me as a whole; now, by definition, my consciousness cannot know these from within. The *other* is therefore at once constitutive of human beings and fundamentally asymmetrical with respect to human beings: human plurality finds its meaning not in a quantitative multiplication of "I"s but in the fact that each one is the necessary complement of the other.

The sociological and Marxist period reaches its culmination in the three books originally attributed to Bakhtin's friends and collaborators. In opposition to subjectivist linguistics and psychology, which proceed as if man were alone in the world, but also in opposition to the empiricist theories that are limited to knowledge of the observable products of human interactions, Bakhtin and his friends declare the primordial character of the social—language and thought, constitutive of mankind, are necessarily intersubjective.

It is in these same years that Bakhtin makes an effort to lay the groundwork for a new linguistics, or, as he will say later on, a "translinguistics" (today we would call it "pragmatics"), whose object is no longer the utterance, but the speech process, that is, the verbal interaction. After criticizing structural linguistics and formalist poetics, which reduce language to a code and forget that discourse is above all a bridge between two people, themselves socially determined, Bakhtin formulates positive propositions for this study of verbal interaction in the last part of his *Dostoevsky* and in his lengthy essay "Discourse in the Novel." In particular, he analyzes the way in which, within the novel, the various voices are interwoven with that of the explicit subject of enunciation.

The historico-literary period begins in the middle of the nineteen-thirties; it consists of two major books, one on Goethe and one on Rabelais, of which the second alone has reached us (only a few excerpts from the first have survived), as well as a long general essay that introduces the notion of chronotope. Bakhtin observes that literature has always played upon the plurality of voices present in the consciousness of the speakers, but in two different ways: either the discourse of the work is homogeneous in itself but is globally opposed to the general linguistic norms, or else the diversity of discourses ("heterology") is represented *within* the text. This second tradition is the one that particularly attracts Bakhtin's attention, as much outside literature as inside it: hence his studies of popular festivals, carnival traditions, the history of laughter.

Each of these vast explorations may be judged within its own field, but it is also clear that they all share in a common project. This project cannot be reconciled with the individualist ideology, which is responsible for so many of Bakhtin's other assertions, and Bakhtin is right to remind us that Dostoevsky is at the antipodes of the "culture of fundamental and definitive solitude" (*Estetika*, p. 312), of the idea of the self-sufficient being. In order to differentiate the two doctrines, Bakhtin sometimes contrasts "personalism" with "subjectivism": the latter is limited to the "I," the former depends upon the relation between "I" and "the other" (see p. 370). And the comparison that seems to evoke Dostoevsky's world view best for him is not in harmony with his other theses, but postulates the irreducibility of the transindividual entity: "If we were to seek an image toward which this whole world gravitates, an image in the spirit of Dostoevsky's own worldview, then it would be the church as a communion of unmerged souls, where sinners and righteous men come together" (*Dostoevsky*, pp. 26-27). But the church is not a simple confrontation of voices having equal rights; it is a place qualitatively distinct from the individuals that occupy it, and it can exist only by virtue of a common faith.

"Superman" exists—but not in the Nietzschean sense of being superior; I am superman for the other, as (s)he is for me: my external position (my "exotopy") gives me the privilege of seeing him or her whole. At the same time, I cannot act as if others did not exist: knowing that the other can see me radically determines my condition. (Wo)man's social nature grounds her (his) morality: not in pity, or in the abstraction of universality, but in the recognition of the constitutive nature of the interhuman. Not only is the individual not reducible to the concept, but the social too is irreducible to individuals, no matter how numerous. And one can imagine a transgredience that could not be mistaken for superiority pure and simple, that would not lead me to transform the other into an object: that is what one encounters in acts of love, confession, pardon, or active listening (see *Estetika*, p. 325).

Some Christian echoes are evident in this language. We know, too, that in his personal life Bakhtin was a believer, an Orthodox Christian. The rare explicit references to religion in his published works make it possible to reconstruct his position as follows. Christianity is a religion that breaks radically with previous doctrines, and especially with Judaism, in that it no longer sees God as an incarnation of the voice of my consciousness, but as a being outside myself who provides me with the transgredience I need. I am to love the other and not myself, but he can and must love me. Christ is the other made sublime, a pure and universal other: "What I must be for the other, God is for me" (*Estetika*, p. 52). The image of Christ, then, at once furnishes the model for human relations (the asymmetry between "I" and "thou," and the necessary complementarity of "thou") and embodies its extreme limit, since *he is only other*. This interpretation of Christianity can be linked to the Christological trend that lives on in the Russian religious tradition and was very familiar to Dostoevsky. Now Bakhtin declares that what Christ is for human beings, Dostoevsky is for his characters (which, as we can see, by no means amounts to putting him on the same level with them): "It is, so to speak, God's action with regard to man, allowing him to reveal himself to himself right to the end (in an immanent development), to condemn himself, to refute himself" (p. 310).

The originality of this interpretation of the absolute other, which we owe to Bakhtin (or perhaps to Dostoevsky), can be assessed if we compare it to another well-known formulation, the one Rousseau gives in speaking of himself, in the abandoned preface to the *Confessions* in which he sees himself as pure other. Rousseau situates himself in the perspective of self-knowledge, a task that confronts all men; and he proposes his own life as capable of serving as reference point: "Here is what I want to try to do: in order to learn to appreciate oneself, one needs to have at least one point of comparison, so that each of us can know himself and another; and that other will be myself" (*Oeuvres complètes*, I, 1149). The important difference is not in the human or divine nature of this universal mediator: Bakhtin's Christ is a sufficiently human figure. Nor does it lie in the fact that Rousseau chooses this role for himself, whereas Bakhtin assigns it to someone else. The essential difference is that, in Rousseau's passage, the other intervenes only as the object of comparison with a self that has already been entirely constituted; whereas, for Bakhtin, the other participates in the very constitution of the self. Rousseau sees the other as necessary only in the process of coming to know a preexisting entity; Bakhtin's Christ plays out his role in an interaction that establishes the human. In Rousseau's world, made up of self-sufficient atoms (as described in this text), the relationship between men is reduced to comparison; Bakhtin's world (and Dostoevsky's) is familiar with —and requires—lateral transcendence, in which the interhuman is not merely the void separating two beings. Now one of these views is not only more generous than the other, it is more true. Sartre said as much in *Saint Genet*: "For a long time we believed in the social atomism bequeathed to us by the eighteenth century, and it seemed to us that man was by nature a solitary entity who entered into relations with his fellow men *afterward*. . . . We now know that this is nonsense. The truth is that 'human reality' 'is-in-society' as it 'is-in-the-world'" (p. 590).

Thus the absolute does find its place in Bakhtin's system of thought, even though he himself is not always ready to recognize it, and even though it is a question of a transcendence of an original sort: no longer "vertical" but "horizontal," or "lateral"; no longer one of essence but of position. Men accede only to values and meanings that are relative and incomplete, but they do so with the plenitude of meaning, the absoluteness of value, as their horizon; they aspire to a "communion with the *higher value* (at the extreme, absolute)" (*Estetika*, p. 369).

We may now return to the starting point and reexamine Bakhtin's position with respect to the history of aesthetics—no longer as he formulates it himself, in one text or another, but as it derives from his most original philosophical choices. Where does literature fit in? and what about criticism?

For the first question, we must begin with an observation: in practice, Bakhtin did not limit himself to criticizing the formalist definition of literature (in order to replace it with another); instead, he simply gave up looking for literary specificity. Not that this task lost all meaning in his eyes; but its meaning exists only in relation to a particular history (of literature or criticism) and does not deserve the central place that has been attributed to it. Something else now seems much more important to him: all the links woven between literature and culture, the latter construed as the differentiated unity of the discourses of an epoch (*Estetika*, pp. 329-330). Hence his interest in the "primary genres" (quite like Brecht's), that is, in the forms of conversation, public speech, more or less rule-governed exchanges. Rather than "construction" or "architectonics," the literary work is above all a heterology, a plurality of voices, an echo and anticipation of discourses past and to come; it is both a crossroads and a meeting place, and thereby loses its privileged position. Unfaithful to his own earlier program, Bakhtin never studies entire works, nor does he close himself off inside one single work: to tell the truth, the question of architectonics no longer even comes up. The object of his literary analyses is something else again: the status of discourse in relation to present or absent interlocutors (monologue and dialogue, quotation and parody, stylization and polemics), on the one hand; the organization of the represented world, particularly the construction of time and space (the "chronotope") on the other. These textual characteristics are directly linked to a conception of the contemporary world, but they are not limited to this, since people of later periods seize upon them and discover new meanings in them. Bakhtin's object is indeed transtextuality, no longer in the form of Formalist "devices," but as something that belongs to the history of culture.

As for criticism, Bakhtin announces (more than he practices) a new form, one that could well be called *dialogic criticism*. We can recall the break introduced by Spinoza's *Tractatus theologico-politicus*, and its consequences: the transformation of the text studied into an object. For Bakhtin, such a positioning of the problem dangerously distorts the nature of human discourse. To reduce the other (here, the author studied) to an object is to fail to recognize his principal characteristic, namely, that he is a subject, that is, someone who speaks—exactly as I do in commenting upon him. But how can we give him back his discourse? By recognizing the kinship of our discourses, by seeing in their juxtaposition not that of metalanguage and object-language, but the example of a much more familiar discursive form: dialogue. Now if I accept the view that our discourses are in a dialogic relation, I also agree to raise once again the question of truth. This does not mean returning to the situation that existed prior to Spinoza, when the Church Fathers could openly refer to truth because they believed they possessed it. Here one is aspiring to seek the truth rather than considering it as given in advance: the truth is an ultimate horizon and a ruling idea. As Bakhtin says: "It should be noted that both relativism and dogmatism equally exclude all argumentation, all authentic dialogue, by making it either unnecessary (relativism) or impossible (dogmatism)" (*Dostoevsky*, p. 69). For dialogic criticism, truth exists but we do not possess it. Thus we rediscover in Bakhtin a connection between criticism and its object (literature), but this connection does not have the meaning it has for the French writer-critics. For Blanchot and Barthes, literature and criticism resemble each other in that both lack any relation to truth; for Bakhtin, they resemble each other because they are both committed to the search for truth, and neither is privileged with respect to the other.

This view of criticism has some important repercussions for the methodology of all the social sciences. The specificity of the human world, as Montesquieu had already noted, is that human beings obey laws and *at the same time* they act freely. Conformity to the law makes them subject to the same analysis as natural phenomena— whence the temptation to apply the methods of the natural sciences to the study of mankind. But to be content with that would be to forget the double character of human behavior. Alongside of *explanation* by means of laws (to speak the language of turn-of-the-century German philosophy that Bakhtin borrows), it is necessary to practice *comprehension* of human freedom. This opposition does not coincide precisely with the opposition between natural science and social science, not only because the latter in its turn has to do with explanation, but also because the former, as we know today, makes use of comprehension. It remains true, however, that the one predominates in the first area and the other in the second.

The critic's task is threefold. At a first level, it is simply a matter of establishing facts, and here the ideal, Bakhtin says, is accuracy: collect material data, reconstitute the historical context. At the other extreme of the spectrum we find explanation by means of laws: sociological, psychological, even biological (*Estetika*, p. 343). Both are legitimate and necessary. But in between the two, as it were, is situated the most specific and the most important activity of the critic and researcher in the social sciences, and that is interpretation as dialogue, the only interpretation that makes it possible to rediscover human freedom.

Meaning is in fact this "element of freedom piercing through necessity" (ibid., p. 410). I am determined as a being (object) and free as meaning (subject). To model the social sciences on the natural sciences means reducing men to objects that do not know freedom. In the order of being, human freedom is only relative and deceptive. But in the order of meaning, it is by definition absolute, since meaning arises from the meeting of two subjects, and since that meeting begins again and again, eternally (ibid., p. 342): once again Bakhtin's thought rejoins Sartre's project. Meaning is freedom and interpretation is its exercise: this indeed seems to be Bakhtin's final precept.

6

Knowledge and Concern:

Northrop Frye

The most appropriate image for Northrop Frye's lengthy intellectual career would be familiar to all Vico's disciples, Frye included: a spinning motion tracing wider and wider circles, spiraling around a fixed axis while frequently traversing new territory. Frye is a prolific author whose practice spans at least four different critical genres: the monograph (he has eight to his credit, including one on Blake, three on Shakespeare, and one on Milton); the essay (six collections to date, of which three are of particular interest here: *Fables of Identity*, 1963; *The Stubborn Structure*, 1970; and *Spiritus Mundi*, 1976); the brief lecture series devoted to a particular theoretical subject (five volumes so far); finally, the major work of synthesis: *Anatomy of Criticism*, in 1957 and, in 1982, *The Great Code*. A single outlook is expressed in these twenty-odd works; there is no identifiable temporal break in the series. Yet the fact that Frye's thought is of a piece in its broad outlines does not mean that his works are internally consistent; in other words, there may be no contradiction between one book and another, but that does not mean that each book is free from internal tensions. Following a pattern that will be familiar to my readers by now, once again I am going to try to make a distinction between what stems from the Romantic heritage in Frye's thought and what transcends that traditional conceptual framework. Betraying the letter of a work the better to see its spirit, then, I shall introduce a break where for the author there is only a long series of barely discernible displacements, whether in focus, in emphasis, or in the degree of adherence to a particular thesis.

CRITICISM I

Frye's first response to the question "What is criticism supposed to do?" can be summarized in few words: it is supposed to become a science. This requirement is not formulated with the intention of frightening the layman; it is, rather, a statement based on common sense (that is a rare commodity in the area of literary studies, however, and so the statement is shocking). Since critics readily agree that the object of literary studies is a better knowledge of the literary works studied, it follows that a critical work must not be written as if it were a poem, that a critic ought to try to make his concepts unequivocal and his premises explicit, that he should practice hypothesis-making and result-checking. This principle might even seem self-evident, if we were to judge by the critics' usual source of income (they teach at universities) or by the aridity of their style, which makes their work inaccessible to the uninitiated.

But if we accept this primary evidence, we must draw at least two conclusions from it, according to Frye: the science of literature has an obligation to be both systematic and internal. As he writes at the beginning of *Anatomy of Criticism*: "The presence of science in any subject changes its character from the casual to the causal, from the random and intuitive to the systematic, as well as safeguarding the integrity of that subject from external invasions" (p. 7).

He must therefore wage his battle on two fronts, changing adversaries and allies as he goes. On the one hand, he is opposed to the tendency that has predominated in literary studies in North America (Frye being Canadian), that is, New Criticism: to be sure, this type of criticism is internal, but its practitioners study one work after another, without any sense of the broader entities— genres, or even literature in general—to which these works belong; nor do they have any sense of the structural principles that operate in more than one poem or novel. Frye's position here re-sembles that of any practitioner of the social sciences—anthropol-ogy, psychology, linguistics—who does not study one phenome-non and then another in a compartmentalized fashion, but instead looks for structural regularities.

The other battlefront, however, is the livelier one; this is where Frye struggles—in company with the New Critics, as it happens—against the specialists in those very same social sciences; now the struggle concerns not the method but the object. What Frye objects to on the part of his colleagues who are vassals within one branch or another of philosophy, psychology, or anthropology is that their approach is external, and that it neglects the specificity of litera-ture. The science of literature has to derive its principles from liter-ature itself, and it must achieve independence instead of settling for the role of colony or protectorate subject to a powerful mother-land. Referring to his own early days as a critic, Frye writes: "It seemed to me, entering this situation a generation ago, that the first thing to look for was a basis for critical principles within criti-cism itself, trying to avoid the kind of externalized determinism in which criticism has to be 'based on' something else, carried around in some kind of religious or Marxist or Freudian wheelchair" (*Spiri-tus Mundi*, p. 5). For every external approach necessarily fails to recognize the specificity of the literary form as well as that of the poetic meaning, and remains incapable of grasping the complex, often contradictory, relation between the literary work and its milieu.

The internal approach, on the other hand, situates the work in the context appropriate to it, that of literary tradition (for us, that of the West), with its multiple conventions—its generic forms, its narrative schemas, its ways of signifying, and its sets of stereo-typed images—which pass almost intact from one work to an-other; to these sets Frye gives the name "archetypes," using the word both broadly and in a purely literary sense (so that it is more or less equivalent to Curtius's *topoi*). Critical compartmentalization is a mistaken approach, for, when we read a literary work, we are always reading much more than a single one; we enter into com-munication with literary memory—our own, that of the author, that of the work itself; the works we have already read, and even those we have not read, are present in our reading, and every text is a palimpsest.

Frye's specific contribution, up to this point in our study of his work, thus lies neither in the fact that he requires an internal approach to literature, since that is the dominant critical ideology (that of the New Critics), nor in the fact that he favors a systematic attitude, since that is a matter of common sense; his contribution lies in the fact that he has managed to combine the two, an undertaking that was not self-evident. In so doing he rejoins—consciously—the poetic tradition, as it has existed since Aristotle but also as it has been reworked in our day. Here we cannot fail to juxtapose Frye's work with the evolution of literary studies in France, even though that evolution came about some ten years after Frye's first important writings and even though—the paradox is familiar—at that time the works of the Russian Formalists were known in France, but not those of Northrop Frye. Beginning in the mid-sixties, the renewal of poetics in France was carried out in the name of the same two requirements: that criticism be internal and that it be systematic. Thus we may be allowed to call Frye a "structuralist," if such a classification has any interest, even though Frye says he did not know the word when he wrote *Anatomy of Criticism.*

Once this common framework has been recognized, a series of significant differences can be observed. In France, the study of metaphor and rhetorical figures was undertaken in order to describe a linguistic mechanism; when Frye studies them, his aim is to catalog the most persistent metaphors in the Western tradition. French poeticians have studied narrative in order to understand how a plot is formed or presented to the reader; Frye on the other hand records and classifies the favorite plots of two thousand years of European history. I am forcing the opposition somewhat, to be sure; but without stretching the facts we may say that Frye is more interested in substance, while the French "structuralists" are oriented toward form; he writes an encyclopedia, they produce a dictionary in which the definitions are cross-referenced, referring to each other rather than to an object that remains external to them (namely, literature); he is panchronic, in that he perceives—here he is faithful to Eliot's precept—the simultaneous presence of all literature, whereas they are achronic, since in the last analysis they are studying the faculties of the human mind (the capacity to symbolize or to narrate). In the end, the object of knowledge, for Frye, is not man but men; the opposite has been true in France. The differences of course are considerable, but they nevertheless allow co-habitation within a single conceptual framework, one that we may represent in terms of complementarity rather than contradiction.[1]

One striking consequence of Frye's general orientation is his re-fusal to leave room for value judgments within literary studies. This refusal constitutes the nerve center of the "Polemical Intro-duction" to his *Anatomy of Criticism*. Incorporating value judg-ments ("this is a beautiful poem," "this is a dreadful novel") within the program of literary studies, Frye holds, is like including the happiness of citizens in the Constitution, as one of society's objec-tives: happiness is desirable, but it is out of place in this context. What Frye means to warn us against is the illusion that we can ar-rive at judgments deductively, on the basis of knowledge (he is warning against the confusion between fact and value, which has been stigmatized in the social sciences since Weber's time). The value judgment exists before the work of acquiring knowledge is undertaken, and continues to exist afterward; the two do not merge, however, nor is there continuity between them: knowledge is oriented toward the object of study, whereas judgment is al-ways, and exclusively, oriented toward its subject. "In knowledge the context of the work of literature is literature; in value judge-ment, the context of the work of literature is the reader's experi-ence. . . . When a critic interprets, he is talking about his poet; when he evaluates, he is talking about himself, or, at most, about himself as a representative of his age" (*The Stubborn Structure*, pp. 66, 68).

It does not follow that one must renounce judgment. Frye him-self does not deprive himself of that pleasure, but there is no con-tradiction here; one must simply not claim that what "ought to be" is based on what "is." Unlike the poetic arts of the Renaissance, to-day's poetics tells how works are, not how they are supposed to be.

But there is perhaps something misleading in the simplicity with which Frye settles the question of the way facts are related to val-

---

[1] In 1970 I devoted the first chapter of *The Fantastic: A Structural Approach to a Liter-ary Genre* to a "structuralist" critique of Frye. In addition to being a rather cursory study, this text declares its loyalty to the very principles Frye espouses, as I took care to note, while interpreting them in a more extreme fashion: in short, I criticize Frye for not being internal enough or systematic enough. The debate now seems to me to be situated between two variants of "structuralism."

ues, knowledge to judgment. It does not seem appropriate to subject that epistemology to a critical examination here; let us nevertheless remark that, by "judgment" and "value," Frye is referring exclusively to aesthetic appreciations that concern the *beauty* of the work alone. Now an aesthetic attitude of this sort is in itself highly restrictive, and it paves the way for the eventual rejection of all judgment: the work of art is already cut off from other types of discourse and its apprehension cut off from other types of judgment. It is reserved for disinterested contemplation alone, and this cannot lead beyond the work itself. Literary texts, however, are shot through with cognitive and ethical ambitions; they exist not only to produce a bit more beauty in the world, but also to tell us what is true about this world, and to speak about what is just and unjust. The critic, too, may formulate not only aesthetic judgments (the least "concerned" of all—they may as well be left to the daily press and the juries that award literary prizes), but also judgments as to the truth and rightness of the works.

To be sure, Frye himself is not unaware of these other dimensions of literature. In *Anatomy of Criticism*, he even postulates a level of meaning common to all works, a level that he calls the tropological or moral meaning (borrowing a term from traditional biblical exegesis): literary works are read within a context of social communication, as precepts for our everyday actions. In *The Well-Tempered Critic*, Frye writes: "It is not necessarily naive to write 'how true' on the margins of what we read; or at least we do not have to confine our contact with literature to purely disinterested and esthetic responses" (p. 141). But when he attempts to apply this observation to the form of literary studies themselves, the result is disappointing: he is content to transpose that distinction between two aspects of literature into two phases of reading: when reading is immediate (or "naive," or "invisible"), one looks for beauty; when it is mediated (or "sentimental," or "visible"), it has truth as its object, and that is what the critic works toward. But this "truth" is nothing but the establishment of the facts; along the way, the ethical and cognitive dimensions of literature have been lost.

Returning to the fundamental distinction of philology (Spinoza's precept: seek meaning, not truth), Frye declares that "the academic aim is to see what the subject means, not to accept or reject it" (*The Great Code*, p. xx), and he refuses to join the critics who are waging moral battles using those tin soldiers they call "Milton" and "Shelley." Where moral issues are concerned, the only judgment permitted the critic is the one that links a given authorial utterance to that author's overall value system: "the only moral criterion to be applied to them is that of decorum" (*Anatomy*, p. 114); in other words, he shuts himself up in a radical relativism. We may follow Frye in his concern to show that there is no continuity between the establishment of facts and judgments of value (the one will never *lead* to the other); we may join him in refusing to see the one substituted for the other, and nevertheless view criticism (like the rest of the social sciences, moreover) as an activity with two facets, knowledge *and* judgment; at that point, articulation between these two facets becomes a necessity.

But let us leave that question dangling for the moment.

LITERATURE I

If the influence of the Romantic ideology on Frye's "first" critical project was not necessarily obvious at a glance, his "first" answer to the question "What is literature?" reveals its roots at once: as evidence, there are references in *Anatomy of Criticism* to Mallarmé or his disciples Valéry and (to a certain extent) T. S. Eliot. Literature is defined by the autonomy of its discourse, which opposes it to utilitarian language: "Wherever we have an autonomous verbal structure of this kind, we have literature. Wherever this autonomous structure is lacking, we have language, words used instrumentally to help human consciousness do or understand something else" (*Anatomy*, p. 74). Poetic activity is intransitive. "The poet *qua* poet intends only to write a poem" (ibid.). The poetic symbol refers to nothing outside itself; its meaning is the place it occupies in the structure (in that, poetry is like mathematics); the weakening or disappearance of external ("centrifugal") relations is compensated for by the reinforcement of internal ("centripetal") relations: words are no longer signs, but "motifs."

When he speaks of autonomy, Frye always implies: "with respect to a heterogeneous series." A constitutive element of a work is not autonomous; on the contrary, it is strongly linked to all the other elements. And, if the work itself is autonomous with respect to nonliterature, it is, on the other hand, entirely dependent on the literary tradition: only the experience of literature can give someone the idea of creating a literary work. Poets imitate Homer, not nature. "The new poem, like the new baby, is born into an already existing order of words . . . Poetry can only be made out of other poems; novels out of other novels" (ibid., p. 97). All textuality is intertextuality, and the question of "originality" or "influences" is most often poorly formulated: "the real difference between the original and the imitative poet is simply that the former is more profoundly imitative" (ibid.).

The main lines of Frye's approach, presented in summary fashion here (an approach to literature that is internal but systematic; only literature, but all literature) determine the form of what is probably his most popular work, *Anatomy of Criticism*. This is an encyclopedic and synoptic work, a sort of superclassification that makes room for all aspects of literary works, but that unequivocally refuses to interpret them or to situate them in relation to social history; it is an inventory of literary forms, in the broad sense of the word "form," which includes thematic configurations, levels of meaning, types of imagery, and generic conventions, each of these categories being itself subdivided into two, four, or five subcategories illustrated by examples derived in turn from an encyclopedic culture. This taxonomy could of course be improved at one point or another (and Frye himself did not hesitate to modify it), but it will never become anything else: it is a taxonomy, that is, a tool for thinking rather than thought itself.

LITERATURE II

We have seen that the Russian Formalists came to reject their point of departure (the affirmation of the autonomy of literature) precisely because they had used it as a working hypothesis. Something similar happens with Frye, even though the break in his case is less clean. Upon looking closely at literature, as he is required to do by his own initial postulates, Frye discovers that literature does not exist! More precisely, he makes two related observations (and he is already doing this in *Anatomy of Criticism*). First, he observes that literature is defined variously according to its historical and social contexts, that no possible structural definition of the literary object exists (see *Anatomy*, p. 345), and that literature is a fundamentally heterogeneous object. His second observation, which is only an extension of the first, is that literature cannot be cut off from the other discourses operating in a given society (ibid., p. 350, and earlier, p. 104): "literariness" is found outside of literature, just as "nonliterariness" is present within it.

It is the first of these two observations that determines Frye's interest in a particularly heterogeneous literary genre, the Menippean satire or "anatomy" (he shares this interest, for reasons that are not irrelevant, with Bakhtin). But he returns even more frequently to the second observation. Whereas in *Anatomy of Criticism* he was able to state that studying second-rate literature could not lead very far (cf. p. 17), in *The Stubborn Structure* he writes:

> I wish all teachers of English, at every level, could feel that they were concerned with the whole of a student's verbal, or in fact imaginative, experience, not merely with the small part of it that is conventionally called literary. The incessant verbal bombardment that students get from conversation, advertising, the mass media, or even such verbal games as Scrabble or cross-word puzzles, is addressed to the same part of the mind that literature addresses, and it does far more to mould their literary imagination than poetry or fiction. [Pp. 84-85]

In short, "the area of literature should not be restricted to the conventionally literary, but expanded to the entire area of verbal experience" (ibid., p. 85). And, if Frye believes he has influenced the evolution of literary studies, it must be precisely in this sense, in passing beyond the restricted notion of literature: "the scholarly revolution which I have helped to agitate has resulted in weakening the distinction between classical and popular literature" (*Spiritus Mundi*, p. 22). Wherever one stands on this question of influence, one thing is clear: in his own work, Frye does not shrink from speaking of riddles and incantations, Bob Dylan's lyrics and student slang.

The difference between this assertion and the preceding one (*Literature I*) is considerable, even if it is inappropriate to speak of change in chronological terms. Whereas Frye requires on the one hand that criticism be based on principles that are internal to literature, he asserts on the other hand that nothing is external to literature, so long as it has to do with the imaginary. Whereas in one place he recommends that a literary work be related above all to the context provided for it by other literary works (a diachronic context, that is), he enjoins us elsewhere to work out the relationship between the work and its nonliterary verbal context (a synchronic context). And not even exclusively verbal: in fact, everything that stems from culture is relevant to the comprehension of literature. Here Frye has ceased to be a theoretician of literature in order to become a theoretician of culture; in this new context, literature will still find a place, but after this circular movement, its place is no longer quite the same. We shall thus have to detour by way of the global image of culture that Frye is sketching out, in particular in his book *The Critical Path* (1971).

One thing is self-evident at the outset: human beings live simultaneously in two distinct universes, nature and culture. The world of nature, that of time and space, is made up of objective data that are independent of human will, and in it mankind is just one element among others. The world of culture is a world that human beings have created for themselves and of which they will always remain the center (it is, then, a geocentric and anthropocentric world); human culture is an incarnation of the values (desires, hopes, fears) of human society. A universe whose only characteristic is that of being real, on the one hand; a universe that is an ideal become real, on the other; a world of indifferent nature, and a world of self-interested individuals.

Mankind's immersion in these two very different environments inspires two equally distinct attitudes. The most general way of designating them is in terms of *freedom* on the one hand, *concern* on the other. Concern is a term that Frye borrows from the existentialist tradition (*engagement*, commitment); but the meaning he gives it differs from the one it had, for example, in Sartre's writings (this is already apparent from the opposition with "freedom"): it is all that connects us with the society in which we live, the world of our own culture, and that contributes to its integrity. Freedom, or lack of concern, or detachment, is an attitude of disinterested examination of the phenomena that surround us, an awareness of the natural world in which we are submerged.

These two attitudes are supported by different aspects of human life and, in turn, they crystallize in distinctly different social forms. It is clear, for example, that every valorization of the social at the expense of the individual creates a terrain that invites the various forms of concern; conversely, interest in impartial knowledge of the world correlates with the flourishing of individualism. Concern is essentially conservative, since it requires adherence to social values; lack of concern is "liberal," in that it allows the individual and his own reason to decide where everything belongs. Concern thrives in a context of oral culture that favors the maintenance of traditions; the civilizations of the written word, on the contrary, facilitate the isolation of the individual and his direct confrontation with nature. The clearest opposition is perhaps the one that involves the nature of truth in each case. For the attitude of concern, truth is a truth of authority, or of revelation; it coincides with social values, and the corresponding human reaction is belief. For the attitude of freedom, truth is necessarily a truth of correspondence, or of equivalence, a relation between phenomena and discourse rather than between discourse and values; the human behavior that derives from this is knowledge.

When the attitudes of concern and freedom are manifested through language, they give rise to two principal types of discourse that Frye calls *mythology* and *science*. Science, especially as embodied in the natural sciences, objectifies the world, including the inner human world; it elevates impartiality and detachment to the rank of the cardinal virtues, and the only arguments it recognizes are empirical verification and logical reasoning. "Mythology" is a term that Frye also uses in a broad sense: it refers to the set of discourses that express the relation of man to values. "A mythology is . . . a cultural model, expressing the way in which man wants to shape and reshape the civilization he himself has made" (*Spiritus Mundi*, p. 21). Others would have chosen "ideology," and Frye knows this (see *The Critical Path*, p. 112); but he prefers the root "myth," which suggests that these discourses are, predominantly, narratives. Mythology is a product of the imagination and an expression of the ideal, but so too is the world of culture; mythology is thus nothing other than the verbal expression of a culture.

Neither of these two worlds, or attitudes, or types of discourse, can be reduced to the other. But the human mind aspires to unity, and it has therefore always tended to assimilate one of the two to the other. The classical reaction is the one that subjects knowledge to belief and nature to culture. At the dawn of humanity, myths were perhaps considered not only expressions of an ideal but also descriptions of the world. We readily take our desires for realities, and we prefer to believe in the harmonious and intelligible world presented by myths rather than to seek empirical truth. This supposedly primitive attitude has clearly persisted into our day, and in the course of history it has taken the form of major ideological systems that subordinate freedom of knowledge to commitment to convictions; thus in Christianity or, more recently, in Marxism (these two examples always go hand in hand for Frye), science is deduced from a philosophical vision. The desire to establish a Marxist biological science is a case in point. "When we hear that it is more important to change the world than to study it, we know that there is, once again, a social movement on foot to subordinate all philosophical myths of freedom to a new myth of concern" (*The Critical Path*, p. 53).

But a specifically modern reaction to the duality of the human condition can also be identified: it consists in seeking to eliminate concern in favor of freedom, to replace mythology by science. Science is originally an attitude toward nature; but, since it is at the same time a social phenomenon, it becomes in turn the nucleus of a new mythology, an internally contradictory mythology, since, unlike Christianity or Marxism, it affirms a myth of freedom. This myth makes us believe that every concern or commitment, every ideology, is condemned to extinction in the near future, as new areas are annexed by science. One of the consequences of this conviction is precisely the assertion that myths are only an immature science: "Early students of mythology . . . liked to think of it as primitive science, because that view implied such a flattering contrast between primitive visions of nature and theirs. . . . This attitude was mainly a by-product of a European ideology designed to rationalize the nineteenth-century treatment of non-European peoples" (*Creation and Recreation*, p. 7). Now this sort of assimilation is no less illusory, and no less dangerous, than the preceding one: it is based upon a confusion between fact and value, between nature and culture, and it does not allow us to take into consideration the specifically human properties of our world. We should not have to choose between the freedomless world depicted by Orwell in *1984* and the world devoid of concern portrayed by Huxley in *Brave New World* (see *The Critical Path*, p. 55).

Thus Frye never tires of insisting on the simultaneous necessity of the two, mythology and science, concern and freedom. Concern without freedom degenerates into anxiety; freedom without concern engenders indifference. Nonetheless, we must not dream of some sort of synthesis of the two: "It may be significant that really thoroughgoing efforts to 'reconcile' the two kinds of reality turn out to be cannibalistic ones: in Hegel knowledge ultimately swallows faith, as in the *Summa contra Gentiles* faith ultimately swallows knowledge" (ibid., p. 58). The two attitudes are not always in contradiction; sometimes there are analogies between them, or they may tend to converge, or even meet by chance in passing; but, since their natures are different, they can never coincide. Antithesis and tension are thus healthier than synthesis: let us not envy the Cyclops' single eye. As human beings, we need both discourses, for in fact we live in both worlds at once: mythology does not serve us in our relation with impersonal things; science is likewise of little use in the dialogue between "I" and "thou." "As long as man lives in the world, he will need the perspective and attitude of the scientist; but to the extent that he has created the world he lives in, feels responsible for it and has a concern for its destiny, which is also his own destiny, he will need the perspective and attitude of the humanist" (*The Stubborn Structure*, p. 55).

Democracy, which is the social form in which we live, is clearly situated on the side of liberty, tolerance, and individualism. Does this mean that all concern has disappeared, or has to disappear? Certainly not; but the role that science plays here modifies the position of concern. A mythology that takes belief alone into account, or—and this amounts to the same thing—one that claims for itself the truth of authority as well as the truth of correspondence, is necessarily a *closed* mythology. But a society that recognizes the necessary coexistence of freedom and concern, of science and mythology, may have at its disposal an *open* mythology, and that is the only kind to which democratic society should aspire. Such a mythology is nothing other than "a plurality of myths of concern, in which the state assumes the responsibility for keeping the peace among them" (*The Critical Path*, p. 106). This does not mean, as it is sometimes too hastily supposed, that in such a society all values are relative (i.e., that they depend upon point of view alone), nor does it mean that all truth of authority is abandoned. What is modified is the function of that truth: rather than being a prior obligation, truth becomes the common horizon of a dialogue where different opinions come into contact; it is what makes such a dialogue possible. And Frye even proposes some reference points making it possible to evaluate the various myths of concern that circulate in our society: their compatibility with charity, or with respect for the life of others, as with intellectual honesty and thus finally with the results of science.

How does a mythology manifest itself, concretely? In traditional societies it finds expression in myths and in the various forms of religious practice. In modern societies this role is assumed by what we call culture, with the arts and literature in particular at its center. Hence the affinity between religion and literature: not because the latter arises from the former or should replace it, but because both are varieties of mythology, adapted to different societies. Literature—to which we are returning after this long detour—is not a degraded form of science, not a description of the world, but an expression of the values of a society, an imagined world. The function of literature is that of "providing a society with an imaginative vision of the human situation," Frye writes ("Literature and Myth," p. 35), and also: "literature is the 'great code' of concern" (*The Critical Path*, p. 128). It is clear that, though Frye's thought may never have undergone radical shifts, a certain distance separates this assertion from the view of literature we saw earlier, in which literature finds its goal in itself. Any reduction of the arts to a purely aesthetic function of contemplation is mistaken, for it neglects this essential social dimension. The role reserved for the arts in democratic societies is qualitatively new, furthermore: it is that of a laboratory in which new myths of concern are being freely prepared. It is not by accident that the arts are repressed in societies that live under the rule of a unique concern, as do totalitarian societies. Not only does literature need society (it is social), but (democratic) society too needs literature. "By itself, literature cannot prevent total destruction, which is one of the many possible fates of the human race; but without literature that fate would, I think, be inevitable," Frye concludes (in an unpublished lecture, "Literature as a Critique of Pure Reason," 1982), perhaps echoing the passage with which Sartre ended *What Is Literature?*: "The world can very well do without literature. But it can do without man still better" (p. 291).

For nearly two thousand years, Frye thinks, Western Europe expressed its concerns through a vast set of myths; these myths are still vigorous today, even though Rousseau and the Romantics,

Marx and Freud have contributed new mythological elements. This set of myths has its source in the Bible, in the Judeo-Christian tradition which from the time of its creation has succeeded in absorbing the other myths present in the collective memory: those of King Arthur like those of classical mythology. The Bible, as Blake said, is "the Great Code of Art," proposing a model of space, from heaven to hell, and of time, from the genesis to the apocalypse; all the European poets used it, whether they were aware of doing so or not. We can see more clearly now where the unity of Frye's critical work lies: his first book, *Fearful Symmetry* (1947), is a monograph on Blake, and the most recent, *The Great Code* (1984), is an exploration of biblical mythology. In literary criticism, it seems, the object studied often takes over the will of the subject doing the studying: just as Bakhtin remained all his life a sort of spokesman for Dostoevsky, all Frye's work serves to amplify Blake's intuition and make it explicit.

CRITICISM II

In *Anatomy of Criticism*, Frye defines his project as "the systematic study of the formal causes of art" (p. 29). If we take his other writings into account, we should add: "and a free meditation on the social effects of art." But he himself is ready to make the correction, in *Anatomy* as elsewhere: "Criticism will always have two aspects, one turned toward the structure of literature and one turned toward the other cultural phenomena that form the social environment of literature. Together, they balance each other: when one is worked on to the exclusion of the other, the critical perspective goes out of focus" (*The Critical Path*, p. 25). That is why Frye refuses to identify himself with any school, as member or even head, and furthermore that is why he rejects as illusory the plurality of "methods" that characterize contemporary criticism: the only difference is in the part of the object to which one is attached. Understanding a literary text, he writes elsewhere (*The Stubborn Structure*, p. 88), never amounts to anything except relating it to different contexts: that of the author's other works and the rest of his life; that of his time; that of literature taken as a whole. A personal preference for the study of one context rather than another does not mean that it has exclusive relevance; the various critiques of a work may, once again, complement rather than contradict each other.

But how is criticism to be situated with respect to the opposition between concern and freedom, between mythology and science? On this issue Frye hesitates. On the one hand, he knows that criticism, like all the social sciences, like political theory or philosophy, is an integral part of the mythological structure proper to society, even if, just like the rest of the humanities, it also obeys rules of empirical verification and logical reasoning: it participates in fact in the establishment of a society's system of values. But on the other hand, true to his interpretation of science as a product of the attitude of freedom and not of concern, he refuses to attribute to the scientist any responsibility other than the exact description of his object. It might be possible to surmount this apparent contradiction in Frye's statements by going back to its cause, that is, to the complexity of the object described. It is true that these disciplines, and criticism in particular, belong at one and the same time to the sciences and the arts; not, as we saw already with Bakhtin, because criticism requires an "artistic" writing, but because even as he is obeying scientific constraints, the critic takes a position with respect to the values that are the subject matter of the literary texts themselves; or, in any case, he ought to be doing so. As Frye himself reminds us occasionally, "the only knowledge that is worth while is the knowledge that leads to wisdom, for knowledge without wisdom is a body without life" (*The Stubborn Structure*, p. 15). But can one aspire to wisdom if one is satisfied to situate each author in relation to his own particular ideal, as the author of *Anatomy of Criticism* advised us to do? If we are thus drawn into aporia, it is because Frye's initial dichotomy was too radical (which does not mean that it must be entirely eliminated). Values do not arise from empirical verification; that is a fact. But is it therefore inevitable that they be established by authority alone? Contrary to the adage, it is possible to *argue* over values and tastes; now this possibility itself implies a reference to the universal and to truth, which is no longer incompatible with the scientific spirit.

I believe that in reality Frye has chosen to reconcile knowledge and wisdom, knowledge and concern, rather than allowing himself to be locked into a monistic conception of his task; he has even gone fairly far in the direction of the artist and thus of the moralist, if we are to judge by the form and style of his writings. Not that everything in them is above reproach. His text often gives the impression of presenting in simpler terms, of "popularizing," ideas of which the rigorous version will never be made available. Furthermore, his works are curiously repetitive: I am inclined to attribute this less to the obvious facility with which he writes than to the somewhat naive conviction that his readers, like his listeners, are always new ones, and that he must therefore go back to the beginning and explain everything all over again; whatever the explanation, in each new book we discover that the preceding one was only a rough draft. We may regret this state of affairs, but we cannot help observing that Frye proceeds on the basis of a perfectly justified conviction, namely, that pedantry of style can destroy freedom of thought. This is why his systematic study has been complemented, as I indicated, by free reflection: specialized jargon is reduced to a minimum, the notes have disappeared, analyses of other works having to do with the same subjects are rare. The context recreated by Frye's works is that of a dialogue, not that of an impersonal study. He is speaking to a listener who is well disposed but not well informed. And although after finishing one of Frye's books the reader may not always have the impression of having learned a great deal, one nonetheless feels that one has been in contact for a time with a mind endowed with the rare quality of nobility.

7

Realist Criticism: Correspondence with Ian Watt

Except for two articles published in *Poétique*, Ian Watt's work has not been translated into French, This can be explained, though not excused, by the fact that up to now Watt has dealt mainly with English literature, although he has also ventured into the realm of general anthropological theory, as collaborator on a widely noted essay on the role of writing in history ("The Consequences of Literacy," with Jack Goody, 1960, reprinted in J. Goody, ed., *Literacy in Traditional Societies*, 1968). Moreover, Watt has not published abundantly: his work is limited to two books, *The Rise of the Novel* (1957), a study of the "birth of the novel" in England through the work of Defoe, Richardson, and Fielding, and *Conrad in the Nineteenth Century* (1979), the first of two projected volumes of a monograph on Conrad; in addition, he has written a dozen or so major articles. The reason for this limited output is inherent in the very nature of Watt's procedure: he is not a theoretician but an empiricist, and unlike the theoretician, the empiricist of necessity reads a great deal and writes little.

But Watt's two books are two masterpieces of literary criticism. This is why I have chosen Watt's work as an example—a particularly successful example—of a kind of critical enterprise that could easily be overlooked if programmatic utterances and theoretical reflections alone were to be taken into account; in fact, the enterprise illustrated here by Watt absorbs the efforts of a large majority in the critical profession. The task involves patient commentary, the restitution of the meaning of words and syntactic constructions, a search for information of all sorts—all subordinated to a single goal, a more complete understanding of the text under study. This kind of criticism does not shout its agenda from the rooftops, but an agenda there must be, nevertheless, if one only takes the trouble to look for it. As it happens, I am acquainted with Ian Watt; thus I decided to send him my description of his work, inviting him to make a statement in response. Our exchange of letters follows.

Dear Ian,

Let me share with you some of the ideas that your critical writings have given me.

I propose to use the term *commentary* to describe a text that is produced in response to another text in order to make the latter more intelligible. The commentator's fundamental procedure is always essentially the same: he relates the text he is analyzing to other elements of information which make up the text's context. What are the essential contexts to which one refers in reading a page? Schleiermacher, the founder of modern hermeneutics, distinguished between two types. On the one hand, the reader needs to know the language of the period, which might be symbolized by a dictionary and a grammar book; Schleiermacher used the label "grammatical" for interpretation carried out along these lines. On the other hand, the reader has to situate the passage he is analyzing within the corpus to which it belongs: the work from which it is excerpted, other works by the same author, and even the author's life history; Schleiermacher called this kind of interpretation "technical."

Schleiermacher's terms are no longer used to make this distinction, so I shall replace them with others: I shall speak of *philological* analysis in the first case (restitution of the language of the period) and of *structural* analysis, in the broad sense, in the second case (explication of intertextual relations). But these two contexts have not been found sufficient, and others have been added to the list: of these, I shall be concerned here with two that may be seen in some respects as extensions of Schleiermacher's. On the one hand, there is what I shall call the *ideological* context: it consists of those other discourses—philosophical, political, scientific, religious, or aesthetic discourse, or representations of socioeconomic realities—that are in use alongside the literary discourse; this context is therefore both *synchronic* and *heterogeneous,* contemporary and nonliterary. It is sometimes called the "historical" context, but that use of the word is paradoxical, since in fact any temporal dimension is excluded; the label would actually be better suited to another major context that I shall simply call the *literary* context in order to avoid confusing the issue. Here we are dealing with the literary tradition, with what writers and readers remember: this tradition is crystallized in generic conventions, narrative and stylistic stereotypes, more or less immutable images. This second context is thus at once *diachronic* and *homogeneous.*

What sorts of relationships obtain among these diverse contexts? Here we have to distinguish between what is theoretically possible and what actually occurs. In practice, modern specialization requires us to choose one context at the expense of the other, with a view to increasing our own competence. But in principle it is not easy to see on what grounds these successive relationships need to be declared mutually exclusive. Literary works (like other kinds of works, obviously) are quite clearly dependent on *both* their ideological *and* their literary contexts; furthermore, it goes without saying that both philological analysis and structural analysis should be part of any attempt at a better grasp of a work's meaning. Thus it is both useless and detrimental to set these various perspectives at odds, claiming the right of monopoly for each; if some have strayed onto that path, it is because they have mistaken the means for the end. Instead of allowing the scholarly efforts undertaken within each of these perspectives to contribute to the understanding of literary works, some critics have reified the various viewpoints, turning them into competing ideologies with a totalizing cast. Nevertheless, it is good to discover that the critical perspectives in question are mutually compatible, not only in principle but also in fact; and this is precisely what your critical work demonstrates.

The first chapter of *The Rise of the Novel* begins with a double query concerning the novel, and all the rest of the book constitutes a reply: "How does it differ from the prose fiction of the past, from that of Greece, for example, or that of the Middle Ages, or of seventeenth-century France? And is there any reason why these differences appeared when and where they did?" (p. 9). It is already clear that these questions pertain to several of the contexts mentioned above. Philological competence is taken for granted, and thus not even mentioned; but the first question brings to mind both the structural perspective (the identification of the novelistic genre, its formal description) and the literary perspective (the confrontation of the novelistic form with literary tradition), whereas the second is oriented toward the ideological context, since it relates the genre to other contemporary phenomena.

And the entire book carries out these diverse inquiries simultaneously. On the one hand, it describes the formal features of the novelistic genre as contrasted with earlier prose texts: these features include the choice of an original rather than a traditional plot; the representation of changing phenomena rather than immutable essences; interest in the life of individual people as evidenced by a new type of character name; the particularization of time, which leads to the interior monologue of the twentieth century; the particularization of space; the use of language as "a purely referential medium" (p. 28), and so on. On the other hand, the book analyzes the important ideas contributed by Descartes and Locke, and by the religious revolution of the Puritans, and at the same time it analyzes the transformations of social and economic realities themselves, since these realities, in the form of discourse or images, are equally present in the minds of the authors and readers of the day (for example, the evolution of marriage in eighteenth-century England is described in statistical terms).

The same thing is true of your other writings. You analyze each of Conrad's works (here we have the case of an individual writer rather than a genre) at length on its own terms; but your analyses are preceded by a reference to the major ideological oppositions of the period (between the Victorian ethic and a rising nihilism, between religious nostalgia and a scientistic ideology), along with their echoes in aesthetic thought proper (the impressionist and symbolist movements); furthermore, you continually confront these works with other literary texts, contemporary and otherwise. A briefer analysis of Henry James identifies the features of his style first of all: "a preference for non-transitive verbs; many abstract nouns; copious use of 'that'; a certain amount of elegant variation to avoid piling up personal pronouns and adjectives such as 'he,' 'his' and 'him'; and the presence of a great many negatives and near-negatives" ("The First Paragraph of *The Ambassadors*," p. 255); this is extended by a discussion of James's empiricism and his individualism, and of skeptical relativism, which dominates not only James's thought but more generally that of the second half of the nineteenth century.

My description may make your juxtaposition appear mechanical, but nothing could be further from the truth. The explanation, I suggest, is the following. In each of your books you forge a *lingua franca*, a kind of Esperanto into which you translate the various discourses you are analyzing. This intermediary language is the language of *ideology*; I am using that term here to designate the translation of philosophical or religious or political ideas and also of literary forms into everyday language. In this sense it is akin to what Montesquieu called "the spirit of nations," an ideological substratum that is produced through the combined influence of all social institutions and that influences those institutions in turn. To be sure, if the first kind of conversion, the translation of other types of discourse into ideological discourse, merely confronts you with the ongoing problem of deciding what level of abstraction is appropriate, the second kind, the translation of literary forms into ideology, brings out an exceptional gift for interpretation on your part. With apparent ease you write sentences like the following: "[Defoe's] total subordination of the plot to the pattern of the autobiographical memoir is as defiant an assertion of the primacy of individual experience in the novel as Descartes's *cogito ergo sum* was in philosophy" (*The Rise of the Novel*, p. 15); or this: "the novel requires a world view which is centered on the social relationships between individual persons" (ibid., p. 84); or again: "the most obvious and demonstrable features of James's prose style, its vocabulary and syntax, are direct reflections of his attitude to life and his conception of the novel" ("The First Paragraph of *The Ambassadors*," p. 271).

The hypothesis underlying an analysis of this sort is that literature is just one form of ideology among others. This hypothesis — a minimal one — must not be confused with more ambitious claims. It would be going too far, for example, to assert that a relation of cause and effect obtains between an already constituted social ideology and literature. "Both the philosophical and the literary innovations [of the eighteenth century] must be seen as parallel manifestations of larger change — that vast transformation of Western civilization since the Renaissance which has replaced the unified world picture of the Middle Ages with another very different one" (*The Rise of the Novel*, p. 31). It is even imprudent to believe that the ideology in a book is a faithful representation of the ideology in the surrounding world. "In any case the greatest authors are rarely representative of the ideology of their period; they tend rather to expose its internal contradictions or the very partial nature of its capacity for dealing with the facts of experience" (*Conrad in the Nineteenth Century*, p. 147). But if the author is not satisfied to follow the dominant voices of his time, he nonetheless enters into argument with them; in order to understand him, we need to be familiar with those voices in turn.

You propose to restore the meaning of the work in itself, no more and no less, with the help of a detailed analysis of the text and of a broad investigation of its contexts; as you say yourself, "the primary commitment must be to what may be called the literal imagination—the analytic commentary restricts itself to what the imagination can discover through a literal reading of the work" (ibid., p. x). Such a project may appear outdated today, at a time when "skeptical relativism" has gained much new ground. Rather than argue over the theoretical possibility of your project, I for one will settle for observing its existence in fact; anyone who does not believe in it should read the hundred thirty pages you have devoted to Conrad's *Heart of Darkness*.

But I am struck at the same time by another fact. Let us say that for you the critical ideal is faithfulness alone, the exact representation of one part of the world (constituted by the productions of the mind). Now you discuss this project in your books, not in connection with your own enterprise—on the contrary, you are very sparing with programmatic declarations—but in connection with those writers who constitute the particular subject matter of your work, the realists. A good number of these writers deny that their works may be perceived in themselves: the works exist as pure transparency; they exist only in order to transmit a segment of reality. These are writers "whose prose aims exclusively at what Locke defined as the proper purpose of language, 'to convey the knowledge of things', and [their] novels as a whole pretend to be no more than a transcription of real life—in Flaubert's words, 'le réel écrit'" (*The Rise of the Novel*, p. 30). They seek to eradicate all traces of a design that might be attributed to them: the reported facts are not presented in order to illustrate some idea on the author's part, but simply because they occurred. "This is the kind of participation which the novel typically induces: it makes us feel that we are in contact not with literature but with the raw materials of life itself as they are momentarily reflected in the minds of the protagonists" (ibid., p. 193).

You come close to recognizing this parallelism yourself. As you analyze one of Conrad's stories, *The Shadow-Line*, you try to discover Conrad's philosophical position, and you write: "Conrad is not concerned to tell us that the various general features which he discerns in the experience of the narrator are inherently good or bad, but that they are there" ("Story and Idea in Conrad's *The Shadow-Line*," p. 147). This is the realist position in literature: to show, without judging. But on the immediately preceding page, you write, in connection with your own analysis: "Whether the ideas I have attributed to *The Shadow-Line* are true or interesting, and whether (and how) Conrad made them seem so, are not directly within my present purview" (ibid., p. 146); needless to say, the question will not be dealt with elsewhere either. Here, then, we are faced with the realist position in criticism; once again the writer is content to show without judging. Is that why, when you refer to your own book, *The Rise of the Novel*, twenty years after its publication, you call it "a work of realist criticism" and you declare "the necessity of realism in literary criticism" ("The Realities of Realism," unpublished talk, 1978): not criticism of realist works, but realist criticism of works?

Critics do allow themselves to be very much influenced by the subject of their research (its subject, indeed, rather than its object): Bakhtin was influenced by Dostoevsky, Frye by Blake, you by the realists; Blanchot was similarly influenced by Sade, Jakobson by Khlebnikov, Mallarmé, and Baudelaire. . . . Schools of criticism are modeled on literary trends. The reason for this is that critical activity is (at least) twofold: it offers a description of the world, on the one hand (in this way it can be compared to science), and it is an ideological activity on the other (in this it is like literature). So far, so good.

But the program of "realist criticism," whether explicit or implicit, poses a different problem. When structuralist criticism presents its work as perfectly objective (that is, as depending only upon its object) and transparent, it remains in harmony with its own conception of the literary work: such a work is already viewed as an artefact that is exhausted in its immanence, as an object that can be explained only in terms of itself. The immanence of literature has as its counterpart the immanence of the critical work. The same cannot be said, however, of criticism that is sensitive to the ideological context. In fact, this latter sort of criticism is clearly opposed to the realist program. The realist writer claims that his work is justified only by the existence of the things he represents; he admits to no project, and consequently to no ideology; he does not judge, he shows. Ideological criticism demolishes this claim: far from being merely a faithful reflection of the real, the realist work, we learn, is also the product of an ideology (the author's)— whence the relevance of the study of the context. But, having carried out this demonstration, realist criticism (a subspecies of ideological criticism) adopts—perhaps unwittingly—the credo that has just been demolished and in turn conveys the following message: the work I have produced has as its only justification the truth that it contains; it is a "slice of life," "*le réel écrit*," it has neither project nor ideology, it settles for representing without passing judgments. But why would what was true of literature not be true of criticism? How does it happen that the ascendancy of ideology, so strong in the one instance, stops in the other instance at the threshold of the enterprise?

To be sure, enclosure within immanence can be no more than a project: the critic cannot prevent himself from judging. Yet there is a difference between the judgments for which the author accepts responsibility and those that come across surreptitiously. After presenting Defoe's praise of solitude, you add: "In his narrative . . . Defoe disregarded two important facts: the social nature of all human economies, and the actual psychological effects of solitude" (*The Rise of the Novel*, p. 87); thus we learn that you pass judgments on this subject that differ from Defoe's. When you report Conrad's ideas on the function of literature, you cannot keep from commenting: "History has remorselessly apprised us of the objections to these high claims: that literature does not really do these things; . . . and that 'human society' is not in fact 'bound together' by literature or by anything else" (*Conrad in the Nineteenth Century*, p. 80). When Conrad bases his human pessimism on a geological fatality, you retort: "We can logically object that the life of a planet is after all much longer than that of a man, and that

Conrad is really confusing two wholly different orders of temporal magnitude" (ibid., p. 154). This is where criticism stops being pure presentation and becomes, by means of dialogue, a shared search for truth; but one would like to be able to benefit more directly from your own wisdom.

"Wisdom and truth" in fact constitute part of your "patent preoccupation" in your writings ("The Realities of Realism," p. 18), as they do of a large part of realist literature itself. There is a tension proper to realism, between its program of pure presentation and its natural propensity to judgment, such that you find yourself led, in *The Rise of the Novel* and elsewhere, to distinguish between two types of realism, which are in fact realism of presentation and realism of assessment. Up to now, only the first type has been in question. It is the second type, however, that is characterized by "contact with the whole tradition of civilised values," "a true grasp of human reality," and "a wise assessment of life" (*The Rise of the Novel*, p. 288). In reality, every realist author practices the two simultaneously: "Some form of evaluation is always inextricably connected with any writer's presentations" ("Serious Reflections on *The Rise of the Novel*," p. 214). The difference is only one of intention, but that "only" is crucial: unlike Defoe's, "Fielding's words and phrases intentionally invoke not only the actual narrative event, but the whole literary, historical, and philosophical perspective in which character or action should be placed by the reader" (ibid.).

Thus your work—and with it the best part of what is called historical criticism—oscillates between realism of presentation and realism of assessment, between the "immanentist" program and the practice of dialogue, between concern for truth of correspondence and concern for wisdom. I would have liked to see your work more firmly committed to the second path, yet I confess that I am also attracted to the spirit that prefers to keep a low profile and that leads you to write (in "The Realities of Realism"): "I cannot believe that we are required to spell out all our postulates in black and white."

Cordially,

Tzvetan

Correspondence with Ian Watt

Dear Tzvetan,

Like other authors, I suppose, there's nothing I like more than being taken notice of by critics, except perhaps having the opportunity to say how these critics have failed to do full justice to my merits. Of course, you have done justice, and more; your account of my work seems to me not only substantially right, but also a very perceptive conceptual synthesis of the various aspects of what I've tried to do as a critic. Still, there are a few other things that might be mentioned.

Your title was something of a shock: am I a "realist critic" *tout court*? Of course I've been called a "sociological realist" in print, and my basic reaction to that; as I said in that talk you mention, was "a yawn followed by a plea of *nolo contendere*." Actually, that talk is still unpublished because the occasion of giving it required me to affirm a general critical position, and I didn't really want to. In any case my full title was: "Flat-footed and Fly-blown: The Realities of Realism"; the two adjectival phrases with which I began were meant as an ironical acknowledgment of the pedestrian and out-of-date nature of my critical position.

In what sense is my "critical position" "realist"?

Studying the relation between the real world and the literary work is not, in my view, the only proper aim of literary criticism; so I wouldn't like to be classified as a "mimetic critic," which is what some have called Auerbach. This is not, of course, to assert that studying the modes of literary representation is not a useful thing to do, as Auerbach, among other things, magnificently shows. Naturally I don't accept the absolutely opposite position either: the assumption that the relationship between the literary work and the world is a completely useless study—useless on the theoretical grounds that the world is completely heterogeneous whereas literature is not. I agree that the relation between the world, and either the literary work or the language it uses, cannot be fully analyzed or described. Less happily, I am even willing to agree that if one is going to try to found a scientific critical system it may be advisable, as a matter of method, to ignore the relation between the work and the world. But I do not agree that there is no relation whatever between the work and the world, or between the work and the words we use to describe it; on the contrary, I believe that much of the best literary criticism is concerned with that relationship.

Obviously, I accept that this view entails some methodological difficulties, and that in some areas of literary study they are probably insuperable. But I would rather write in the other literary areas anyway; and in those, at least, the vast Western tradition of philosophy which runs counter to common-sense assumptions about reality leaves me totally unperturbed. On what grounds? Most simply, that literary criticism is essentially a social rather than a philosophical activity, and that in that area epistemological skepticism need not be accepted, or even considered. What I am attempting to do is largely, to use I. A. Richards's phrase, "Practical Criticism."

I can't, then, grumble too seriously about the term "realist"; I would, though, like to suggest that "historical" and "sociological" should be added. You acknowledge the historical tendency in my work when you talk about how "historical criticism" always oscillates between the concern for truth of "presentation" and the concern for wisdom of judgment. You say, and I suppose rightly, that you wish I had concerned myself more with the wisdom side of the dichotomy, and done more with what, in *The Rise of the Novel*, I call "realism of assessment" (p. 12). But there was a genuine difficulty. The basic thesis of the book was founded on the great—one might even say the naive—seriousness with which both Defoe and Richardson took what I called "realism of presentation", this alone went far to explain what was historically new, in the sense of "chronologically unprecedented," in the "rise of the novel." From this point of view, at least, "realism of assessment" was, after all, a feature of narrative which the novel, if it had the quality at all, certainly shared with earlier narratives and other literary genres. I had to introduce the concept itself, of course, when I came to Fielding, but my treatment of it was, or was intended to be, rather conspicuously incomplete. That I had no intention of rejecting the importance of "realism of assessment" as such, however, was suggested by the presence of two of the book's ten chapters—those on *Moll Flanders* and *Clarissa*. They were much less historical or sociological than critical, and I believe that the writing made it clear that I felt that I was giving my own personal "assessment" of the two works; at least I was patently free to make analyses and judgments about the moral value of actions, characters, or an author's comment. I suspect, incidentally, that one reason many readers haven't been aware of the extent to which I actually engage with questions of ethical and social judgment is because of what you—originally and I think rightly—call my use of a personal *lingua franca* which mediates the "ideological" and the "literary" languages.

I have written directly about the moral and social value of literature in a short essay called "Literature and Society." There, speaking about the didactic value of great writing, I wrote:

> . . . the works of Sophocles and Shakespeare, Goethe and Tolstoy, are essentially didactic only in the sense that our social and moral awareness is increased by imaginative participation in the works of those who have been supremely responsive to the realities of human experience: realities, of course, which always have a very important social component.
>
> From this perspective the literary opposition between the Realist and Naturalist insistence on the literal description of the actual social worlds, and the Parnassian and Symbolist reassertion of the artistic autonomy of imaginative creation, is seen to be a good deal less than absolute. For, although there is an age-old divergence between those who see man as essentially a social being, and those who insist on his individual uniqueness, the force of the contradiction begins to disappear the moment a writer puts pen to paper: as W. B. Yeats put it, "art is the social act of a solitary man." [Pp. 312-313]

The passage ends by considering one element of criticism which is certainly nonrealist and even nonsocial, but is, nevertheless, in its own way, moral:

> It is a social act, however, of a very special kind, and one which reminds us that "literature and society" can be a misleading phrase in yet another way, because it suggests a more absolute distinction between the two terms than is actually the case. If only because, in one perfectly valid sense, literature *is* its own society: it is the subtlest and the most enduring means which man has devised for communicating with his fellows; and not the least of its functions is to give those who have learned its language something that no other society has ever afforded. [P. 313]

At a rather high level of abstraction, then, I assume that some literature, at least, should be treated as autonomous, and not from the point of view of some mimetic, referential, historical, or social category; but it remains aesthetic and moral.

The moral tradition in general is, of course, long established

117

among English critics, from Matthew Arnold to F. R. Leavis. I remember, as part of the final examination for the B.A. at Cambridge, taking a paper called "The English Moralists." It sounds stuffy and provincial, but the questions actually began with Plato and Aristotle, and ended with a rich mixture of modern English and Continental philosophers, novelists, and poets. Looking at literary works from a definitely, though not exclusively, ethical point of view is typical of many English critics, including myself; I remember one of my American friends commenting that my recent book, *Conrad in the Nineteenth Century*, was merely "More Watt on Life." I don't particularly mind the ironic aspersion; it seems to me to be appropriate for the teacher. As I wrote in an article giving my views on teaching:

> . . . many of our best students really want an absolute system of truth; and many of our most influential modes of criticism, from formalism to structuralism and semiotics, have in common the assumption that what we ought to do is extract some kind of changeless universal pattern from the particularities and contingencies of the literary work. But we surely don't need Blake or Arnold to tell us that it is the concreteness of literature which is its characteristic strength. The engagement of the individual's mind, senses, and feelings, not with a universal model which the teacher or the student has brought along, but with the stubborn resistance of the particularities of the other, or, to use Arnold's terms, of the "not-ourselves," exercises the imagination, and is thus the main general source of the educational value of reading literature, as Coleridge put it in the eleventh lecture on Shakespeare, "the imagination is the distinguishing characteristic of man as a progressive being." ["On Not Attempting to Be a Piano," p. 14]

My concern with social and moral values, incidentally, wasn't a matter of the writer's having, or not having, a didactic purpose. I went on to say that the kind of imagination which Coleridge presumably had in mind was that which, as he wrote, had the effect of "carrying the mind out of self." That, Coleridge thought, was the main educational function of literature, and as I agreed with him I ended the talk:

> [Literature] Department classes should be classes for the reading— and the real reading—of literature that really is literature, and then for writing about it in a way that, in its own appropriately humble manner, attempts to be literature, or at least not to demean it. . . . This

simple, unambitious, and old-fashioned program . . . seems to me the natural outgrowth of the imperatives of our subject, and of the reasons for our commitment to it. One reason for that commitment was suggested a hundred years ago by Turgenev in a brief prose poem on his personal feelings towards his own language, a passage which Russian schoolboys, I believe, still learn by heart. Turgenev invokes the greatness, power, truth, and freedom of his language, and then reflects: "Without you, how could one avoid falling into despair at the sight of all that goes on around us? Yet it is impossible to believe that such a language was not given to a great people." [P. 15]

Two last points occur to me. You quote me as saying that "I cannot believe that we are required to spell out all our postulates in black and white." This reluctance to state one's premises is partly because of my empiricism, or my skepticism about philosophical methods in general; but also because of my particular belief in the function of critical writing. It is relatively humble: Sartre said of *L'Etranger* that it is a translation from the original silence; and I would risk the addition that good criticism is only a supremely responsive and illuminating paraphrase of what others have so translated. It is also humble in what topics it permits itself to address. This critical reticence may just be a reflection of the English notion of polite manners in public discourse; but there are surely some positive advantages in not, for example, speaking directly about the truth or the values of a work of literature; one of them is that it leaves more for the reader to do on his own. I suppose I write about literary values as such only when I think I can assume a community of belief with my readers.

This is not to deny your view that my idea of criticism is too "self-sufficient"; I certainly tend to circumscribe the area in which I am presenting myself to the reader more narrowly than many critics. It is partly a question of reducing theoretical matters to a minimum; and, if I may mention a personal view, one paradoxical result of this is that my writings are rather popular with many readers of criticism but that at the same time I am not regarded as a critic at all by some of my colleagues. A Conrad scholar, Andrzej Busza, was puzzled by this, and once asked me about the antipathy my "method" aroused in some other critics; I answered: "Le bon sens n'a jamais fait école."

One illustration of this may make my position clearer. Some years ago, I had to face some serious objections from my American publisher who, at least until my letter, didn't want to publish my Conrad manuscript. I wrote to him in part:

> The full critical justification of my Conrad enterprise which the Editorial Committee asks me to add to my preface would not be particularly difficult to do (examples are available in most doctoral dissertations); but, through its necessary abstractness, over-simplification, and implied self-importance, it would remove the book from the particular literary sphere where I think it belongs; and if I began the book with such a statement, I would immediately bore, offend, or deter many of my readers, since I would in effect be saying, "This is where I stand on the various principles which we critics have been quarrelling about over the centuries. Pay very close attention because it's the price of admission to the book that follows." But in fact I don't think it is; and so I don't believe anyone is entitled to assert as a general principle that every book of criticism should contain "a forthright statement or explanation of the rationale of its critical method." I stand with Samuel Johnson in rejecting "the cant of those who judge by principles rather than perception."

Lastly I should also add that, if one also considers my actual personal tastes in reading, my empiricism is rather more apparent than real; or at least, my empiricism is partly qualified by a fairly wide knowledge of critics and thinkers of very different persuasions from my own. I mention my debt to Ivor Richards and Theodor Adorno in the preface to *The Rise of the Novel*; and when the Modern Language Association asked me to describe my attitude to teaching, I turned back to my memories of the French poet Francis Ponge. I will end by quoting another part of the essay, "On Not Attempting to Be a Piano." The passage begins with an extreme form of realistic particularity, but then considerably expands its range of meaning:

> I have always found my own attitude to literature, and to the institutional context with which that attitude coexists, much simpler, much more intuitive, and much less amenable to discussion or theoretical formulation, than it seems to be for most of my colleagues. If I look for an image that can bridge this gap between the public and the private . . . I must go back some three decades, and to the Parisian left bank, where I found myself again [in 1946] after an absence of seven years in the army. In the talk I heard then, four new words struck me. I soon got tired of the first three: *Engagé. Authentique. Absurde;* but the fourth—*Les Choses*—seemed somewhat less fly-blown. I started read-

ing Francis Ponge's prose poems [in *Le Parti Pris des Choses*] about "things" with enormous interest. I remember particularly a newspaper article about a talk Ponge had given called *Tentative Orale* [1947]. His "attempt at a speech" circled amiably around his dislike of the common hyperboles about literature, his sense of being sickened at general theoretical and public propositions, and how in his own writing, finding it impossible to put the great literary subjects into words, he had determined, like a man at the edge of a precipice, to fix his gaze on the immediate object—a tree, the balustrade, the next step —and try to put that into words instead. It was a charming anti-talk, especially its ending. "So we haven't had a lecture?" he commented. "Perhaps not. Why did you ask me?" Then he concluded: "Dear table. Goodbye!" At this, Ponge leaned over and embraced the table; then he explained: "You see, if I love it, it's because there's absolutely nothing in it which allows one to believe that it takes itself for a piano."

I would like my own activities as a student and teacher of literature to be as simple and yet comprehensive as Ponge's gesture. It should contain the same four necessary constituents: an intellectual recognition of just what I am modestly but directly attending to; an aesthetic appreciation of the object of my attention for what it exactly is; a direct commitment of my feelings to that object; and lastly, perhaps incidentally, an attempt to express all of the first three things in words. The collective enterprise of the students and teachers in an English department, I take it, should also be a joint engagement with these four constituents; and its rationale would be only that, as Ponge puts it, in his "Notes for a Shell," language (*parole*) and the monuments created out of it are the things which are most perfectly adapted to the human mollusk, and enable him to experience and express his fraternity with the objects of his world.

To which I can now only add that I have never tried to be a piano.

Yours,

Ian

8

Literature as Fact and Value: Conversation with Paul Bénichou

I first "met" Paul Bénichou's work while I was studying the history of ideologies in France: his commentaries on the authors I was reading—La Rochefoucauld, Jean-Jacques Rousseau, Benjamin Constant—struck me in each case as particularly judicious. Later, I became familiar with his major works, *Morales du grand siècle*, *Le Sacre de l'écrivain*, *Le Temps des prophètes*, and I noted that in Bénichou French literary and intellectual life between the seventeenth and the nineteenth centuries had found a historian of uncommon merit, whose work deserved to be better known not only as an irreplaceable introduction to the field, but also for its exemplary historical analyses. In addition, I was attracted by the absence of any preoccupation with "purity" (he never seemed tempted to reduce literature to "pure poetry"): in his critical writings, literature was only the center of a broader field made up of public discourse.

To what can we attribute Bénichou's critical acumen? Needless to say, the factual content of his work is abundant and reliable. He has not limited his reading to the major works; he has read the minor works as well, and even the contemporary press. But this much, clearly, is not enough; even mentioning such a preliminary requirement would be superfluous if others did not tend to neglect it now and then. To my mind, Bénichou's "secret" is to be found elsewhere: in the concern for truth that underlies his analyses. The truth in question here is no longer simply a matter of accurate information; it is the horizon of a search in which both writer and critic are engaged. The best way to discover a writer's "intention" is to accept the role of interlocutor (and not to be satisfied with a faithful reconstruction—one which by that very token ceases to be faithful), thus to take a stand on the ultimate rightness of the author's position, and in so doing to invite one's readers in turn to commit themselves to the quest for truth, rather than to present readers with a well-constructed object destined to produce an admiring silence.

In all fairness I ought to add that, while I find Bénichou's work exemplary in many respects, I also have some reservations, the most important of which—and the only one that raises a question of principle—concerns his relative lack of attention to the structure of literary works themselves, to their rhetorical, narrative, and generic modalities. (However, in the course of our conversation he replied, as I expected he would, that the question was not really one of principle but one of personal inclination and choice which needn't be explored further.)

Bénichou's general ideas on literature and criticism constitute only a very small portion of the half-dozen volumes that make up his entire work. That is why I felt it would be useful to analyze his undertaking by examining both his statements of principle and his concrete studies. But I found myself in some doubt as to the form this analysis should take. Speaking of criticism, and of his own criticism, Bénichou says: "If I sometimes make bold to decipher in literary texts what their authors perhaps did not put in them knowingly, it is in the hope that they would accept the discovery, if they were here" (*L'Ecrivain et ses travaux*, p. xiv). I decided to follow his precept and to submit to him my own interpretation of his thought, so he could express his agreement or disagreement and answer the questions to which my reading gave rise. More often than not, the author on whom a critic is working has long since become inaccessible to this kind of inquiry; I was fortunate enough to be living in the same time and place as my author.

We met one cold winter morning, in the Latin Quarter. Paul Bénichou agreed to the idea of an interview; we worked out the following text together, without seeking to minimize our differences.

Thus our text not only takes a certain idea of criticism as its subject but also illustrates it.

LITERATURE

Definition

TZVETAN TODOROV: In defining the object of your work, you have rejected the two most influential definitions of literature: the "classical"—or, more precisely, the Aristotelian—definition, according to which poetry is a representation by means of language, whereas painting is a representation by means of images, and so forth; and the "Romantic" definition, which holds poetry to be an intransitive use of language, an art of language. Your point of departure was a different conception of literature, a much broader one, in which nothing separates it abruptly from "everything that is written for the public" (*L'Ecrivain*, p. x). What is most striking, first of all, in your approach, is that it does not start with the nature of the product but with its use (a diary, as Tynianov said, belongs to literature in certain periods and not in others). (But is there no elective affinity between function and structure?) And the result speaks for itself: in your books you have dealt with Mallarmé and with popular poetry, with both Corneille and Pascal.

You criticize earlier definitions for reducing literature to an art, that is, to a pure object of aesthetic contemplation. "Literature . . . cannot be limited to simple 'manners of speaking'" (*Man and Ethics*, p. 178); "literary fictions [are] far from being simple distractions of civilized life" (*L'Ecrivain*, p. x). (But is art what is really at stake here, or merely the Romantic conception of art? Is painting nothing but art, in this narrow sense of the word?) Literature is art but it is also something else, through which it is related not to music and dance but to the discourse of history, politics, and philosophy. It "involves . . . sentiment and imagination" (*Man and Ethics*, p. 178); it is a way of "taking a stand on the world and the human condition" (*L'Ecrivain*, p. x), "a writer usually reinforces values" (ibid., p. xv). Literature is a way of taking a stance with respect to the values of society; let us say, in a word, that literature is *ideology*.

All literature has always been *both*, art *and* ideology, and it would be useless to look for pure substances: this is the lesson, for example, of Romanticism. "The authors of systems are . . . brothers of the poets. One cannot be unaware of this fraternity, still less deplore it, while imagining a pure Romanticism that protected art from an adulterous admixture of ideology: that would no longer be Romanticism but something else, something that is nowhere to be found" (*Le Temps des prophètes*, 1977, p. 566).

If we suppose that this is the way things are, could not literature be defined as the intersection of public discourse (and thus of ideological discourse) and of art? Although we would still have to come to an agreement about the meaning of the word "art" itself.

PAUL BENICHOU: I should simply like to say one or two things about this problem of definition. In general, and in our critical studies in particular, I am not very much in favor of definitions. To define literature itself, especially, seems to me the height of difficulty. Any definition of this sort is likely to fall short of the mark or else to go too far. The one you quoted earlier, the one that calls literature "everything that is written for the public," is too broad. The one thing in its favor is that it draws attention to the impossibility of providing a definition with precise contours. The one you point to next, the one that makes literature out to be an "art of language," evokes only a very restricted aspect of what is being defined. The same criticism can be leveled, to a lesser degree, against the definition that you propose in the end: the encounter between ideological discourse and art. As it does not give the slightest idea, for example, of what a play or a poem might be, this definition is a ghostly one, so to speak. It does, however, have the advantage of positing two of the realities that are more or less bound to be present in every literary work, provided that the notion of *ideology* is stripped of any pejorative nuance. It is important to stress this, because such a nuance has been attached to the word *ideology* from the outset: "empty and harmful thought," in the language of the French counterrevolution; then, in Marxist language, "thought subservient to material interests under a false appearance of autonomy." On the contrary, "ideology," as an activity of the mind positing values, has to be envisaged in the fullness of its role, as one of humanity's fundamental faculties.

Art and Ideology

T.T.: If we accept (if only as a first approximation) such a definition of literature, we can expect the "ideological" and "artistic" aspects of the work to be treated in a balanced way. This turns out not to be the case, however, for, in your books (perhaps in reaction to an earlier situation?), "literature is considered principally as a vehicle for ideas" (*Le Sacre de l'écrivain*, 1973, p. 18), and you announce that you are interested only in "the ideas that literature conveys" (ibid., p. 466). In fact, when you analyze the ideology of someone like Corneille (in *Man and Ethics*, for example), you draw it entirely from the plots of his plays, from his characters and their statements, without ever offering the slightest comment on genre, composition, style, meter, and so forth. Are these elements of the work accidental and arbitrary? Or, even though they conform to their own organizing principles, do they escape the ascendancy of ideology? You never analyze a literary work in its entirety, either: does this mean that that level of structuring, halfway between the isolated element (a line, an episode, a theme) and the global universe of the writer, has no relevance for the identification of the writer's thought?

It is true that you offer some clarifications as to the nature of the "ideas" in question, which make them out to be something other than pure ideas. What interests you in fact is not a given idea as it can be found in some theoretical work, but that same idea compromised, as it were, in an individual existence, in certain particular forms, in the attachment to certain values. This position was already expressed and illustrated in *Man and Ethics*: "the true import of a doctrine or theory lies in the human intent that inspires it, in the conduct to which it leads, and in the nature of the values it defends or condemns, [much more than in] the speculative aspect of a statement or creed. . . . To give meaning to the debate and human relevance to the conflicting arguments one must look for the profound motives, that is, *passion* that actually produced them" (pp. 77-78).

However, when you are analyzing an author such as Mallarmé, you seem to adopt a different attitude. Here you establish solidarity between poetic technique and thought, between "form" and "substance": "There is no discontinuity between the 'grammarians' debate' to which Mallarmé's syntax gives rise, to use his own expression, and the meditation encouraged, from further and further away and secretly, by the 'reflection from underneath' that Mallarmé admits is 'almost inseparable from the surface given over to routine'" (*L'Ecrivain*, p. 76). One finds the same position in a more recent study ("Poétique et métaphysique dans trois sonnets de Mallarmé," in *La Passion de la raison*, 1983), in which you are seeking "the profound motivations of Mallarmé's obscurity" (p. 415), and in which, after analyzing the construction of a poem in detail, you conclude that "the strange structure of the sonnet confirms, in a way, the metaphysics that the sonnet professes. . . . In short, Mallarmé's very technique here gives form to his negation of the soul" (p. 414).

Is this difference in treatment deliberate?

P.B.: I do not believe I have ever thought that ideology, in literature, deserved more attention than art. In the very passage you are quoting, I stated that "[the perspective] *I have adopted* seems to shed light in particular on the ideas that literature conveys." The words I am stressing made it clear that I was not defining an ideal criticism but a personal choice. And I went on to develop at length the idea of a necessary conjunction, in literature, between ideas and perceptible forms. The fact that I myself have concentrated principally on what is called the "history of ideas" corresponds to my own mindset and to the preferences of my own curiosity; that is all. Moreover, it seems to me that the expression "history of ideas" does not do justice to what I have tried to do: for *ideas*, which are abstract by definition, cease to be so when they are embodied in a literature and are given corporal form.

It is true that I should be generally inclined to believe in the relative primacy of thought over forms, to the extent that a more or less clear ideological intention is what seems to me most often to be the driving force behind the perceptible materials of the work. But in no way do I exclude the possibility that the opposite may occur. This argument is not fundamental, as it has to do only with the relative proportion of influence, which has little chance of being fixed, between two equally necessary components.

You say that I never analyze the organization of a work taken as a whole. I have done this, however: for example, with Racine's *Phèdre* (in *L'Ecrivain*). To be sure, I was considering the characters of this tragedy in the general context, the folkloric and literary context, of the earlier versions of the fable that constitutes its subject. But this preliminary research seemed indispensable in order to shed light on the construction and the organization of the Racinian *Phèdre*, in which I wanted to show the close relationship between a world view and the arrangement of the formal materials. I went still further in another case, that of Corneille's *Rodogune*. I attempted to show how a proposed scenario, adopted by the author of this tragedy with formal elegance and paradox in view, had given a new orientation to the conception of the characters' personalities and to the very meaning of the drama. This study, which was the topic of a lecture at the Ecole Normale in 1967, has not been published to date, so you could not have taken it into account.[1] Unfortunately, I have not had the time to devote to further studies of this sort.

Where poets are concerned, the question seems to me no different. As for the Romantics, I have often looked at the ideas that emerge from the whole of their work rather than the construction of one or another of their poems, and I am in the process of preparing a collection of studies of this sort. But there is no poetic thought, no matter how broadly conceived, that is not tied to formal realities. In studying a particular poem, one cannot avoid considering its verbal organization. That is true for every poet, and Mallarmé is no exception; but, having made his technique a screen that he erects between the meanings of his poems and the reader, he is more imperious than other poets in obliging the critic to penetrate that technique—vocabulary, syntax, metaphors, all arranged in a deliberately atypical way and requiring close examination. All my life, here and there in articles and with my students, I have studied poems, tragedies, and novels. But I have chosen rather to write books on writers, or even groups of writers, considered through their works taken as a whole. At the level of technical devices and forms, such a choice allows only general observations; I do not believe I have neglected to make these whenever they did not seem self-evident.

One more point. I have devoted a good deal of time to studies of French and Spanish oral poetry (traditional or "folkloric" poetry), and in this area I argue—rightly or wrongly—that ideology is of little interest. This poetry (the Hispanic *romancero*, French songs

[1]This study has since been published (in *Le Débat*, 31 [1984]), 82–102.

from the oral tradition) brings from the Middle Ages to our day notions and types that have been in unbroken favor; the variations to which this poetry has been subjected over the centuries by historico-social evolution are all too obvious and hold no surprises; they are unimportant in comparison with the permanence of the subjects treated, the schemas of fable construction, and the judgments that more or less explicitly accompany the various situations of love, betrayal, adultery, murder, or war. On the other hand, this poetry is of the greatest interest in terms of the devices of formal creation that it displays: under the effect of the infinitely renewed play of variants, the order of narrative, the organization of incidents, the details of features and expressions are seen to be modified, diversified, sometimes changing or ruining the poem, sometimes introducing new beauties and new poetic horizons. Through this investigation I have learned the full literary importance of the material, of its relatively independent existence, and of its arrangement. And it is true that this arrangement, to a great extent, is organized and reorganized exclusively, especially in oral poetry, through the automatic play of associations. We have to recognize, however, that the consciousness of those who transmit it retains control of what takes place outside this consciousness and would come undone without its interventions. It is not a matter, here, of an original ideological project, but of that artisanal consciousness that aims in all poetry at relevance and beauty, and that is required just as decisively of the intellectual poets of "high" literature.

Determinism and Liberty

T.T.: Your work is that of a historian, which implies that you believe in the existence of a strong relationship between a literary creation and its time; you have always been interested in the relationship between literature and society. But your position on that issue seems to me rather complex, and it needs to be presented quite carefully.

I shall begin by isolating a position that I shall call the "first" one, less because it happens to be particularly well represented in your first book than because, in its simplicity, it constitutes a convenient point of departure. This position consists in an unreserved adherence to the idea of a social determinism where literary works are concerned. In *Man and Ethics,* you write that "moral thought, whether explicit or only obscurely present, has its natural roots and its sphere of action in men's lives and interrelationships, especially when such thought emerges in widely read literary works"; and you define your project as an attempt "to discern the many forms this relationship assumed" (p. vii). The metaphors you use are revealing in themselves: men's lives form the roots, their works are the consequence of these lives; literature is like the clothing of a body that it conceals and reveals at the same time.

Your analyses in *Man and Ethics* often follow this principle. For example, you describe Montesquieu as an "interpreter of aristocratic traditions," and you add in a note that "this characteristic stands out in all his work, one might almost say in every line he wrote" (p. 47). Here it might be said that the "almost" comes to mute *in extremis* the categorical character of "all" and "every." The same with Racine: "At the time they [his tragedies] appeared, it could hardly be otherwise" (p. 160). Furthermore, the entire vocabulary of your book attests to the same adherence to the idea of a rigorous determinism, and thus, on the surface, to the idea of a parallelism between literature and society: literature "was steeped" in the social ideology, which in turn "permeated" it (p. 2); the one was "echoing" the other (p. 4) or was "embodied in" the other (p. 19); the one "evokes" the other or is modeled on "the likeness" of the other (p. 20), "bears the imprint" of the other (pp. 46–47), translates the other (p. 49), "expresses" it (p. 55), and so on.

This "first" position comes to be modified, however, by various "temperaments" that end up making you take a qualitatively different position; these all make their appearance as early as your first book.

In the first place, in *Man and Ethics,* after declaring the existence of a relationship, you note that "there is no lack of contrary examples" (p. 52). Conscious strategies give the lie to our expectations based on social determinism: Corneille knows how to practice "the precaution of the dedication" (p. 60), and human beings themselves are not coherent and homogeneous, for they are subject to a multiple determinism which, in the last analysis, makes the result of each particular determinism uncertain. "Corneille the flatterer by training and by profession is always found alongside of Corneille the enemy of tyranny by inclination and by eloquence" (p.

71). You observe, too, that determinism is exercised more strongly in certain works than in others: "Racine's tragedy is perhaps less representative than Corneille's in the sense that it is less spontaneously and less directly the expression of a social environment and a moral tendency" (p. 167). You account for these exceptions and these degrees of "representativeness" by substituting the idea of a (favorable) condition for that of causality: "Actual events of the time did not influence literary works in terms of precise details, but in terms of general conditions and atmosphere" (p. 63); "he was working within the limits his age set for him" (p. 159); "the conditions that made it possible . . ." (p. 178).

P.B.: What you say is correct, in that I have never been a determinist in the true sense of the word, which implies a *necessary* linkage between causes and effects and presupposes the existence of *laws*. Furthermore, as I see it, of the disciplines that we call "social sciences" [Fr. *sciences humaines*], not one is capable of establishing such laws. If, like many others, I have thought I could see instances in which society has had an influence upon literature, these have taken the form of more or less plausible causal relationships whose degree of obviousness, in the case of individual works and authors, defies strict demonstration and precise measurement. Determinism, which is one of the postulates of human research in the natural world, an unquestionably fruitful postulate in this area, cannot be rigorously applied, it would seem, to man's investigation into his own works.

My first book, which you single out in seeking evidence of my "determinism," was written in the years before World War II, and I am quite willing to recognize that my view of the relationship between society and literature was more naive then than it is today: let us say that I was more "Marxist" then than I am now, although in my book I instinctively avoided making any explicit profession of faith on that subject.

T.T.: Alongside this determination of literature through its social context, which is thus both synchronic and heterogeneous, you have concentrated in some of your other texts on describing a diachronic and homogeneous type of determination. Here I am thinking first of all of the studies (of which you have just reminded us) that focus on the relationships between a popular song and its earlier versions. But you have not limited yourself to this traditionally circumscribed terrain; you have wanted to extend the methods of the folklorist to "high" literature, "to the whole set of literary themes, motifs, and schemas in use in the cultural tradition to which the author belongs" (*L'Ecrivain*, p. 167), and you have provided illustrations of this project in your study of some of the traditional subjects of tragedy. Finally, in your work on the history of ideas, carried out for example in *Le Temps des prophètes*, you seem to have adopted a similar viewpoint: each idea appears as the transformation of another one that had been formulated earlier; once more, the pressure exercised by tradition comes to rival the pressure produced by the immediate social context.

P.B.: Naturally, social causality is not the only influence to act upon literary creations so as to pressure them to respond to the needs and the problems of a given era; literature exists only in forms that have their own tradition and their own developmental logic, which is relatively autonomous. This point, too, seems self-evident to me. And ideas are also transmitted forms, in their way.

T.T.: Perhaps those first two "temperaments" can be seen as clarifications of the initial hypothesis; they make it more flexible and more complex without negating it outright. The same cannot be said, however, for certain other "temperaments," which modify the very substance of the initial hypothesis. Early on, in *Man and Ethics* you note the impossibility of reducing values to facts and thus of deducing a society's ideal on the basis of its reality; now that ideal is found in literature rather than in society itself. "Society is the realm of real man, and literature the realm of ideal man, and . . . one does not and cannot completely overlap the other" (p. 26). We are led astray, in literary studies, when we become interested in what you call "men's lives and relationships," if we take that to refer to some social and economic reality. "Sociological criticism . . . is wasting its time when it calculates the influence of economic realities on literature. . . . The passions of men in society, of the social groups they form, are what supply literature with its tasks and its nourishment. . . . It is this psychology, which is at the same time, and irresistibly, an ideology, that is, the constitution of values and a complex of judgments, that supports writers" (*Le Sacre*,

p. 465). The crucial relationship is thus not between society and literature but between social ideology and literature.

P.B.: Here we are dealing with an obvious proposition that is less often formulated but that seems to me no less important. If a society acts upon literature, it is through the influence brought to bear on authors by the collective psychology and the diffuse ideology of their contemporaries, by *mentalités*, as we say today, rather than through the direct influence of the forms of production and economic life. Literature is created according to moral traditions, old and new passions, needs, and ideals. Economics and technology, if they have any influence on letters, can exercise it only in a mediated and more or less remote manner, by acting upon the public mind. For literary studies, these connections lie in the background. We are attempting to keep in mind what historians are discovering in these areas, and to profit from their findings. But our own field lies further downstream, so to speak: it is the field of ideas, values, forms, and works.

T.T.: But how does one become aware of this ideology? By reading the philosophical, political, scientific, and even (why not?) the literary writings of an era. Let us go even further: literary works are often precisely the ones that present the richest and most nuanced picture of an ideology, so much so that what one learns from other sources is finally less important than what can be learned from literature itself. "We are thus obliged . . . to settle for what has been written and published in this domain, that is, to take literature itself as the chief witness to the suggestions that it has taken from the public mind, and to form our intuitions according to the greatest possible number of these testimonies. . . . These means put literary criticism in the position of teaching historians of society at least as much as, if not more than, criticism can learn in return" (ibid., pp. 465–466). The change here is considerable, since it is no longer a question of setting two entities, "social ideology" (or "public mind") and "literature" in a deterministic relationship, however nuanced, but of analyzing a single entity, the-ideology-of-literature. The reversal is perhaps comparable to the one we find in the work of Dumézil who, if I understand correctly, has stopped seeking the roots or the projections of the trifunctional ideology in one society or another and has settled for describing this ideology as such. All this does not mean, of course, that the effort to recognize the ideological aspect of literature is being abandoned.

P.B.: We would have a truly vicious circle here, if it were possible to imagine that writers are the exclusive and absolute creators of the thoughts they express. In fact, we have ample evidence, if only in the fate of literary works and the testimony of criticism, of the fact that writers' thoughts and those of their characters correspond to contemporary ways of seeing and feeling. Alongside the works themselves, we read treatises on morality and manners; we read notebooks, memoirs, correspondences, political speeches, chronicles; in short, we read works that are more or less close to literature or more or less foreign to it, works in great numbers that inform us about the way people lived and thought in a given period of history. We should like to be informed more amply and completely as to the state of mind, at a given moment, of each sector of society. But we are ill informed. I meant to say only that the documentation on this subject supplied by literary works themselves is, until further notice, by far the richest and the most meaningful that we have. About whom does it inform us? Not only about the authors, but unquestionably, as well, about their typical readers, about their public. The extent of that public in relation to the population as a whole is hard to assess. We may suppose that all those individuals who were more or less reflective and who had the means, through education, condition, and character—that is, an appreciable segment of society—were interested in literature and provided or suggested its themes, in earlier times as today. This view is quite inadequate, but it fits the state of our knowledge. Who will venture a social description of the theatre-going public? Who will go beyond the limits of literature for the literate to assess the dissemination of chapbooks, oral literature, traditional tales, songs? Historians are more and more interested in this broad aspect of the past; they are undertaking detailed inquiries, according to their own methods and means, into what people once thought and felt, and we can only congratulate them and welcome their results with interest.

T.T.: The most radical critique of social determinism is yet to come. Its point of departure is not, this time, a factual deficiency (the empirical difficulties of establishing the relationship), but a disagreement of principle: you now find objections that can be raised "against any system or school that claims to reduce thought to vital necessities" (*L'Ecrivain*, pp. 50–51). Here, too, we find the declaration already formulated in *Man and Ethics*: "Social man needs to conduct himself by something much broader than his own immediate interests" (p. 242). "Man the thinker is able to imagine more justice, happiness, truth, and greatness than he has before his eyes" (p. 244). The horizon of the debate may have broadened, at this point: the ideal is irreducible to the real, and values cannot be deduced from facts; to speak of determinism while remaining ignorant of liberty amounts to encouraging the renunciation of liberty. Such a statement is false, its utterance dangerous (as soon as it is supported by a sufficiently strong State apparatus). "Objective existence, considered by itself and as the only reality, would fully justify—how is it that this goes unnoticed?—contempt for law, oppression, and cruelty; more precisely, there would be no grounds in objective existence for condemning these things. Tyrants know this, and they pretend to know man from this perspective alone, like a machine to be manipulated, without personal reality and without rights" ("A propos d'ordinateurs. Note sur l'existence subjective," in *Commentaire* 19 [1982], 456). This can be observed in a particular case, the attacks carried out against liberal ideology and the doctrine of human rights: "It may be said that by limiting the discussion to the economic order, by maintaining that liberty has never been anything but the right to enrich oneself at the expense of others, by taking this tack to hurl anathema against the individual, one implicitly accredits a dictatorial philosophy" (*Le Temps des prophètes*, p. 16). But this is also the general truth of the human condition: "By its very nature, the human spirit in any century transcends society and history; it rejoins the humanity of the epochs that have preceded and of those that will follow, and communicates with them" ("Réflexions sur la critique littéraire," in *Le Statut de la littérature*, 1982, p. 5).

Now every society includes a group of individuals who are, so to speak, professionals of the mind; consequently, what they produce cannot be reduced to some social determinism: we know these people as intellectuals. "Man is made in such a way that he can step outside himself in order to view his conduct in terms of absolute values; there would be no intellectuals if this were not the case. . . . Men of thought, writers and artists, are in some degree by virtue of their function the judges of society even as they are its mainstay" (*Le Sacre*, pp. 19–20). Thus Montesquieu, if he is a true writer, and Racine, a true artist, cannot be reduced, in their work, to the milieux from which they arose. This is not merely a matter of circumstance, but a permanent characteristic of the man of ideas. "Thus we expect of intellectuals universal formulas, distinct from interests and circumstances, valid for everyone and forever" (ibid., p. 19).

At the end of this itinerary, I would say that your "new" position no longer consists in choosing between determinism and freedom (in favor of determinism), but in thinking the two simultaneously. Having always done the work of a historian, you do not hesitate to write: "Shall I confess that I consider self-evident the existence of a more or less constant human nature, within a reader's memory, so that from the Bible to Montaigne and from the *Iliad* to Baudelaire, the vast communication that supports us and includes us all is possible" (*L'Ecrivain*, p. xv); nor do you hesitate to express your faith in "the perfectibility of mankind" (*Man and Ethics*, p. 245), thereby rejoining the hopes of a Rousseau along with those of Condorcet and Constant. Literature itself is governed by this antinomy; it "is at once circumstantial and exemplary, in other words dependent and sovereign, like the human mind itself" ("Réflexions," p. 5).

P.B.: This last point is really the only one that poses a problem, because it challenges a certain scientific mindset. Yes, the object of our studies is something more than an ordinary *object*. It transcends the factual order; it brings into play creative consciousnesses and values that are the texture of literary works; knowledge of this object requires faculties other than those that lead us toward knowledge of nature. Can historians themselves be satisfied with rendering an account of an order of things and of its evolution, and, where they see new values coming into being, describe the event as if they were biologists or naturalists? Nothing is less certain, or more difficult to imagine: in the process of recounting man's story, they are constantly faced with what goes beyond raw nature, in man, attesting to the freedom to choose goals and soliciting the subjective judgment of the narrator. It is their task in particular, however, to deal with the bulk of material facts and events, with the necessities and the hazards of the life of nations; the responsibilities of the human spirit are not really their business. We critics, on the other hand, deal more or less exclusively with men's ideas about goodness, justice, or beauty, and, however much we may wish and claim to be historians, history is only of relative concern. You are correct in thinking that becoming conscious of such a situation, with the consequences it implies for our own undertaking, means not only bringing a corrective to a doctrine of causality, it means recognizing that no causal putting-into-perspective exhausts the meaning of a literary work, and it means assigning to the study of literature a position that differs from the outset from the position of the natural sciences. It clearly does not follow that in this study there is no criterion of truth: for at the root of our interpretations there are many facts to gather, much information to verify, and, in our interpretations themselves, there is much intuition and judgment to put into play in order to attain the adequate degree of plausibility which, in things human, takes the place of certitude.

CRITICISM

Critical Methods?

T.T.: With respect to contemporary criticism, you have taken a position that is itself critical: this is how I should like to approach your thinking on the subject. The first general reproach you address to the contemporary critical debate is that you observe in it a belief in a sort of verbal fiction called "method." Critics "think they are talking about method," tend to "christen every discovery a new 'method'" (*L'Ecrivain*, pp. xii–xiii), whereas in fact the issue is entirely different. If I decide to carry out a sociological analysis of literature, or to adopt a psychoanalytical approach, I have no particular method at my disposal; I choose rather to concentrate on only a part of the object (literature) and sometimes I adopt a set of hypotheses concerning this part. Nothing in all this corresponds to what a method ought to be, namely, a "way of approaching a truth, in which the nature of that truth is not presupposed" ("Réflexions," pp. 4–5).

If it were just a matter of an inappropriate use of the term, the damage would be trivial. What is more serious, though, is that each of these "methods" has a totalizing ambition. Critics are quite ready to insist on the "organic," "integrating" aspects of a literary work; they find separations distasteful; they would like to base their views on "a single glance," and see only "a single sequence"; they valorize the "wholeness" of the work, the "unity" and "solidarity" of its elements; they aspire to a "total illumination" (*L'Ecrivain*, pp. xii–xiii). Now such generalizations are necessarily false, since a literary work, like any empirical reality, cannot be grasped exhaustively from any single, necessarily partial, point of view: "By trying to achieve a total vision, one would necessarily be deceived" (ibid., p. x). Methodological fervor must therefore not prevent us from acknowledging with humility that criticism is, necessarily, "always incomplete," and from seeking a better equilibrium between faithfulness to the facts and coherence of the system, between "sensitivity to the works and aptitude for reasoning about them" (ibid., p. xiii).

P.B.: Yes, I believe that the word "method" is misused today, because it suggests the idea of a scientific project; in fact, it is used to designate preconceived systems of interpretations and arbitrary undertakings that are sometimes, I think, at the opposite pole from the scientific spirit.

New Criticism?

T.T.: We do not agree so completely on the subject of your second charge. You think that the "new" criticism has brought nothing new, that the ideas and hypotheses have been the same for two hundred years, and perhaps even longer (*L'Ecrivain*, pp. x–xi). Without even going into the heart of the argument, one can be astonished: do you believe that criticism totally escapes the historical and ideological determination which has such a strong hold on literature itself? Even supposing that the elements of each doctrine have remained identical, what about their internal articulation, the hierarchy that they constitute? Are these of no importance? Is it not possible, for example, to observe in literary criticism an evolution parallel to that of other social sciences, from interest in the historical inscription of a literary work to interest in its internal organization—an evolution that consists only in a shift of emphasis, but that nevertheless comes about more or less simultaneously in almost all the countries of Europe and for this reason might not be without significance?

P.B.: I do not think I have really said that "new criticism" had nothing new to its credit. To be sure, discussion on this issue is difficult, given the vagueness of the notion of new criticism itself. In fact this label is applied to quite diverse tendencies: thematic, Marxist, psychoanalytical, structuralist, semiotic, and so on. And it is beyond question that most of these labels either had already been used by previous generations or else had some precursory seeds, under other names, in traditional criticism. That criticism was not completely unaware of psychological or social references on the one hand or of the consideration of themes or forms and figures on the other. It is true that, in each of these directions, our era has launched new undertakings, whose fruitfulness would have to be determined in each case, but which, from one school to another, are far from coinciding.

Where, then, does the unity of the new criticism lie? Its often observed penchant for system and totalization cannot be the basis for any unity among the various schools, but is rather a source of difference and warfare. And yet we see the new criticism, like the old, often tending to merge and combine several theoretical approaches, in varying dosages. What is more striking, and what establishes an air of kinship among all the varieties of the new criticism, is on the one hand their apparent lack of concern, in certain of their interpretations, for the manifest signification of texts, and on the other hand their predilection for a specialized language impenetrable to the ordinary reader. Is there a desire here to imitate what happens in the hard sciences, whose modern results are in fact situated at an ever-greater distance from the perceptible evidence and are formulated in a special language? But these sciences base their results on a series of difficult experiments and abstract deductions which distance them from ordinary knowledge and language and authorize them to do without the adherence of the uninitiated. Literature, on the contrary, is based on widely shared subjective experiences; it constitutes part of the ordinary relations of humanity; it implies a vast communication. By affecting a status analogous to that of the sciences, literary criticism runs the risk of ruining its own truth and of losing contact with its object. Obviously I am describing extreme defects and consequences, which the best of the "new critics" have of course been able to avoid. One cannot say as much for the mass of disciples and imitators.

Having said all this, I think it possible, as you do, that our era may have manifested a general tendency to emphasize the "internal organization of works" rather than their "historical inscription," and that this is the general spirit of new criticism. We must still note that the earlier criticism is not essentially historical. For centuries, it took no notice of history, as it were; and, even when it came to be called literary history, it was unable to neglect the configuration of a work or a page, taken in themselves: it was the founder of literary history (Lanson) who created, in France, the religion of the "explication de texte."

Extrinsic Criticism?

T.T.: There is also a third general reproach that is often found among various critics of criticism but that is surprising, coming from you: this is the condemnation of recent criticism because it introduces concepts extraneous to the field of literature. You deplore "the often brutal intrusion of foreign disciplines and terminologies in a field of study as delicate as ours, which collapses before them" (*L'Ecrivain*, pp. xii–xiii); you are suspicious of systems "inspired . . . by disciplines and hypotheses foreign to literature" ("Réflexions," p. 4). If this kind of attack is surprising in your case, it is because earlier you had declared that there are no watertight boundaries between literature and "everything written for the public," so that it is hard to see what might be "foreign" to literature. Furthermore, when you yourself practice literary analysis, your conceptualization seems to me neither more nor less "foreign" to literature than that of other critics; on a single page of *Man and Ethics*, for example, I note the terms freedom, servitude, judgment, free choice, will, reason, ego. One cannot have it both ways: either literature is taken in a narrow sense, but then one cannot really say that these notions belong to such a delicate field; or else literature is taken in its broad sense (yours) and your notions fall within it, but then so do those of the other critics.

P.B.: I think I have already responded in part to this objection. I quite agree that, in a way, a sociological or anthropological or linguistic treatise may be part of literature in the broadest sense. It does not follow that successful undertakings in these fields may be fruitfully transported into literary criticism. To be sure, criticism always uses concepts that it applies to texts, and this usage is not peculiar to modern criticism; all criticism uses notions dear to the heart of the commentator to characterize the works under study. But what notions? You pull out of my work those of freedom, servitude, will, reason, ego, and so on, and you could mention many others. You should observe, however, that these notions are familiar to the authors themselves; they are the raw material of literature, as it were, like common sense. Can the same be said of the concepts that linguistics or psychoanalysis have needed to introduce in their research? Literature is naturally unaware of them, and literary usage welcomes them charily; their massive intrusion into criticism has something traumatic about it.

Not that I have any objection in principle to the possible exchanges between literary criticism and neighboring disciplines. On the contrary, one ought to be well disposed, I think, toward every new inspiration in the reading of texts. But every enterprise has to be judged in the end by its results. Now the results have appeared to be peculiarly uneven: brilliant and convincing sometimes, and with some authors, but, to a disquieting extent, farfetched or totally negative. If one sees things this way, why not say so?

Structural Criticism

T.T.: In the wake of these general criticisms, you also direct some remarks at certain particular tendencies of contemporary literary studies; you focus especially on structural, psychoanalytical, and sociological criticism. Your first comment on the subject of the "structuralist method" seems to me to arise from a misunderstanding, since you accuse it of being external, "drawn from a foreign source," like other types of criticism, whereas in the same sentence you identify it through a definition of literature as a pure "organization of verbal forms or signs" ("Réflexions," p. 4). This definition is subject to serious challenge, but it certainly cannot be accused of reducing literature to something external to it.

But your questioning goes further than this. Structural criticism, precisely because it is "internal," seeks to exclude from its object any consideration of the work's intention and any relationship between that work and social values; in other words, it considers the work as an object, or "as a thing, [and] chooses to consider only the organization and arrangement of the materials that it comprises" (ibid., p. 9). Now if such an exclusion indeed serves the critic's interests, by providing him with homogeneous and easily observable material, it does a serious disservice to the empirical object itself, that is to the literary work, by amputating several of its essential properties. "Disenchanted or fervent, a literary work is always the tendentious message that one subject emits for other subjects; it lives on a relationship of influence and purpose that objective science, as it defines itself, has no way of mastering" (ibid., p. 20). Transposed to the scale of global knowledge of human beings, "this reduction, in order to offer up man to the scholar's gaze, would amount to denying him, along with all subjectivity, consciousness and will as our intuition makes them known to us" (ibid., p. 9): this is clearly too high a price, and one is allowed to refuse to pay it. But if this is the way things are—and here we encounter Bakhtin's criticism of the Formalists or the structuralists once again—"any attempt to suppress or to ignore the intersubjective character of the literary message risks being nonsense from the very outset" (ibid., p. 20).

What you are condemning here is the philosophy underlying structural criticism, the idea of the self-sufficient text. But this condemnation seems to me to apply less well, or not in the same way, to the *practice* of structural criticism. To wish to study the work as a combination of materials is hardly reprehensible in itself, if it means that every element of the work (all its "raw materials") must above all be set into relation with its other elements, since the element finds its meaning only in its context. The requirement becomes exorbitant only if it is paired with the totalizing ambition we spoke of earlier. For structural relations to be relevant is one thing; for them to be the only relevant relations is something else again, since that would mean excluding any relation to the synchronic context, and, beyond that, any relation to universal human values. Is it not appropriate, rather than to exclude all research into the organization of the work, to see it as a necessary though not sufficient phase of literary criticism?

P.B.: The contradictory stance you attribute to me concerning my appreciation of structural criticism is not that at all. For it is a fact that some have believed that the literary work could be treated as a "pure organization of forms or signs" only through a method indeed "drawn from a foreign source," from natural history, or linguistics, or anthropology: not an undertaking to be condemned in itself, but one that carries with it the obvious risk of failure. For the rest, I prefer simply to repeat what I said, at the beginning of this exchange of ideas, about the value of studying the organization of literary works, but in connection with their meaning and the author's intention.

The Critique of the Unconscious

T.T.: Your reservations regarding criticism that grants a privileged place to the unconscious to the detriment of consciousness can be explained in part by the tendentious use that is often made of this so-called determinism. The simplest case is the one in which the critic attempts, as you say about Rousseau, to probe a heart in order to deprecate a doctrine (*L'Ecrivain*, p. 50): literary psychoanalysis is in such cases only a rejuvenated variant of biographical criticism, which must be faulted not for establishing certain facts but for attributing to them a disproportionate role, for reducing the value of someone's thought to the causes that gave rise to it.

But there are also other reasons that lead you to resist certain forms of criticism based on the unconscious—thematic or psychoanalytic criticism that aims to expose and glorify the "unthought" of the text rather than of its author. You are particularly clear about this when you deal with Michelet. Identifying certain obsessions or noting preferences for one substance or another are not in themselves illegitimate acts; they become illegitimate, however, when they entail the systematic elimination of any reference to the doctrines professed by the author, or when they are even accompanied by the stated deprecation of those doctrines. The exclusion of any part of the author's work is arbitrary to begin with; but the denigration of the author's conscious thought implies that one takes the freedom and will of the subject to be negligible. "The elementary universe of sensations and instinctive appeals" (*Le Temps des prophètes*, p. 498) is indeed present in the author; but is it not somewhat presumptuous to seek to wipe out in one stroke the author's entire effort, which consists in converting these sensations into language and thus into an appeal addressed to others? Does not thinking the "unthought" of authors such as Rousseau or Michelet amount, in spite of everything, to demonstrating a certain condescension toward them?

The hierarchy between conscious and unconscious that you postulate contradicts one of our current commonplace assumptions: "Images in literature have value only through the passions and the desires that the author's tendentious ego invests in them; these are another name for his ideology. The imaginary universe is oriented by thoughts and ulterior motives. . . . Michelet's nausea grows out of his principled condemnations" (ibid., pp. 489–499). Today we are much more likely to say that the value of ideology lies only in the images, that thought is oriented by the imaginary universe, and that principles arise from nausea. Is it simply a question of reversing the prevailing hierarchy, or must one instead seek to conceive in a different way of the antinomy formed by consciousness and the unconscious?

P.B.: I have no objection in principle to psychoanalysis, either. The psychology of writers generally has some relevance to their world view, even to their choices and formal predilections, and it cannot be excluded from the purview of criticism. The psychology of the unconscious, a traditional element of our culture like psychology itself, has had an assured place in literary criticism for a long time. It misses the mark when, in place of the author's discourse, another discourse that the author would not have recognized is substituted, one whose presence in the author's work is conjectured by an external authority. Now the claims of this authority to a true knowledge of the literary domain are necessarily problematical. Should they be confirmed, the reworking that psychoanalytic criticism imposes on the content of the work would remain foreign to literature, whose realm is above all that of conscious exchanges among minds. It is true that in his commentary the critic may be led to go beyond the manifest meaning of the work; he has always had to do this, for the text does not simply speak, it suggests without saying, it veils what it does not want to say. But the critic, in this order of ideas, can act only with a measured audacity, and in a plausibly imagined complicity with the author and with the reader whom he hopes to enlighten. Beyond that, the arbitrary is likely to flourish.

To answer your last comment on this subject, I do not know what is the real hierarchy between the conscious and the unconscious, nor do I know the merits of the currently prevailing views as to the meaning of this hierarchy. But I know that literature lives chiefly in the light of consciousness, and dies without it. No man, even a psychoanalyst, could bear to live—the period of his own analysis excepted—with an interlocutor who saw something hidden behind each of his remarks and judged it appropriate to inform him of this. What would make life impossible would likewise kill literature.

Sociological Criticism

T.T.: This form of criticism is closer to you than the others, to the extent that it offers a thematization of the relation between literature and society, a relation that has always interested you as well. You report that early on you felt yourself attracted by "historical materialism" ("Réflexions," p. 3); the "Marxist variant of this enterprise" seems to you "truer and more penetrating in its foundations than the others" (L'Ecrivain, p. xi), and you think that "every sociological analysis of the works of the mind is led to use the notion of class" (Le Sacre, p. 18). As we have already seen, however, you keep your distance from this form of criticism as well. Can you clarify your position?

P.B.: Sociological criticism also runs the risk of substituting the external authority of the sociologist, or the commentator who believes he is invested with it, for that of the author, and in so doing risks distorting the meaning of literary works. We have already spoken of this way of approaching literature, of its legitimacy and its dangers. As far as the use of the notion of class in this type of criticism is concerned, its appropriateness may vary depending upon the periods studied. I must say that, contrary to what one might expect, this use seems more called for when one is dealing with the seventeenth century than the nineteenth. What I think I was able to do in Man and Ethics turned out not to be feasible in my studies on the Romantic era, and I have had to reflect on that difference. During the Old Regime, the nobility, the court, and the legal profession could each have a different world view. In the nineteenth century, between the upper bourgeoisie, the middle class, and the lower class, nothing of the sort holds true—nothing so clear-cut, at least. Political behavior differs, of course, but the general philosophy is in large part shared, especially in the first half of the century: a more or less pronounced lay spiritualism, generally liberal, progressive, and humanitarian in orientation; analogous values recognized all along the social scale; the same ideal types, masculine and feminine, occupying people's imaginations. Something similar had indeed existed in the seventeenth century, to the extent that Christian beliefs, piety, and ideals reigned throughout society. In that highly compartmentalized society, however, each social milieu was able to develop its own ethic, in relation to its own particular condition. This would have been difficult in the more unified society produced by the French Revolution: with no theoretical barrier separating the classes, it was possible in principle to climb up the full length of what was a single social ladder. From this point on, when we look at literary works, we are led to consider less their possible roots in a certain social class than the project they suggest and the situation of this project within the process of social evolution as a whole. On the other hand, the observation of a certain ideological *consensus* within society (a Christian consensus for many centuries, then a progressive and humanitarian consensus) sheds the light of a spiritual power upon human existence; it allows us to understand the role of inspiration and guide that poets, writers, and thinkers saw themselves playing in the nineteenth century, as they formulated and maintained the various versions of the common ideology.

Research Practices

T.T.: We have just been talking about various critical orientations; now there is one aspect of criticism which, without being an "orientation" in itself, is found (or ought to be found) at the root of all the others: that is the accumulation of information, or erudition. Your works, especially those that come after *Man and Ethics*, are impressive in terms of the breadth and sureness of knowledge they display. How did you go about your task, in concrete terms?

P.B.: I'm happy to talk about that. I prefer to focus on my work on French Romanticism, which took the longest time; I shall leave aside the books and articles on other subjects that preceded the Romanticism project or that occasionally led me to interrupt it. Before explaining how I worked, I should tell you what my starting point was, and how it evolved. Originally I had in mind a study on poetic pessimism in the post-Romantic generation (Baudelaire, Banville, Leconte de Lisle, Flaubert, and their literary milieu). But as soon as I started reading, I understood that this pessimism was a kind of reaction against the enthusiasm and the faith of the preceding generation, and that I would have to look to that generation of writers in order to understand what happened next. In fact, I found I had to go back even further, as the problem had its source in the role that the philosophers of the Enlightenment saw themselves playing with respect to human destinies. The scope of the task was worrisome but at the same time exciting; still, I saw no way to cut it down while complying with the demands of truth.

My work consisted first of all in constructing a card file—I began this around 1950—of texts and references having to do initially with the condition of the poet and writer and with the prevailing ideas about this condition, during a period running approximately from 1760 to 1860. I began to notice as I worked that the problem of the mission or sacred "calling" of literary figures appeared and became explicit only in connection with historico-social conditions and modes of thought and belief that extended far beyond this particular problem. My documentation grew apace. I had a great deal to read, excerpt, and classify. In particular, I spent a long time going through a very large number of magazine collections, both general and literary: this aspect of information-gathering had often been neglected because of the low rate of return, but in the process I discovered and understood many things. In this way I gathered together, little by little, over a period of many years, what I thought should furnish the substance of my work. I filed this material according to summary criteria, by authors and generations of authors, titles and categories of periodicals, connections with schools of thought, and so forth, without allowing these classifications to prejudice in my mind the order I would follow in my books. I was not seeking to control all this material in the process of assembling it: that would have been a fruitless effort, as the vastness of the field and the unforeseeability of the future harvest made premature syntheses useless. I simply allowed partial or provisional schemas on my subject, or certain of its aspects, to form in my mind; I took notes on these schemas and thought about them, thinking that, if nothing contradicted them, they might lead me to go back to earlier research and complete it, and they influenced the future course of my work.

When I considered myself sufficiently well informed to set about writing, I was at least convinced of the legitimacy of establishing a chronological framework by periods, and I had acquired some relatively specific ideas about what I had to say. During the summer of 1968 I began to write a volume on the period 1760–1830, which appeared in 1973 under the title *Le Sacre de l'écrivain*. To write this book I had to bring the material I had assembled on that period up to date, revise it, and make drastic cuts and reclassifications, several times over; during these operations I learned many things from my own notes, as I found information that I had collected over a period of years brought together for the first time. I was then able to see the definitive outline of this first grouping take shape, along with the book's order and, finally, the internal development of each chapter. In short, I had to deploy the long patience of the researcher and organizer before giving myself over to the inspiration of the writer, who gives the work its final form. I imagine many scholars will recognize their own procedures in mine. For my part, I do not see how a work of vast synthesis, in the history of "ideas," could be carried out in any other way. But of course I am not setting myself up as an example: everything depends on the temperament and habits of the scholar. I proceeded the same way, starting with documentation I had already collected, for the period 1830–1836, which produced two volumes: one of them, *Le Temps des prophètes*, which has already been published, deals with the authors of general doctrines, while the other, which I am in the process of completing, focuses on the poets. Paradoxically, my information on the generation after 1848—the one that first interested me—remains unused up to now: man proposes and time disposes. I hope that my documentation will provide me with the material for a new book.

Submitting to Others

T.T.: Your positive program for criticism has two facets that at first appear incompatible: submitting oneself to others and speaking for oneself. Submitting to another, that is, to the author studied, is the first gesture the critic makes: he has to do his best to establish the meaning of the text he is studying; this is his "method," as well. "One ought not to speak of 'method' in the strict sense, in literary criticism, . . . except for the approach that consists in gathering sufficient information, in manipulating this information correctly, and in interpreting it plausibly, that is, in avoiding the mental zone in which the undemonstrable and the irrefutable are one" ("Réflexions," pp. 4–5). The critic, like the writer, starts with preexisting texts; but whereas the writer is appreciated for the transformation he imposes on those texts, the critic, on the contrary, gets credit ony if he reduces that transformation to a minimum: the ideals of intertextuality practiced by the latter and the former are at opposite poles. "It is appropriate . . . that the fear of inventing should be the highest of virtues [on the critic's part]" (ibid, p. 20). The critic's ideal is the establishment of truth, in a first sense of the term (the truth of correspondence, or equivalence). What the critical work achieves concretely is not truth but plausibility (or, as people used to say, verisimilitude). But, if the ideal cannot be achieved, it still has to act as a regulatory principle for research, as a horizon making it possible to choose one's orientation.

This faith in truth as a regulatory principle has been hotly debated in our time; our contemporaries prefer to believe that "everything is interpretation." You do not deny the interpretative character of the critical task, but you do not want to settle for this observation, either: "No one dares to say that any interpretation whatsoever is legitimate" (*L'Ecrivain*, p. xiv). The reason for this hermeneutic optimism is that language and literature are not individual and arbitrary games, but social conventions that serve communication and permit understanding between one man and another. "Language . . . is in spite of everything the link among men, and with the precious and severe aid of philology, the link among centuries. . . . The uninterrupted exchange, through the generations, of authors and public is the very postulate of literature, which is based upon understanding" (ibid., pp. xiv–xv). That is why it is possible to establish rules for interpretation: "Mallarmé demands to be read first of all according to grammar, and interpreted through the closest possible reading of the text. . . . Mallarmé's thoughts are at once veiled and signified by his text; let us at all costs avoid adding our own" ("Poétique et métaphysique," p. 414).

As you have written, "whoever seeks to define an author is tempted to integrate him illegitimately with his own personal order, to make him the precursor, admirable and yet incomplete, of his own thoughts" (*L'Ecrivain*, p. 414). I sometimes wonder whether it is indeed possible to escape this temptation entirely. I am not thinking of the naive assimilation in which, through a back-and-forth motion that bears a close resemblance to running in place, one first attributes one's own thoughts to a writer and then goes on to rejoice when one discovers how close the writer is to oneself. I am thinking rather of the fact that the very categories of analysis never coincide perfectly with those of the text being analyzed, and that every interpretation is also an inclusion (the double meaning of the word "comprehend" provides a good illustration of this ambiguity). It is possible to avoid imposing one's own assertions on the writer; but can I abstain from putting my words in his mouth?

P.B.: I quite agree with everything you say about my "hermeneutic optimism." As for the temptation on the critic's part to integrate an author into his own personal order, if only by applying his own categories of thought to the writer, I think as you do that it is difficult, by the nature of things, and perhaps not desirable, to avoid it altogether. But one must remain in control. And consciously: one must not cheerfully give in to misunderstanding.

Speaking for Oneself

T.T.: The movement of empathy and submission to the author being analyzed constitutes only the first aspect of critical activity; the other, complementary aspect requires, on the contrary (on the contrary?) that one assume one's own voice, since by ignoring it one is locked into another variant of objectivism. The author belongs to his time; how could the critic escape from that relation? In *Man and Ethics*, you state that "the interest we feel for the history of thought almost always springs from the desire to make some new use of it" (p. 245); and, in *Le Temps des prophètes*, you present that position-taking as a prescription, not just a description. "*Objectivity* in the face of problems that have remained current ceases to be conceivable, even, for the simple reason that man and his present condition are not *objects* for us. To appreciate as an outsider, without reference to any value, a currently unresolved human situation or issue is all too obviously impossible" (pp. 566–567). The historian's ideal cannot be objectivity, but only honesty or probity.

As soon as the critic's subjectivity is taken into account, the critic can no longer claim to limit himself to mere description; he must at the same time take responsibility for his own judgments. "We do not cease to judge ideas when we describe their meaning and their source" (*Man and Ethics*, p. vii). You are thus going beyond the philological project based on the Spinozan separation of meaning and truth and on the consequent exclusion of all research having to do with truth. In your case, the critic once again has to deal with truth, but in a different sense of the term: an ethical rather than a descriptive truth. This new concern for truth comes into play at two levels. It is first of all indispensable in the actual analysis of an author's thought, in order to discover the weaknesses, the incoherencies, the difficulties of that thought. Thus you do not hesitate to speak of the "fundamental flaw in all aristocratic literature" (ibid, p. 44); similarly, analyzing Rousseau, you speculate about the very basis of the debate that he embarked upon: "Are we to believe that the imagination of happiness has ever replaced . . . happiness itself?" (*L'Ecrivain*, p. 42). Your reading of Jouffroy is transformed into a veritable dialogue: "A doctrine of progress is implied . . . Let us admit this; but we are told . . . Let us suppose . . . But the idea . . . And the liberal philosopher sees himself reduced to arguing, like so many others before him, over the notion of a free necessity" (*Le Temps des prophètes*, p. 32).

The concern for truth intervenes at a higher level also, no longer in order to analyze the author's thought but to frame the dialogue in which the critic finds himself engaged—not as a means, but as an end: literature and criticism converge here after having been separated for so long. You write, for example: "In all societies known up to the present, the nature of things requires that what one adds to love one subtracts from virtue" (*Man and Ethics*, p. 32), or: "There is no objective formula for social goals that is not thoughtless or fraudulent" (*Le Temps des prophètes*, p. 567). Here you are expressing, to be sure, a position that characterizes you as a historical subject; but you are also proposing this position as a transhistorical truth, as a possible ground for agreement between yourself and other people: your utterance here aspires to universality.

P.B.: While I accept your observations, I should like to add some clarifications about the notions of dialogue and truth. The critic has, as you say, the right to intervene subjectively to impute to the author's project, as it is manifested in the literary work, a lack of consistency or a lack of plausibility. There is much to be said on this subject. The lack of strict consistency—even the internal contradiction that can be detected in a literary work—may not be, properly speaking, an imperfection, but rather a sign that is laden with meaning: there are innumerable steps in the gamut between pure inconsistency (or what appears as such) and the ambiguity that reveals the profound nature of a problem or a human being. As for the lack of plausibility, this is understood in relation to a human experience more widely attested than the author's discourse; but here too the objection raised by the critic may not really be an objection, may lead him only to emphasize some originality on the writer's part, and lead to the justification of the writer at a deeper level. It is clear to what extent, in these critical proceedings, the search for the author's meaning and the evaluation of his thought may be intertwined. It is the critic's job to forge ahead *as far as he can* toward these reconciling outcomes; and if he cannot entirely succeed, then it is his job to say why.

As for taking an ethical stand vis-à-vis a literary work, that is something else again. Here it is a question of the values that the work is accrediting, values whose legitimacy may be subject to question. Thus it is obviously desirable for the critic to have wide horizons and to make it his business, in this area, to ask the questions rather than answer them. Nothing obliges him to take a stand between Corneille and La Rochefoucauld, or Voltaire and Rousseau, or Hugo and Baudelaire. It is up to him to make his own preferences known, if he believes that these preferences will make his criticism more explicit. The interhuman communication in which he is engaged forbids him to make excessive space for his own persona; by the nature of his work, he is all things to all people. But being an informer and an interpreter does not make him any less a subject, and he has the same right to judge good and evil as any author, or the public. Should the profession that attaches him to literature separate him from humanity? That would be the ultimate absurdity. It is natural for the critic to raise questions when issues arise that involve his own conscience, or when he feels that his commentaries would otherwise lack truth or merit.

T.T.: Perhaps your critical position might be summarized (unless I am becoming unfaithful in turn and overprivileging the system) as an attempt, first of all to bring to light, then to articulate, a certain number of antinomies: between determinism and freedom, the universal and the particular, contextual fidelity and the systematic spirit, the conscious and the unconscious, knowledge and judgment, the self and the other. . . . You do not aspire to synthesis, however; instead you aim to recognize a limited validity in each of the options represented by these concepts, depending upon the point of view adopted. This undertaking seems to be supported by certain philosophical choices. How would you define these choices, and what role do you see for philosophy in the exercise of our trade?

P.B.: You are right to say that I articulate antinomies, but I do so after noting them, or, to put it more accurately, after undergoing them: in particular, the one that shows the mind to be at once dependent and sovereign, or the one that opposes the light of consciousness to the obscurity of motives, or the one that opposes the order of values to the order of facts and causes. These antinomies in fact can be reduced to the opposition between objective existence and the existence of the human subject, an opposition that cannot be resolved either by the chimerical suppression of one of the two terms integrated with the nature of the other, or by the production of a third term, for which nothing at all supplies the idea. This is neither an aspect nor an episode of the life of the human mind, but its principal definition. Let us therefore welcome the contraries in our studies and attempt to accommodate them side by side in our criticism as in ourselves.

You ask me about my philosophical choices. Not being a philosopher by profession, I shall respond to the extent that reflection about the human condition is natural in each of us. The idea of transcendence with respect to the world and man seems to me highly problematical. It is human subjectivity that includes a transcendence, it seems to me, in that it takes itself invincibly to be transcendent and—in spite of all doctrinal professions to the contrary—experiences itself as such. It is a fact that everything that constitutes and distinguishes the human subject, in particular the exercise of knowledge and the conviction of free will, and everything that links the human subject with others—culture, law, morality—transcends the factual order and can be conceived on the purely objective level only through the verbal rejection of what is self-evident. The idea of a transcendence enclosed in the intimate sense of man may seem paradoxical; it is perhaps even philosophical nonsense, but this nonsense, if that is what it is, encompasses all that we know of ourselves, without any subtractions or additions.

You ask me, too, what role a philosophy can play in the exercise of our trade. Literary criticism, strictly speaking, has no need to philosophize except about itself; and even here, many have been able to keep silent on this point without disqualifying themselves in their practice of the profession. It is not very easy to keep silent today: too many questions have been raised which lead one to take a position. It seems to me that the points I have just made in answering your last question, if they are not absolutely indispensable to the exercise of criticism, may perhaps help to conceptualize its vocation and its scope. They show a large and continuous commerce within literature, a commerce that is intersubjective by nature, humanly transcendent in content and universal in scope, owing to the fact that it is concerned in principle with the universality of subjects. This is no different, after all, from saying something that has long been considered self-evident: that literary studies are "humanities."

9

A Dialogic Criticism?

Everyone knows how hard it is to accept criticism directed at oneself. Either your critics are being aggressive (but that is because they don't know you and aren't trying to understand you; they are upset because you are different from what they would like you to be; they reject you so completely that you no longer feel personally implicated); or else they are (or have been) close to you (but now you are dealing with an emotional rift, and the pain of it outweighs all other considerations: what counts is that you don't love each other any more, not that you yourself may have this quality or that one). Or else the critics continue to love you and thus tell you nothing that you might interpret as a basic challenge: they have accepted you for what you are, whatever their private opinions. It is enough to make one wonder how one ever learns anything at all about oneself on the basis of what others say. But perhaps I am speaking only about myself? And yet, when I take the trouble to think back over my own intellectual itinerary, the memory of two encounters comes to mind, encounters that did bring about change in me, as I have come to realize long after the fact.

At first glance, these two meetings have only superficial features in common. Each took place in the aftermath of one of those occasions that make up an indispensable aspect of my profession: lectures given abroad. Such occasions are part tourism, part spectacle (one is visiting and letting oneself be visited at the same time); personal affinities may arise, and one may also hear acerbic criticism, but generally speaking, nothing that happens has very deep personal impact. The two lectures I am referring to took place in England, a country I rarely visit. And, regrettably, I remember the effect the words spoken had on me much better in each instance than I remember the words themselves.

The first of these encounters occurred in London a little more than ten years ago. I had given a talk on something or other at the French Institute, and during the reception that followed I was introduced to a man older than myself. He had bright blue eyes; the glass of whisky in his hand was drained, I believe, rather quickly. It was Arthur Koestler. I had read *Darkness at Noon* while I was still in Bulgaria; the book had made a strong impression on me. As is the custom, the conversation had nothing to do with my lecture, but rather with the fact that I myself came from an Eastern European country under Communist rule. At the time I professed an attitude toward politics that I had adopted during my adolescence in Bulgaria, one that is shared by many of my generation, I think: an attitude made up of fatalism and indifference. Given that things cannot be other than what they are, this attitude holds, the best approach is one of complete detachment. I was expressing my indifference, then, in conversation with Koestler, presenting it as a position of lucidity and wisdom. I cannot recapture the precise wording of his response, but I know his reaction was made up of politeness, firmness, astonishment, and total disagreement. And upon seeing him I suddenly felt that his very existence was proof that my own words were false. Here was a man who had not adopted a fatalist attitude. He did not challenge or reproach me in the course of the conversation, but he seemed to have a tranquil assurance that he was right because he was who he was.

The second incident took place at Oxford. This time I know that my talk had to do with Henry James and "structural analysis of narrative" (at the time, I knew what that meant). I had been invited by a college whose master was Isaiah Berlin. At that point I had not read anything by that enchanting philosopher and historian, but he was warm and eloquent, and I was seduced at once. He offered me his hospitality (as he must have done other lecturers), and I shall never forget the night we spent in his house, a veritable museum; this time I was the one with a glass of vodka in hand. He refilled it obligingly, all the while telling me anecdotes (they have since been published) drawn from his memories of Pasternak and Akhmatova. He had sat silently through my lecture, and at one point, later in the evening, said something like this: "Henry James, yes; narrative structures, yes, of course. But why don't you look into things like nineteenth-century nihilism and liberalism? All that's quite interesting, you know."

I am well aware that these reminiscences are particularly telling for me alone; the events in question, so insignificant in themselves, take on meaning only in connection with other personal experiences. At the time, moreover, I paid no attention to these two incidents. Only retrospectively, and of course because my memory retained these incidents among countless others, have I discovered that they were important to me; retrospectively, I have begun to look for common features and to muse about what distinguishes these incidents from all the rest. In the two responses addressed to me, I heard something like a reproach and a recommendation. And yet I did not set them aside, as I usually would have, assigning them to the categories of incompetence, ill will, or partisan fervor. No doubt that had something to do with the identity of my interlocutors, who were both well-known and respected individuals; but it also had something to do with their kindness and good will—or perhaps simply their (British) politeness, which I mistook for something else. I tell myself now, too, that both of those men knew what it was to be uprooted, had experienced cultural otherness, as I had, and that because of this they both were better able to live personal otherness, that state in which one acknowledges the other while keeping one's distance.

The fact remains that these two conversations, however trivial, had an unquestionable influence on me. If I were to attempt a rather crude translation of the way I have come to understand them, I would say that in each case I was brought to an awareness of the nonnecessary, or arbitrary, nature of my own position. What I heard Berlin say was that literature is not made up of structures alone but also of ideas and history; Koestler's message as I took it was that there were no "objective" reasons to choose to give up the exercise of freedom. These statements are self-evident, of course; yet they have to be received in a particular way in order to be fully assimilated.

These propositions, along with other factors of which I remain ignorant, led me to revise my ideas about the nature of literature and the role of the critic. As it happened, they fell in fact upon prepared ground. During those same years, curiosity had led me to read a number of ancient works bearing upon my major preoccupations at the time, symbolism and interpretation. I had read these works of rhetoric, hermeneutics, aesthetics, and philosophy of language without any historical project in mind; instead, I was looking for remarks that might have remained "valid," insights into metaphor, allegory, or suggestion. But during my reading I began to realize that it was harder than I had expected to keep the systematic project separate from the historical one. What I had until then viewed as neutral instruments, as purely descriptive concepts (my own), now appeared to me as the consequences of some specific historical choices, which might have been made differently; moreover, these choices had corollaries—"ideological" ones—that I was not always prepared to assume. I have already referred to these articulations in the introduction to this book.

Thus I became aware of two things as I read through those old books: first of all, that my frame of reference was not the truth at last revealed, the tool that makes it possible to measure the degree of error in all earlier views of literature and commentary, but rather it was the result of certain ideological choices; second, that I was not enthusiastic at the idea of being caught up in all the implications of this ideology, whose most familiar faces are individualism and relativism.

But was there any other possibility? To reject these premises would presumably mean an even less tenable return to the earlier form of criticism (though it was not always called "criticism"), which would have to be labeled *dogmatic* to distinguish it from the *immanence* claimed by the moderns: there literature, no longer opposed to other human verbal productions, was to "sign up in the service of the truth," as Augustine said about eloquence. Would commentary in turn have to accept being the servant of a dogma, knowing in advance what meaning had to be found in each text, or at the very least determining the value of that meaning in terms of some preestablished principle?

Having been trained in Bulgaria, I in fact knew that form of criticism very well, even though I had not practiced it except in high school essays. That situation was quite different from the one I found in France when I arrived there in 1963; "theory of literature" ranked among the disciplines that the philology student at Sofia had to master (I still recall how the face of the dean of the faculty of letters at the Sorbonne suddenly froze when I asked him in halting French, in 1963, who taught literary theory there). But the literary theory in question in Bulgaria—which permeated courses in literary history, needless to say—might be boiled down to two basic notions: "the spirit of the people" and "the spirit of the party" (*narodnost* and *partijnost*). Many writers had the former attribute, but only the best possessed the latter. What writers were supposed to say was known beforehand; all that remained to be determined was the extent to which they would succeed. I think this early training is what awakened, by way of contrast, my initial interest in the Formalists.

Those who hold the "immanentist" position, like those who hold the "dogmatist" one, it seems to me, have always sought to present the adversary's position as the only possible alternative to the one they occupy themselves. The dogmatic conservatives claim that any renunciation of their values is tantamount to giving up all values; the "immanentist" liberals claim that any search for value leads to obscurantism and repression. But do we have to believe them?

The answer to this question came to me, as might be expected, in a roundabout way. After I became a French citizen, I began to feel more acutely than ever the fact that I would never be a Frenchman like any other, because of my simultaneous participation in two cultures. A double belonging, an interiority and an exteriority: it can be experienced as lack or as privilege (I have consistently inclined toward the optimistic view), but in any event it sensitizes one to the problems of cultural alterity and the perception of the "other." I had just conceived of a vast project on that subject when, during another series of lectures, in Mexico this time, quite by chance, I discovered the writings about the conquest of America by the earliest conquistadors. That dazzling example of discovery— and ignorance—of the other preoccupied me deeply for three years. Now as I think back on those topics, I find that I encounter my literary problem once again, although projected on a much larger scale, since here what is in question is the opposition of the universal and the relative in the ethical order. Does obedience to the spirit of tolerance that dominates our mind (even though it may leave our behavior intact) require that we refrain from making any judgment about societies other than our own? And on the other hand, were we to maintain certain values as universal, could we avoid crushing the other in a preestablished mold (our own)? The alternative obviously brings to mind the conflict between "immanentists" and "dogmatists."

What has impelled me to declare that impasse an illusory one is, I think, my more or less fortunate experience as an exile. The choice between possessing the truth and giving up all claim on it does not exhaust all the possibilities that lie before us. Without turning one's back definitively upon universal values, one may posit them as a possible area of agreement with the other rather than as an a priori certainty. We may be aware that we do not possess the truth without giving up our search for it. The truth may be a common horizon, a set of directions for the journey, rather than a point of departure. Instead of abandoning the idea of truth, one may change its status or function, making it into a regulatory principle behind the exchange with the other, rather than the content of the program. In the last analysis, understanding between representatives of different cultures (or between the parts of my own being that stem from one culture or the other) is possible, if the desire for understanding is present: we can go beyond mere "points of view," and it is in human nature to be able to transcend one's own partiality and one's parochialism.

To return to criticism and literature, I must say that this conviction has led me to view them differently. Giving up the search for truth (still in the sense of wisdom and not of correspondence to the facts), the "immanent" critic rules out all possibility of passing judgment; he explains what a work means but does not take that meaning seriously, in a certain sense: he does not respond to it, he acts as if ideas concerning human destiny are not involved. This is because he has transformed the text into an object that it suffices to describe as faithfully as possible; the "immanent" critic contemplates Bossuet and Sade with the same benevolent eye.[1] The "dogmatic" critic, for his part, does not really allow the other to express himself: he swallows the other whole, since the critic himself embodies Providence, or the laws of history, or some other re-

---

[1] I note that Sartre said the same thing, but with the intention of rejecting any universalist perspective. "Rousseau, the father of the French Revolution, and Gobineau, the father of racism, both sent us messages. And the critic considers them with equal sympathy" (*What Is Literature?*, pp. 25–26).

vealed truth; he allows the other to serve only as the illustration (or the counterillustration) of some unshakable doctrine that the reader is expected to share.

Now criticism is dialogue, and its own interest is best served by recognizing this openly; it is a meeting of two voices, author's and critic's, and neither has the advantage over the other. However, critics of various persuasions find common ground in their refusal to recognize this dialogue. Whether consciously or not, the dogmatic critic, followed in this by the "impressionistic" essayist and the partisan of subjectivism, allows a single voice to be heard: his own. On the other side, the ideal of "historical" criticism (a somewhat misleading label, as we saw in connection with Watt) was to allow the authentic voice of the writer to be heard, without anything added by the critic himself. The ideal of identificatory criticism, another variant of "immanent" criticism (as exemplified for instance by Georges Poulet), is to project oneself onto the other to the extent of becoming able to speak in the other's name; while the ideal of structural criticism is to describe the work while completely removing oneself from the picture. But ruling out in this way the possibility of dialogue with literary works and thus the possibility of passing judgment on their truth value is tantamount to amputating one of their essential dimensions, which is precisely that of stating the truth. I recall giving a talk in Brussels on Diderot's aesthetics (these occasions seem to have left their mark to a greater extent than I realized) during which, after presenting Diderot's ideas as best I could, I pronounced them "false" and spoke of his "failure." One member of the audience, a Diderot specialist, intervened: "I agree with your description, but I am surprised by your value judgments. Are you presuming to correct Diderot? Are you not guilty of anachronism?" I think that in his eyes I was lacking in respect for a classical author. But upon reflection (with the advantage of hindsight), I find that he was the one lacking in respect for Diderot, since he refused to discuss Diderot's ideas, and settled for reconstructing them, as if he were putting together a puzzle. Diderot wrote in order to discover the truth; was it an offense to him to recognize this, while continuing the search, with him and against him?

Dialogic criticism speaks not about literary works but to them, or rather with them; it refuses to eliminate either of the two voices involved. The text under study is not an object that must be taken in hand by a "metalanguage," but rather a discourse that is met by the critic's own; the author is a "thou" and not a "he," an interlocutor with whom one discusses human values. But the dialogue is asymmetrical, since the writer's text is closed, whereas the critic's text can go on indefinitely. In order not to load the dice, the critic must allow his interlocutor's voice to be heard with fidelity. The various forms of immanent criticism find their justification here (though along different lines); what better way to contribute to the clarification of the meaning of a passage than to integrate it into broader and broader contexts—first of all that of the work, next that of the writer, then the epoch, finally the entire literary tradition? As it happens, this is precisely what any given "specialist" does. The various integrations are not mutually exclusive, but are either sequentially embedded, or overlapping, or mutually complementary, as Spinoza well knew when he used them as the subdivisions of his new interpretive method. As a critic, I am indeed obliged to choose between one orientation and another (although there are exceptions): not because of any fundamental incompatibilities among them, but because life is short and there is too much else to do. As a reader, however, I have no reason to make an exclusive choice: why should I deprive myself of *either* the competence of a Northrop Frye, who shows me to what literary tradition the image I am looking at belongs (its diachronic context), *or* that of a Paul Bénichou, who reveals to me the ideological ambiance in which that same image was formulated (its synchronic context)?

At this level, then, what the "structuralist" lacks can be made up for by what the specialist in ideologies has to offer, and vice versa. But both of them (I am no longer speaking now of Bénichou or Frye) also lack something else, which is perhaps more important: what we need is not more facts, but more thought. We can deplore the critic's refusal to posit himself as a thinking subject (rather than hiding behind the accumulation of objective facts) and to pass judgments. Taking the opposite course from Spinoza's, or at least from the one indicated by his expressed intentions, we shall not stop, then, with this search for meaning, we shall pursue it through a discussion about truth; not only "what did he say?" but also "is he right?" (Which does not, we can hope, simply amount to saying "I am right.") Although we agree with Spinoza that we must not subject the search for meaning to a truth that would be held in advance, we have no reason to refrain from searching, at the same time, for truth, and from confronting the meaning of the text with it.

That is why I call this kind of criticism "dialogical." The type of truth to which I aspire can be approached only through dialogue: conversely, as we saw with Bakhtin, if dialogue is to be possible, truth has to be posited as a horizon and as a regulatory principle. Dogmatism leads to monologue on the critic's part; immanentism (and thus relativism) leads to monologue on the part of the author being studied; pure pluralism, which is only the arithmetical addition of several immanent analyses, leads to a copresence of voices which is also an absence of listening: several subjects are expressing themselves, but no one of them is taking his divergencies from the others into account. Anyone who accepts the principle of the shared search for truth is already practicing dialogic criticism.

Marc Bloch, one of the fathers of the "new history," used to say: "How much easier it is to condemn or praise Luther than to scrutinize his soul!" I have come to believe almost the opposite, except that I do not see why the two should be incompatible. If we have "scrutinized" well, we need not refrain from passing judgment, unless the object of study is so completely foreign to us that there is nothing left to say. If Luther continues to speak to us, we must continue to speak to him, and thus to agree or disagree with him. Let us not fool ourselves: our judgment will not derive from our knowledge. Our knowledge will help us to resurrect the voice of the other, whereas our own voice finds its source in ourselves, in the ethical responsibility we have taken on. I do not find this an easy task. I have written twice about Benjamin Constant, once in 1968 for *Critique* and again in 1983 for *Poétique*. The difference between the two studies and my preference for the second cannot be attributed simply to the fact that I did a lot of reading in the intervening fifteen years, or that in 1968 I found it easier to generalize; I find also that in my first text I do not have a distinct voice. I claim to be presenting Constant's thought, but naturally I want to say something myself as well, so I attribute my own ideas to Constant. The result is a hybrid voice, but a single one, in which our respective contributions are not clearly distinguished. In the more recent study, I made an effort both to remain more faithful to Constant and to contradict him. It is somewhat comparable to personal relationships: the illusion of fusion is sweet, but it is an illusion and it comes to a bitter end. The recognition of the other as other makes a better love possible.

It is possible to change our image of criticism in this way only if we transform our idea of literature at the same time. For two hundred years, the Romantics and their countless heirs have been ceaselessly reiterating that literature is a language that finds its end in itself. It is time to come (back) to the self-evident facts that we should never have forgotten: literature has to do with human existence, it is a discourse oriented toward—let us not be intimidated by the ponderous words—truth and morality. Literature is an unveiling of man and the world, Sartre said, and he was right. Literature would be nothing at all if it did not allow us to reach a better understanding of life.

If we have managed to lose sight of that essential dimension of literature, it is because we began by reducing truth to verification, and morality to moralism. The sentences of a novel do not aspire to be taken for factual truth, as do those of a history text; let us not belabor the obvious. The novel is not required—even assuming the task is within the realm of possibility—to describe the specific historical forms of a society; that is not where its truth lies. Nor of course is it a matter of saying that the author's ideas are necessarily correct. But literature is always an attempt to reveal to us "an unknown side of human existence," as Kundera says somewhere, and thus although it has no privileged access to truth, it never stops searching for it.

Literature and morality: "how disgusting!" my contemporary will exclaim. I myself, discovering around me a literature subordinated to politics, thought that it was essential to break every link and preserve literature from any contact with what is not literature. But the relation to values is inherent in literature: not only because it is impossible to speak of existence without referring to that relation, but also because the act of writing is an act of communication, which implies the possibility of understanding, in the name of common values. The writer's ideal may be interrogation, doubt, or denial; he incites his reader nonetheless to share this ideal and thus does not cease to be "moral." Propagandistic literature or the *roman à thèse* by no means exhaust the possible relationships between works and values; they may even be said to represent only an aberrant form of such a relationship: that of a dogmatic truth, held from the beginning, that one is merely seeking to illustrate. Yet a work of literature is not a sermon: the forms differ in that what is for the latter an a priori certainty can be for the former only a horizon.

Someone else will retort: at that price literature is no longer anything but the expression of ideas that we are expected to accept or contradict. But such a reaction presupposes that literature is a single thing. Now this is precisely what it is not: it is a formal game of its elements *and* at the same time an ideological entity (as well as many other things); it is not simply a quest for truth, but it is *also* a quest for truth. In this it is distinguished from the other arts, as Sartre and Bénichou remind us, since it "passes" through language, instead of being a structuring of a simple raw material such as sound, color, or movement; there can be no such thing as "abstract literature." We have at our disposal today a conceptual apparatus that suffices (no matter how obviously imperfect it is) to describe the structural properties of literature and to analyze its historical inscription. But we do not know how to speak of literature's other dimensions, and this is a gap we need to fill. Overly deterministic criticism makes the error of postulating that literary works are the expression, or the reflection, of ideology (of the "dominant" ideology, moreover); it then becomes a facile exercise to look for examples that prove the opposite. But if literature is not the reflection of an external ideology, this does not prove that it has no relationship at all to ideology: literature does not reflect an ideology, it is one. We have to know what literary works are stating, not *in order* to discover the spirit of the times or *because* we are already familiar with that spirit and are seeking new illustrations of it, but rather because the statement is essential to the works themselves.

And we come back once again to the proximity between literature and criticism. It is sometimes said that the former speaks of the world, the latter of books. But that is not true. First of all, the works themselves always speak about earlier works, or in any event imply them: the desire to write does not come from life but from other writings. Next, criticism must not, cannot, be limited to speaking about books; in its turn, it always has something to say about life. When it limits itself to structural description and historical reconstruction, it simply attempts to make its voice as inaudible as possible (even though it never entirely succeeds). Yet it can and must remember that it too is a quest for truth and values. The type of truth to which criticism and literature have access is of the same nature: the truth of things rather than of facts, the truth of unveiling and not the truth of equivalence (which the critic is acquainted with as well, but which constitutes only a preliminary truth for him). Many a wrong turn could have been avoided, in criticism as in history or anthropology, if it had only been recognized that, just as Dostoevsky is seeking to state the truth about man although one cannot declare that he possesses it, in the same way the critic is seeking to state the truth about Dostoevsky, with —at least in theory—the same chances of success; at the same time, and inevitably, he too speaks about man. As Sartre said, "prose is communication, a joint quest of truth; it is recognition and reciprocity" (*Saint Genet*, p. 439); but this definition can be applied, word for word, to criticism. Of course criticism and literature have their differences; in the current context, however, it seems to me more urgent to see what they have in common.

Dialogic criticism is standard in philosophy, where scholars are interested in authors for their ideas, but not very common in literature, where critics think it suffices to contemplate and admire. Now the forms themselves are bearers of ideology, and examples of literary criticism exist—although they are rare—that are not limited to analysis, but that argue with their authors, thereby demonstrating that dialogic criticism is just as possible in the literary field: René Girard disagrees with the Romantics, for example, and Leo Bersani enters into a polemic with the realists. In order to be understood, the language of forms requires a certain kind of listening (Ian Watt provided an excellent illustration of this); in its absence, we are forced to fall back upon the author's direct utterances or, worse, those of his characters. But just because some critics are deaf does not mean that literature ceases to speak. Even the least "moral" works take a stance with respect to human values and thus allow a confrontation with the position of the critic. The only case in which dialogic criticism is impossible is when the critic finds himself in complete agreement with his author: then no discussion is possible, and the dialogue ends up being replaced by an apologia. One may wonder whether such a perfect coincidence is really possible, but it is certain that even differences in degree are perceptible: it is easier for me to engage in dialogue (when I dare) with Diderot, whose ideas I disapprove of, than with Stendhal. I must say too, however, that personally I am even more ill at ease when the opposition is radical: war is not a search for understanding.

I should add that the critic who wants to enter into dialogue with his author should not forget that as soon as his own book is published he becomes an author in turn, and that a future reader will seek to enter into dialogue with him. The ideal of dialogic criticism is not the oracular formula that plunges the reader into stupefaction, followed by a bitter mix of admiration for the author and pity for oneself. Once he has become conscious of the dialogue in which he is engaged, the critic cannot remain ignorant of the fact that this particular dialogue is just one link in an uninterrupted chain, since the author was writing in response to other authors, and since one becomes an author oneself from that moment on. The form of one's writing itself is therefore not without importance, since this form must authorize a response, and not mere idolatry.

Is dialogic criticism more appropriate to our times than immanent criticism and dogmatic criticism? I have perhaps given the impression that I think so, by describing the relation between these latter as sequential: first came Patristic exegesis, then philology. But things are of course not so simple, both because societies are not perfectly homogeneous and because history does not unfold according to any linear schema. An "immanent" attitude toward art is found in Quintilian, and the "dogmatic" commentary did not die with the Church Fathers. The contemporary world, in particular, recognizes the plurality of options, and ("dogmatic") Christian or Marxist viewpoints are found side by side today with ("immanent") outlooks that are historical or structuralist in orientation. Human beings are never entirely determined by their milieu; their freedom is their defining characteristic; and I am a living illustration of the weakness of that determinism, since I have found myself in the span of just a few years attached more or less closely to each of the three forms of criticism that I have set out to distinguish here.

And yet it is clear, too, that even if individualism can be detected as far back as the writings of the Stoics, it takes on new vigor in the Renaissance and becomes dominant with Romanticism. The ideologies of a society are hierarchically articulated, and this articulation is significant: I do not believe that it is purely a matter of chance (a pure act of freedom on the part of certain individuals) that the idea of dialogic criticism, by this name or some other, comes to us here and now; nor do I believe that it has reached us because we are more intelligent than our predecessors. The events of the world around us are "favorable conditions" for this criticism rather than its "causes"; but I think I hear them echoing in it. Deliberately mixing the proximate and the remote, the fundamental and the derived, the trivial and the sublime, I shall cite the following: the current absence of any unanimously accepted doctrine; our increased familiarity with cultures other than our own, thanks to mass media and charter flights; the acceptance of decolonization, at least on the ideological level; an unprecedented development of technology; the new type of massacre that the mid-twentieth century has known; the rebirth (birth?) of the struggle for human rights.

I find another indication of this evolution in the contemporary transformations of literature itself (but here I am surely succumbing to a choice that derives from what I seek to find). What seems to me characteristic of this literature is not the inexhaustible autobiographical genre under which it is giving way, but the fact that it openly assumes its own heterogeneity, that it is at once fiction and pamphlet, history and philosophy, poetry and science. The writings of Solzhenitsyn and Kundera, Günter Grass and D. M. Thomas cannot be neatly packaged within previous conceptions of literature; they are neither "art for art's sake" nor "literature of commitment" (in the ordinary rather than the Sartrean sense); rather, they are works that know themselves for what they are, at once literary construction and search for truth.

Dialogic criticism has existed, of course, from time immemorial (like the other types), and if necessary the adjective can be dispensed with, so long as we recognize that the meaning of criticism always lies in transcending the opposition between dogmatism and skepticism. But our epoch—how much longer do we have?— seems to hold out some hope for this form of thought, if only we hurry to grasp it.

APPENDIXES

Some readers' reactions to the French version of this book (*Critique de la critique*) made me think I had not been clear enough about the way the critical position I am defending here relates both to my own earlier views and to those held by other contemporary critics. For this reason, I thought readers of the English version might find it useful to have access to two short texts written after the book's original publication in France and designed to dispel potential misunderstandings. Each of the supplementary texts helps to clarify the relation between my earlier work and the book in hand. The first one, written in response to a review of the book, also spells out the way I perceive what is called traditional literary history. Although some of the issues discussed are specific to the French intellectual context, I think the debate will strike familiar chords for my English-speaking readers as well. The second text, which gives an account of another recent book, also gives me an opportunity to characterize my impressions of contemporary American criticism.

Appendix A

Pseudo-Issues and

Real Issues

In an article in *Commentaire* (no. 30, 1985), Michel Crouzet passes judgment on, among other things, the current state of literary criticism, taking my recent book *Critique de la critique* as a pretext. He touches upon several questions that seem important to me. But whether he is carried away by his convictions or for some other reason, he does not succeed, it seems to me, in situating the discussion on a plane where it might prove enlightening. This has led me to take a fresh look at several of the themes of my book.

EMPIRICISM AND THEORY

Crouzet depicts two diametrically opposed versions of criticism. The modern one, where I am located, is bad; the other—the old one, Crouzet's own—is good: this opposition coincides with the one between (empty) theory and (useful) empirical work, "between theoretical sovereignty and the real works" (p. 649). On the one hand, then, we have the "generalist" who knows nothing, whose work is "secondhand" (p. 650), who believes that his "method" assures him of an answer to everything: in short, we have "teaching and literature contaminated by philosophy" (p.

649). On the other hand, we have the specialist, who does not hesitate to "dirty his hands in the dust of centuries and of libraries" (ibid.), who devotes himself to "empirical or positivist work, to establishing a text, to factual research (sources, biography, events)" (p. 650); this is what leads to real works, "great works, lengthy works" (p. 649). Consequently, Crouzet is astonished that, in spite of certain good intentions, I continue to stick to theory: "What an extraordinary ascetic vocation: always the method and the theory, never the writers. Does boredom never strike, as he goes round and round in the circles of doctrine and ideology? Isn't he a bit fed up with general theories?" (p. 648). "Why, too, does Todorov, weary of a criticism he has wrung dry, settle for announcing a new program? It would be more convincing if he just put it into practice" (p. 649).

This way of presenting the critical situation is, first of all, *empirically* false. The "theoretician" attacked by Crouzet is a straw man, if not a phantom. I cannot ask him to keep up with my publications, but the very book he is reviewing is not—contrary to his allegations and to what ill-informed readers might think—a book of theory, but rather one of history; a (partial) history of twentieth-century criticism. Crouzet limits his focus, to be sure, to the concluding chapter in which I take myself as my own object, as it were. But the fact that he fails to speak of the remaining seven-eighths of the book does not mean that they cease to exist. Now these chapters consist of analyses—empirical analyses—of the work of Mikhail Bakhtin, Northrop Frye, Paul Bénichou, and others. My previous book, *La Conquête de l'Amérique* (1982; *The Conquest of America*, 1984), had nothing to do with theory either (critical or literary), since it consisted of a rereading of narratives describing the conquest of Mexico in the sixteenth century. And the one before that, *Mikhaïl Bakhtine, le principe dialogique* (1981; *Mikhail Bakhtin, The Dialogical Principle*, 1984), was a monograph devoted to a twentieth-century Russian thinker.

Crouzet's image of the other representatives of the critical trends he abhors is equally misleading. He attacks structuralism. Now no one identified himself more proudly with structuralism than Roman Jakobson; would Crouzet accuse him, too, of failing to pay attention to empirical facts? Gérard Genette, another author singled out, has in recent years published two volumes, *Mimologiques* (Seuil, 1976) and *Palimpsestes* (Seuil, 1982), which are monuments of erudition. The great representatives of what was once called in France "new criticism," Georges Poulet, Jean-Pierre Richard, Jean Starobinski, do not stand out in the area of general theory; they have each devoted patient, painstaking studies to particular writers. It is really quite farfetched to assimilate new criticism to "theory" in "general," as Crouzet does.

But the factual error is followed, or preceded, by a more basic confusion. Scholarship is fruitful only if it is at once empirical and theoretical, particular and general. (I took that to be self-evident.) Philosophical "contamination" is no more to be feared than dirtying one's hands through contact with the facts. To shore up his position, Crouzet believes he can draw upon the authority of Leo Strauss, by associating the opposition between empiricism and theory with one of Strauss's distinctions. But Strauss never demanded that critics give up the faculty of thinking. In a text that appears in *Persecution and the Art of Writing*, Strauss distinguishes between interpretation (understanding a text the way its author understands it) and explanation (laying bare implications of a text of which the author himself is not aware) (I cite these statements in *Symbolism and Interpretation*, p. 21). Interpretation is the first step required in every reading. However, that is not a reason to go no further, and in *Natural Right and History*, Strauss describes that same interpretive activity ("understanding people [of diverse societies] in the way in which they understand themselves") as "purely historical and hence merely preparatory and ancillary work" (pp. 56, 57). Anyone who has read Strauss's exegeses knows that he himself practices interpretation and explanation both. One reason, and not the least important, why his texts are so compelling is that he has not fled philosophical "contamination." That is why I can assert, whether Crouzet likes it or not, that "what we need is not more facts, but more thought" (p. 162, above). That does not mean, needless to say, that I am in favor of neglecting facts.

To tell the truth, I doubt that Crouzet himself subscribes to the Manichean opposition between empiricism and theory. His own practice does not tend in that direction: he is the author of valuable books on Stendhal, in which he does not settle for "factual research (sources, biography, events)," but tries to conceptualize the problems that preoccupied Stendhal—which implies that he goes beyond an exclusive focus on the work under analysis. And he even says so, on occasion, in the article in question: "The critic oscillates between the scientific dimension and the humanist dimension, between the mundane biographical details of the individual and the transhistorical or metaphysical signification of a work" (p. 649). In the most "theoretical" text I ever published, *Poétique* (1973; *Introduction to Poetics*, 1981), I for my part stated that "between poetics and interpretation, there is a relation of complementarity *par excellence*. A theoretical meditation on poetics that is not nourished by observations on existing works turns out to be sterile and inoperative. Linguists are well acquainted with this situation, and Benveniste states correctly that 'reflection on language is fruitful only if it deals first of all with real languages'" (p. 21). Is this what Crouzet calls "the structuralist frenzy, the rush to get rid of the obstacle of empiricism" (p. 650)?

Crouzet deplores the "detestable opposition between 'generalists' and 'specialists'" (p. 649). So do I. But then why does he use it? The "correct" opposition is not between empiricism and theory, but between the illusion according to which one might make do with just one of those two terms, on the one hand, and an awareness of the solidarity between the two, on the other hand. We ought to be in agreement on this point. Why does he not say as much, then, instead of wasting his breath on misplaced invective?

THE ORIGINS OF MODERN CRITICISM

In *Critique de la critique*, I attempt to locate the origin of the ideas that have made up the common platform of contemporary critics. I establish a relationship, on the one hand, between the modern idea of literature and the Romantic aesthetic (art is an activity that finds its end in itself); and, on the other hand, between the modern idea of criticism and Spinoza's hermeneutics, as it was to be adopted and adapted by the nineteenth-century philologists (criticism seeks meaning, and is not concerned with the truth of the work). Gérard Genette, in *Mimologiques*, Jean-Marie Schaeffer, in *Naissance de la littérature* (P.E.N.S., 1983) and in "Romantisme et langage poétique" (*Poétique* 42 [1980]), I myself in *Theories of the Symbol* and *Symbolism and Interpretation*—all of us have tried to spell out that hypothesis by analyzing concepts, comparing texts, establishing relationships of influence.

Crouzet tosses these propositions aside without a second glance. If he is to be believed, I create "a nonexistent *Romanticism*," I confuse the modern dogma of "self-referentiality" with the "Romantic sovereignty of art" (p. 648); "no writer, not even Mallarmé or Valéry, can be reduced to this undiscoverable 'Romanticism'" (p. 649). In its place, Crouzet proposes his own explanation, which has two distinctive features. The first is that the origin must be sought close to home in the immediate past and not in the fogs of Jena around 1800. "A little clan of fantastic Saussurians" (p. 649), led apparently by myself, is responsible for these deviations: "the *intransitivity* of literature, formerly a dogma established by Todorov and others" (p. 645). The second is that this plot had not only "theoretical" aims but also political ones: the fight against the "reactionary" "bourgeoisie," in a first phase; and, in the end, "the Socialist Revolution" (p. 641).

This political dimension matters a great deal to Crouzet, and it constitutes the real core of his anlaysis. He paints the following picture. The (French) intelligentsia, wholly given over to "the movement of the left" (p. 641), takes its orders from an all-powerful master: "the intellectual Party [a term used at the turn of the century by Charles Péguy], currently the 'power' of the Elysée Palace [the French "White House," occupied at the time of this writing by the Socialist François Mitterrand] and the rue de Valois [where the Ministry of Culture is located, at the time headed by the Socialist Jack Lang]" (p. 647). Its emissaries are "the P.E.G.C. [undereducated high school teachers] or the Intersyndicale du Supérieur [the left-oriented unions in the universities] and its troops from Collège B [junior professors]" (p. 645). All these incompetents plunge headlong into theory: "the less competent they are, the more 'theoretical' they are; 'narratology' is ideal for minds that are not capable of producing an *explication* of a simple text. . . . Theory, as a means of advancement . . . , was the union's weapon against the 'professors'" (ibid.). From this point on, "the freedom of literary instruction" is "dominated by an ideology and, concomitantly, by all ideologies; Marxism becomes an official component of the denaturing of teaching" (pp. 643–644). The whole thing, that is, the alliance between the unions and structuralism, is spreading throughout the entire world owing to some well-placed connections "in the American Universities" (p. 644).

It is hard to know whether to laugh or cry in the face of Crouzet's diatribe. What has become of his scrupulous respect for the facts, his empiricist passion? Lévi-Strauss is mentioned several times: what is he doing in the socialist squadrons? Does Crouzet not spit rather too ostentatiously on several tombs (in the U.S.S.R.) when he affirms that structuralism, or formalism, "was also a continuation" (p. 643) of the *diamat*, of Marxism-Leninism? The only fact he manages to cite is the Cluny "pact" between [the defunct "avant-garde" periodical] *Tel Quel* and the French Communist Party; but at least its signatories were not Sorbonne professors [which is Crouzet's case], and the project's confusion has causes that are easily understood. Crouzet, for his part, receives it as a revelation and sees in it the acknowledgment of "a program common to the ideological sects and the sect of the left-wing unions" (p. 644).

If Crouzet does not know the facts (in the case in point, the constant hostility between Marxist and "formalist" tendencies, in France as elsewhere), he might at least give some thought to the concepts, and observe that Marxist criticism, which is a historical and causal explanation of facts, cannot be mistaken for formalism, which aims at a phenomenological and internal description of facts; nor can the latter be identified with post-Nietzschean and post-Heideggerian nihilism (quite widespread in France), since this nihilism attacks the principle of reason while formalism defends it. But it is true that Crouzet glides easily from one thing to another: does he not tell us that the postulates of left-wing intellectuals have affinities "with those of Nazism, no less" (p. 642), and that the rejection of "empirical and erudite knowledge" leads straight to "totalitarian engagement" (p. 649)? It is also true that he prefers to talk about the "new criticism," "all tendencies merged into one" (p. 649). But does he not then fall into the level of generality that he was attacking earlier on? In the eyes of Plato, no doubt Marxists and Freudians, formalists and Nietzscheans all look alike (all "moderns"); but from that point of view, I fear, they cannot be distinguished from "empiricists" or "historians" either.

The "power of the Elysée Palace," from this perspective, explains the mutation in literary studies in France (roughly speaking, the change from an external approach—"sources, biography, events"—to an internal analysis of the elements that constitute a

work). But then what can we make of the fact that a similar mutation has taken place, in the twentieth century, in many other European countries and in America? In Russia, we have seen the flourishing of the school known as "Russian Formalism"; in Germany,
the morphological trend of Jolles and Müller, the new stylistics of
Spitzer and Auerbach, the immanent approach of Kayser, the phe-
nomenology of Ingarden and Käte Hamburger. In England, there
have been the linguistic analyses of Richards and Empson; in the
United States, New Criticism and the neo-Aristotelian Chicago
School; in Canada, the mythological criticism of Northrop Frye,
and so on. And what are we to make of the transformation in philology starting at the beginning of this century, in which the historical approach of the neo-grammarians gave way to the systematic
analysis of the linguists? To explain this about-face, must we fall
back upon the Socialist International? or the intervention of Moscow? But Crouzet does not ask that sort of question: if one were to
trust his analysis, moreover, one might believe that *Critique de la
critique* has to do with France alone: he hasn't a word to say about
all the rest (except to mention "a young peasant of the Danube,
fresh from his native Bulgaria" [p. 642]: myself).

What about the arguments Crouzet levels against the thesis of
"Romantic" influence? No individual writer, he says, can be reduced to the Romantic model. I agree with him. There is no reason, however, to require such a reduction. "Romanticism" in this
sense is a schema of thought, a set of motifs, themes, linkages; it
is an "ideal type." The individual, unless he is a pure epigone,
does not settle for repeating the Romantic program; he nevertheless participates in it. Crouzet objects that "'new criticism' has
nothing relativist about it" (p. 648); on the contrary, it is on the side
of dogmatism. —I am not convinced. Stylistic dogmatism is one
thing ("I am right, I alone am right") and this, to be sure, characterizes numerous representatives of Marxism and formalism, although these latter have no exclusive monopoly on it, as Crouzet's
article proves. Dogmatism as a philosophical position is something
else again. For Marxism, everything is historical; transcultural values do not exist: thus we remain indeed within relativism, even
though the latter is taught as a dogma. For formalist immanentism,
the goal of analysis is the description of the meaning of each individual work, without any reference to a transcendent truth: that is
why we are still dealing here with relativism.

There is surely a difference between the "Romantic sovereignty of art" and modern "self-referentiality"; there is also continuity. But falling back upon crude caricatures is not the way to spell out the nature of the relationship, or to confront the real issue.

HUMANISM AND SCIENCE

If Crouzet is to be believed, the intellectual history of twentieth-century France is characterized by an opposition with multiple resonances: left is opposed to right, of course, but also egalitarianism to elitism, scientific instruction to literary instruction, and, finally, science to humanism. Science, or at least its image, thus lies on the left: "At every moment of its history, in all its variants, the French 'left' in the twentieth century has tried to subordinate literary instruction to that of the 'sciences' and to diminish the power of the 'literary spirit'" (p. 644). This was already the case with Lanson, "'scientist,' Jauresian, and socialist" (p. 643), who might have been expected, however, to land on the side of the empiricist historians, for he was "*already* anxious to substitute 'science,' and the scientific method (historical, in this instance) for the purely literary study of texts" (p. 644). The explanation of this alliance resides in the attraction of equality: science squares better with the "hypothetical equality of minds" (ibid.) on which the left depends. That is why the left's struggle consists in a "destruction of 'general culture' in the name of democracy, the subordination of 'letters' to the sciences" (ibid.).

I do not believe that such an opposition is legitimate. Crouzet succeeds in maintaining it only by radically (as it were) distorting the meaning of the two terms, "science" and "humanism." We can follow him when he denounces the assimilation of knowledge of human beings to knowledge of nature; we may still acquiesce when he warns us against exaggerated claims made in the name of science: in so doing, we are not "against" science, but against improper uses of science. When, "in the name of 'scientific methods,' one succeeds in obliterating, in denaturing, in burying the meaning of texts" (p. 643), one is doing bad science, and science itself is not to be blamed. The works of Crouzet himself, once again, grow out of a rationalist and, yes, a scientific spirit.

I am not certain, on the other hand, that Crouzet is a humanist

—or else we are confronting a singular humanism indeed. Rejecting the "hypothetical equality of minds," he has nothing to say in defense of the real equality of rights; now the democracy he assails rests on the latter, not the former. This is how I understand the low esteem in which he holds what he calls my "personalist and 'human rights' preaching" (p. 648); the defense of human rights is indeed incompatible with the philosophical position of the Ancients (that of dogmatism). As is a certain tolerance for the opinions of others and the recognition of a certain plurality in world views (tolerance and plurality which are not, however, as in nihilism, supreme principles, but which turn out to be subordinated to the common quest for truth). Now this tolerance is specifically unacceptable to Crouzet: he has nothing but scorn for the journal *Poétique*, which is hardly a left-wing rag, but which allows itself to welcome "differing, and even contradictory, options" (p. 645) on an equal footing, and without tacking on evaluative commentary.

Contrary to Crouzet's intimations, humanism and science are on the same side of the fence; and I identify with both (without claiming that I have always been worthy of them). Together, they oppose what has to be called political or cognitive obscurantism. Raymond Aron, founder of the journal *Commentaire*, which publishes Crouzet's fanatical outbursts today, said as much in a few telling phrases: "Even if one admits that, logically, the truth of '2 × 2 = 4' is not of the same type as that of 'Thou shalt not kill,' the fact remains that the ultimate meaning of arithmetic equivalence is pertinent to all men, a universality found in a different form in the prohibition against killing. . . . The formal rules of the rationalist ethic . . . are . . . the logical development of the notion of humanity, of the universal society of man, an idea inseparable from the profound significance of scientific truth" (*History, Truth, Liberty*, pp. 361–362). Science does not belong to the left any more than humanism does to the right; but they are both on the side of democracy.

What Does Criticism Need?

In the *Commentaire* article, Crouzet offers an example of what might be called vituperative criticism. Its characteristic features are scorn for facts, the rejection of nuances and distinctions (formalists are confused with Marxists, generalization is totalitarian, Lévi-Strauss is a pawn of the Elysée Palace, and so on), abusive generalization, conceptual amalgamation ("all tendencies merged into one"), ethnocentrism, and the reduction of all thought to simplistic political categories. At the same time, he claims to attack these same flaws in others; in so doing, he illustrates a contradiction between the abstract program and its particular realization, a contradiction for which he would perhaps reserve the name "ideology." Should modern criticism follow this example? I think not.

Crouzet believes that, in *Critique de la critique*, I have been led to repudiate my own earlier work. But that is not true. I have contributed, along with others, toward completing a historical and external empiricism with a structural and internal empiricism; I do not see why I should recant. As Jean Starobinski put it recently, both versions of empiricism have become "philological techniques," on an equal footing. The fact that I must know the meaning of a word in its historical context does not imply that I must fail to know the meaning it takes on in the context of the work itself, or vice versa. "Chronological fields" are not, in themselves, any more or less legitimate than "systematic corpora" (p. 650). *The Red and the Black* is both a novel *and* a work belonging to the first half of the nineteenth century: the incompatibility of these two contexts is illusory. Rather than dreaming about "the immense task of reestablishing literary studies" (p. 650), that is, about wiping out the past twenty years, I should like to see criticism take hold of all available means for increasing our understanding of the meaning of texts, whatever their origin. The best critics do not raise this sort of question: an Ian Watt (it is true that he is not a pure Frenchman), speaking of James or Conrad, is capable of analyzing both style *and* philosophical ideas, formal configurations *and* social data. And Victor Goldschmidt, that exemplary interpreter, used to describe his approach as a "structural method in the history of philosophy." The goal, as Crouzet states, "is what is best, the best work in terms of increased intelligence" (p. 643); it involves contributing, as Genette says, "to the ongoing effort of the human mind, through all the fluctuations of the ideological conjuncture, toward greater intelligibility" (so perhaps they agree after all?).

In *Critique de la critique*, I describe how I came to perceive the "arbitrary" character of some of my own presuppositions. Crouzet pokes fun at this: "does Todorov want to be totally *necessitated* in his research?" (p. 650). The passage in question dealt with the feeling of justification that would arise from the truth of what one says (about science); I noted the illusory character of that feeling. Today I would like my position to be, not "necessitated," but legitimated, by an explicit reference to the values that are my own. What I in turn find to criticize in modern criticism (which never means "among all the critics") is the rejection of transcendence, imprisonment in a search for the meaning of a text while the question of its truth is never even raised. That does not mean—but does Crouzet really believe I think it does?—that one must neglect meaning and settle for stating dogmatic truths. It means rather that one must not stop with the search for meaning; it even means that, in order to do a good job searching, one must also raise questions about the truth of the text. Criticism needs to become aware of the ethical dimension from which it is inseparable: not to the detriment of empirical knowledge of facts, but by freeing itself from the illusions of an empiricism, whatever its nature, that would suffice unto itself.

Here, for me, is where the real issue lies.

Traveling through
American Criticism

When a foreigner visiting France asks me "what's happening in French criticism these days?" I am at a loss: I either keep still or change the subject. I am in the dark about prevailing trends: the people I know are individuals who seem to be following their own separate paths. In the United States, on the other hand, where I spend only a few weeks a year, quite the reverse is true: there, I feel I am observing a coherent picture, and I would have no trouble at all answering the same question about American criticism. I had always attributed this contrast to my own personal vantage point: in France, I lack the distance a good observer needs, while in the United States, where I am a visitor, not a participant, I benefit from the privileged status Montesquieu attributed to Persians in Paris. But this privilege has its drawbacks, too (I lack in-depth knowledge and infallible intuitions), and these might have sufficed to keep me from ever venturing an opinion about American criticism had I not come across Robert Scholes's *Textual Power*. The picture Scholes paints of the critical scene in the United States is so close to my own that it makes me wonder, in my readiness to pat myself on the back, whether the coincidence may not be based on the accuracy of the picture itself.

To formulate my impressions clearly, I need to begin by looking backward. Until roughly 1968, let us say, most American critics seemed preoccupied by one key question: "What does the text mean?" Confronted with a text calling for commentary, they shared the conviction that their most important task was to discover as exactly as possible what the text meant. (They began to disagree as soon as they had to choose one means or another, one approach or another, to finding the answer. Should they pay special attention to historical events contemporary with the book, or to stylistic features? to its author's motivations, or to the rules of its genre?) The only critics who did not share in this consensus were those that might be called didactic (and they were more often journalists than academics, though the two are not mutually exclusive): these critics were generally pursuing some personal goal through their own writing, and they used works from the past without caring much one way or the other about the accuracy of their interpretations.

Structuralism, the most recent arrival on the scene, had not brought about any basic changes in the underlying situation. Whether in Northrop Frye's version or the one inherited from the Russian Formalists, structural analysis, like its predecessors, sought to help find a better answer to the same question. Its approach was to call attention to the internal construction of literary works (which had the side effect of leaving their other aspects unexplored—but that was not unique to structuralism either).

Against such a background, then, the new trend in American criticism that I mentioned above was to emerge. The trend had been labeled *post-structuralism*, a term which strikes me as rather unfortunate: it implies both continuity (otherwise it would mean nothing) and progress (as if what comes after were always an improvement over what went before), whereas in fact we have extreme discontinuity. "Post-structuralism" has developed along two major lines (and in a large number of subsidiary variants and transitional forms) which have one thing in common: they make the earlier question, "What does this text mean?", completely irrelevant. The first—and the more dogmatic and elaborate—of the two main types is called "deconstruction." Oversimplifying somewhat, we might say that deconstruction renders the earlier question moot by invariably answering: "Nothing at all." The second type of post-structuralism, more cheerful but also more naive, is sometimes known by its advocates as "pragmatism." Pragmatism renders the question meaningless by replying: "Anything whatsoever." In the wake of either response, obviously, the question can hardly be raised again; it seems preferable to go on to something else.

Deconstruction appears to be characterized by three interrelated postulates. (1) The world itself is inaccessible; discourse alone exists, and discourse refers only to other discourse. Statements of principle abound. "There is no such thing as an outside-of-the-text." "I don't believe that anything like perception exists" (p. 92). The text "liberates us from the empirical object" (p. 84). The text produces "a structure of infinite referral in which there are only traces" (p. 95). Literature, Edward Said writes, is an "endless naming and remaining of the void" (*The World, the Text, the Critic*, p. 162). (2) Even so, we are not to believe that discourse is better endowed than the world: the latter may not exist, but the former is necessarily incoherent. Deconstructionist commentary always consists in showing that the text studied is internally contradictory, that its intentions are not carried out in actual practice. Thus there is an "insurmountable obstacle in the way of any reading or understanding" (Scholes, p. 78). (3) As no discourse is exempt from these contradictions, there is no reason to prefer one sort over another, or to prefer one value over another. In fact, in the deconstructionist perspective, any value-oriented behavior (criticism, the struggle against injustice, hope for a better world) becomes subject to ridicule.

A good deal might be said about this approach to criticism, and Scholes (like Abrams, Said, and others) does not hold back. The idea that texts are inconsistent is striking first of all for its dogmatism: all texts are implicated equally, with no distinction between literature, theoretical discourse (philosophy, law, ethics, politics) and empirical discourse (the sciences); here, everything becomes "literature." One may wonder, too, whether the deconstructionist idea may not be judged somewhat pretentious: to contradict oneself is human, to be sure, but is it plausible that the contradictions in question could have escaped the notice of thinkers like Plato, Rousseau, or Kant, while they leap to the eye of the first deconstructionist who comes along? When a scrupulous analyst sets out to "think with" Rousseau (as Goldschmidt and Philonenko have done in France, for example), many inconsistencies disappear and the place of the "unthought" is strikingly reduced.

The hypothesis of an inaccessible world is also somewhat overdrawn. It is a commonplace of epistemology, at least since Kant, to recognize the constructed character of knowledge and to challenge belief in a transparent perception of objects; thus both empiricists and positivists may legitimately be criticized. But to go on from there to deny any content whatsoever to perception is a step that ought to be carefully considered before it is taken. As Scholes says, there is something excessive in asserting "that sign-systems affect perception but that the world does not" (p. 164). The discourse of knowledge does indeed have to do with the world, and not just with itself. In this connection Scholes has a delightful example of the independence of the "referent" with respect to the "signifier": the relation between the word "kangaroo" and the thing that jumped up and down around Captain Cook. He quotes eloquent examples of excessive skepticism, and concludes, quite rightly: "From the perspective of deconstruction, there is nothing upon which we can ground an argument for evolutionary biology as opposed to fundamentalist creationism, since both are discourses, with their blindness and their insights" (p. 99). Although literature for its part does not refer directly to particular objects, it is nevertheless not wholly lacking in truth value: if we continue to read Shakespeare today, it is because we have the feeling (even though we cannot explain it) that he offers us a better understanding of "human nature" or something of the sort.

The renunciation of judgment and of values leads to insurmountable aporias, as well. To make their own task easier, deconstructionists seem to have assimilated all values to religious values, thus rejecting the distinction between faith and reason, and they treat reason as an avatar—no more and no less—of God, thus wiping out several centuries of struggle with a single stroke of the pen. Or else they lump everything together under another umbrella-word, "power," which rules out any further distinctions between police-state repression and the exercise of reason, between violence and law. After all this, they can take refuge, without any pangs of conscience, in a "quietistic acceptance of injustice" (p. 79).

Deconstruction is a "dogmatic skepticism" (Eugene Goodheart), and it combines the worst of two worlds. It is skepticism, to the extent that it considers knowledge and judgment impossible, along with truth and justice. But it is also dogmatism, because it decides in advance what each text means—namely, nothing. Deconstructive readings are extremely monotonous, since the result is "always already" known, and since only the means used to reach that result are subject to variation. Deconstruction, according to one of its practitioners, more lucid or more naive than others (Hillis Miller), "is a demonstration that [the text] has already dismantled itself," and each reading "reaches, in the particular way the given text allows it, the 'same' moment of an aporia" (quoted in Abrams, *Theories of Criticism*, p. 25). As Augustine, theoretician of another hermeneutic dogmatism, would say, the path the reader follows is not what matters; his interpretation is correct so long as it leads in the end to the reign of charity. Here the goal is different but the strategy remains the same: "Whatever track the reader follows through the poem he arrives at blank contradictions" (ibid., p. 28). This dogmatic aspect is doubtless what accounts for deconstruction's extraordinary success in academic institutions: the formula has only to be applied to new subject matter to result in an "original" exegesis.

The other major variant of "post-structuralism," pragmatism (whose most prominent representative is Stanley Fish), does not suffer from the same monotony in its results. Its principal hypotheses are the following. (1) A text means nothing in itself; it is the reader who gives it meaning. Here, clearly, we have two propositions. The first is negative ("there are no determinate meanings and . . . the stability of the text is an illusion" [Fish, *Is There a Text in This Class?*, p. 312]), and it links the pragmatists with the deconstructionists, except that their arguments differ. Deconstructionists maintain that discourse as a whole is inconsistent, while pragmatists argue that words have no meaning; the former cast their "suspicion" on the molecules of language, the latter on its atoms. The second proposition, on the other hand, is affirmative: the reader, and thus the critic, may indeed propose and impose a determinate and stable meaning. "Interpreters do not decode poems; they make them" (ibid., p. 327). The text, then, is no more than a sort of Rorschach test allowing readers, like Pirandello's characters, to choose their own meanings: "each in his own way." Of course, in this context, "the notion of a mistake, at least as something to be avoided, disappears" (Abrams, "How to Do Things with Texts," p. 577). (2) What consequences does this choice have for the critical work itself? "It relieves me of the obligation to be right . . . and demands only that I be interesting" (ibid., p. 580). We are far removed from deconstructive monotony here: the field is wide open to creative imagination. (3) More recently, Fish seems to have tempered his relativism into a historicism, claiming that it is not the individual reader who decides what the meaning of the poem is, but rather the group to which the reader belongs: "It is interpretive communities, rather than either the text or the reader, that produce meanings and are responsible for the emergence of formal features" (ibid., p. 14).

The negative part of the first thesis is both empirically false and logically contradictory. It is false because it ignores the social nature of language: neither individuals nor special-interest lobbies are in a position to change the meaning of words. The most idiosyncratic usage, the most audacious metaphor, the most obscure of allusions all presuppose a common language, and this is precisely what dictionaries catalogue (if they did not, it is hard to imagine what they would contain). But the hypothesis is also internally contradictory, for it presupposes that we understand it, while explicitly denying the possibility of understanding. Hence the affirmative part of the statement seems hyperbolic: to be sure, readers necessarily read in a certain way; no reading is transparent. It does not follow, however, that readers produce the complete meaning (and here we return to the problem of perception).

The requirement to write interestingly rather than accurately is shocking only, if at all, because of the field to which it is applied. No one would be scandalized if such a requirement concerned literature itself, even though such a conception, which would raise the detective novel to the summit of the hierarchy, might not seem to do literature full justice. What is called into question by this view of criticism, and in fact of history in general, is its empirical ambition. But the formula is easier to put across when it is applied to criticism. Would anyone dare require historians to give up concern for truth, and only try to be interesting? Would anyone allow interest to be the single guiding principle for the discourse of a judge or a politician? And yet no one is upset about an irresponsible opinion so long as it merely applies to that amusement park known as literature.

Fish's initial conception transforms all reading into that sort of "picnic" Lichtenberg described with reference to Jakob Böhme's works: the author brings the words and the reader supplies the meaning. His later views bring us closer to the Humpty-Dumpty position: it is the master who decides what words mean. In this connection Scholes rightly alludes to the Orwellian world of *1984*, in which the "interpretive community," i.e., the Party, decides on the meaning and nature of past events by constantly rewriting history. To say there there is no difference between facts and interpretations (that is, that "everything is interpretation") is in fact to see force ("the carrot and the stick" [p. 156]) as the only way of imposing one's views. Raymond Aron warned against this confusion long ago: "It can no doubt be maintained, in the spirit of philosophical precision, that every historical fact is a construct and therefore implies selection and interpretation. When applied, these distinctions [facts vs. interpretations] preserve their full implications. It is either true or false that Trotsky played a considerable role in organizing the Red Army; it is either true or false that Zinoviev or Bukharin plotted the assassination of Stalin. . . . Every totalitarian state exaggerates, to the point of absurdity, the interdependence of fact and interpretation" (*History, Truth, Liberty*, p. 345).

Is it appropriate to to bring these two critical tendencies together under a common label ("post-structuralism"), despite their theoretical and rhetorical divergencies? I think it is. They have common roots in Nietzschean philosophy. They have common enemies: on the one hand, universal values, justice, ethics; on the other, truth, knowledge, science. And they have shared affinities: the one revealed by the more or less explicit praise of force (hence the proximity with Harold Bloom, another militant Nietzschean), the other with subjective idealism (the world does not exist in itself, but only in my perception).

In the face of this critical school, what recourse is open to those who continue to believe that literary works have some relation to the world and that some values are better than others, that some are even worth fighting for? Curiously, the only intellectual movement in American criticism that maintains this other position seems to be Marxism, so that the choice boils down to a straightforward one between post-structuralism and Marxism. Scholes himself, who is not a Marxist, has some difficulty differentiating his own position from the Marxist one. Certain coincidences, however, may make us wonder whether the opposition is as radical as it first appears. The idea of an "interpretive community" that would control meaning and interpretation is not foreign to Marxist doctrine, for instance: that doctrine claims that everything depends upon class membership, after all. Communist totalitarianism does not arise from Marxism by accident.

Marxist-inspired criticism claims, of course, that literary works have a relationship with the world. But that is just the starting point; after all, common sense itself indicates that some sort of relationship must exist. Marxist criticism is based on a more specific thesis: what interests it is not the work as representation of the world or statement about it, but rather the world (or a portion of it) as the origin of the work. Marxist criticism is a genealogical criticism; if you say to a Marxist, "the salt is on the table," he never wonders "is it true?" but only "why is she saying that?" It is distinguished from other genealogical criticism (the Freudian version, for example) by its faith in the relevance of the notion of social class. In this game, consciousness always loses to "gut feeling," and every utterance, however universal its intention, is reduced to the particular circumstances of its enunciation; it is necessarily "historical," and that is what counts.

Marxist criticism recognizes the relevance of values, but only certain ones. Those presented as universal or "interclass" values arouse its particular animosity. The rhetorical device most often used to denigrate them consists in a combination of abstraction (liberty is liberalism; individual rights are individualism) and a tendentious particularization (liberalism is the right to fire workers whenever you feel like it; individualism is the right to send your children to the right schools). This is how "liberalism," "individualism," or "humanism" become dirty words. Any attempt to rise above a particular determination is reduced to its humble origins: humanism, for instance, is nothing more than a "suburban moral ideology," in the words of Terry Eagleton (*Literary Theory*, p. 207). Marxism refuses to recognize the distinction of ethics from politics: in its view, politics is a responsible ethics, one that is taken seriously. And so it reduces all striving for values to the defense of group interests: what contributes to the "socialist transformation of the society" (ibid., p. 211) is deemed good, whatever the members of that society may think. And instead of celebrating right and justice, it gives its accolades to the forces of history.

To the universalist aspirations of science, Marxism opposes social and historical determinism; the politics of private interests takes the place of a common ethics. Marxist criticism thus recognizes the relation of literary works to the world and to values, but it rejects universality: truth and justice are grounded in history rather than reason. It is evident, then, that the Marxist opposition to post-structuralism is not as radical as it may have seemed: above and beyond their quarrels over specifics, both are fighting a common enemy called humanism—in other words, in this case, the attempt to ground science and ethics on reason and to practice them in a universal way. Now it is clear why there have been so many attempts to hybridize these two apparently opposed schools of thought: not only because of the superficial desire to be at the forefront of the avant-garde, but also because of deep affinities. Here is a test to try: who said that "the idea of justice in itself is an idea which in effect has been invented and put to work in different societies as an instrument of a certain political and economic power or as a weapon against that power"? No, it was not Terry Eagleton; it was Michel Foucault.[1]

American criticism is thus dominated by what we may as well call by its rightful name, antihumanism. The word may have unpleasant resonances, and it will be objected that its partisans do not usually resemble bloodthirsty ogres. I agree; even Marxists today take pains to dissociate themselves from socialism as it is practiced, and from Stalinist concentration camps. I can bear personal witness to the fact that Paul de Man was a delightful man, and Stanley Fish still is. I am not saying that they themselves are inhuman. I am simply saying that it is not possible, without inconsistency, to defend human rights with one hand and deconstruct the idea of humanity with the other.

What path remains open, then, to criticism today? The one indicated by Scholes might be called critical humanism. Scholes does a good job of highlighting the meaning of the word "critical" that counts here; I will add that that adjective has to serve as a precautionary device against fraudulent uses of the same program. This is not a trivial matter: we know that the humanist camouflage of European colonialism came close to undermining the humanist cause once and for all. Thus the relation of literature and the world has to be recognized: "the whole point of my argument," Scholes writes, "is that we must open the way between the literary or verbal text and the social text in which we live" (p. 24). The relation of both to values has to be recognized as well: "we will have to restore the judgmental dimension to criticism, not in the trivial sense . . . of ranking literary texts, but in the most serious sense of questioning the values proffered by the texts we study" (p. 14).

---

[1] Quoted in Said, *The World, the Text, the Critic*, p. 246.

I should like to hope, though I cannot really believe it possible, that this regrettable episode of contemporary criticism might be quickly forgotten, so that we might begin to look critically at the earlier criticism—but in a different way. The question "what does the text mean?" is a relevant question, and we shall always have to try to answer it, without excluding any contexts, historical, structural, or other, that might help us in the task. But that is not a reason to fail to go beyond it. That question may be carried further by another twofold question, addressed to the response to the first: "Is it true?" and "Is it right?" In this way, we could transcend the sterile opposition between the specialist-critics who know, but do not think, and the moralist-critics who speak without knowing anything about the literary works they discuss. In this way, the critic could finally assume fully the role that is incumbent on him, that of participant in a double dialogue: as reader, with his author; as author, with his own readers—who in the process might even become somewhat more numerous.[2]

[2]Feminist criticism is missing in the overview I have just presented, and I should like to account for its absence. Feminist criticism has undergone a significant development during the period in question: I have not included it not because of any negative judgment, but because it is not defined on the same basis as the other trends considered here. A book of feminist criticism may be at the same time structuralist, or post-structuralist, or Marxist, or humanist; it is not characterized by what the critics call their method, but rather by the choice of certain themes and by the adherence to certain values. I trust that my intentions will not be misunderstood.

WORKS CITED

Abrams, M. H. "How to Do Things with Texts." *Partisan Review*, 46 (1979), 566–586.
———. *Theories of Criticism: Essays in Literature and Art.* Washington: Library of Congress, 1984.
Aron, Raymond. *History, Truth, Liberty: Selected Writings of Raymond Aron.* Ed. Franciszek Draus. Chicago: University of Chicago Press, 1985.
Augustine, Saint. *On Christian Doctrine.* Trans. D. W. Robertson, Jr. New York: The Liberal Arts Press, 1958.
Bakhtin, Mikhail. *The Dialogic Imagination.* Trans. Caryl Emerson and Michael Holquist. Austin: University of Texas Press, 1981. (Partial translation of *Voprosy literatury i èstetiki*. Moscow, 1975.)
———. *Estetika slovesnogo tvorchestva.* Moscow, 1979. (Fr. trans.: *Esthétique de la création verbale*. Paris: Gallimard, 1984.)
———. *Problems of Dostoevsky's Poetics.* Trans. Caryl Emerson. Minneapolis: University of Minnesota Press, 1984. (*Problemy poétiki Dostoevskogo*. Moscow, 1963.)
———. *Rabelais and His World.* Trans. Helene Iswolsky. Cambridge, Mass.: M.I.T. Press, 1968. (*Tvorchestvo Fransua Rable i narodnaja kul'tura Srednevekovija i Renesansa*. Moscow, 1965.)
Barthes, Roland. *Camera lucida: Reflections on Photography.* Trans. Richard Howard. New York: Hill & Wang, 1981. (*La Chambre claire*. Paris: Editions du Seuil-Gallimard, 1980.)
———. *Critical Essays.* Trans. Richard Howard. Evanston, Ill.: Northwestern University Press, 1972. (*Essais critiques*. Paris: Editions du Seuil, 1964.)
———. *Critique et vérité.* Paris: Editions du Seuil, 1966.

——. *The Grain of the Voice: Interviews 1962–1980.* Trans. Linda Coverdale. New York: Hill & Wang, 1985. (*Le Grain de la voix.* Paris: Editions du Seuil, 1981.)

——. "Réponses." *Tel Quel,* 47 (1971), 89–107.

——. *Roland Barthes by Roland Barthes.* Trans. Richard Howard. New York: Hill & Wang, 1977. (*Roland Barthes.* Paris: Editions du Seuil, 1975.)

——. *The Rustle of Language.* Trans. Richard Howard. New York: Hill & Wang, 1986. (*Le Bruissement de la langue.* Paris: Editions du Seuil, 1984.)

Bénichou, Paul. "A propos d'ordinateurs. Note sur l'existence subjective." *Commentaire,* 19 (1982).

——. *L'Ecrivain et ses travaux.* Paris: Corti, 1967.

——. *Man and Ethics: Studies in French Classicism.* Trans. Elizabeth Hughes. Garden City, N.Y.: Anchor Books, 1971. (*Morales du grand siècle.* Paris: Gallimard, 1948; repr. 1980.)

——. "Poétique et métaphysique dans trois sonnets de Mallarmé." In *La Passion de la raison.* Paris: Presses Universitaires de France, 1983.

——. "Réflexions sur la critique littéraire." In Marc Fumaroli, ed., *Le Statut de la littérature. Mélanges offerts à Paul Bénichou.* Geneva: Droz, 1982.

——. *Le Sacre de l'écrivain, 1750–1830: Essai sur l'avènement d'un pouvoir spirituel laïque dans la France moderne.* Paris: Corti, 1973.

——. *Le Temps des prophètes: Doctrines de l'âge romantique.* Paris: Gallimard, 1977.

Blanchot, Maurice. *L'Amitié.* Paris: Gallimard, 1971.

——. *L'Entretien infini.* Paris: Gallimard, 1969.

——. *Lautréamont et Sade.* Paris: Editions de Minuit, 1963. Repr. in coll. "10/18," 1967.

——. *Le Livre à venir.* Paris: Gallimard, 1959.

——. *La Part du feu.* Paris: Gallimard, 1949.

——. *The Space of Literature.* Trans. Ann Smock. Lincoln, Neb.: University of Nebraska Press, 1982. (*L'Espace littéraire.* Paris: Gallimard, 1955.)

Bloch, Marc. *The Historian's Craft.* New York: Vintage Books, 1964. (*Apologie pour l'histoire ou Métier d'historien.* Paris: Armand Colin, 1949.)

Böckh, A. *On Interpretation & Criticism.* Trans. John Paul Pritchard. Norman, Okla.: University of Oklahoma Press, 1968. (Abridged translation of *Encyclopädie und Methodologie der philologischen Wissenschaften.* Leipzig: B. G. Teubner, 1886.)

Brecht, Bertolt. *Brecht on Theatre: The Development of an Aesthetic.* Trans. John Willett. New York: Hill & Wang, 1964. (Partial translation of *Gesammelte Werke,* vol. VII, *Schriften I, Zum Theater.* Frankfurt am Main: Suhrkamp, 1963.)

——. *Gesammelte Werke,* vol. VIII, *Schriften II, Zur Literatur und Kunst, Politik und Gesellschaft.* Frankfurt am Main: Suhrkamp, 1967.

Brik, Osip Maksimovich. "Zvukovye povtory." In *Poètika.* Petrograd, 1919.

Crouzet, Michel. "L'Empire des signes contre-attaqué." *Commentaire,* 30 (1985).

Works Cited

Döblin, Alfred. "Der Bau des epischen Werks." In *Aufsätze zur Literatur*. Olten und Freiburg in Br.: Walter-Verlag, 1963.
——. "Schriftstellerei und Dichtung." In *Aufsätze zur Literatur*. Olten und Freiburg in Br., 1963.
Dostoevsky, Fedor. *The Diary of a Writer*. Trans. Boris Brasol. Santa Barbara and Salt Lake City: Peregrine Smith, 1979. (*Dnevnik pisatelja za 1873 god, Polnoe sobranie sochinenij*, vol. XXI. Moscow, 1980.)
Eagleton, Terry. *Literary Theory: An Introduction*. Minneapolis: University of Minnesota Press, 1983.
Èjxenbaum, Boris Mikhailovich. "How Gogol's 'Overcoat' Is Made." In Priscilla Meyer and Stephen Rudy, eds., *Dostoevsky and Gogol: Texts and Criticism*. Ann Arbor: Ardis, 1979. ("Kak sdelana *Shinel'* Gogolja." In *Poètika*. Petrograd, 1919.)
——. "Literary Environment." In L. Matejka and K. Pomorska, eds., *Readings in Russian Poetics*. Cambridge, Mass.: M.I.T. Press, 1971. (*Moj vremennik*. Leningrad, 1929.)
——. "The Theory of the Formal Method." In Ladislav Matejka and Krystyna Pomorska, eds., *Readings in Russian Poetics: Formalist and Structuralist Views*. Ann Arbor: Michigan Slavic Publications, 1978. ("Teorija formal'nogo metoda." In *Literatura*. Leningrad, 1927.)
Ferry, Luc, and Alain Renaut. "Philosopher après la fin de la philosophie?" *Le Débat*, 28 (1984), 137–154.
Fish, Stanley. *Is There a Text in This Class?* Cambridge and London: Harvard University Press, 1980.
Frye, Northrop. *Anatomy of Criticism*. Princeton: Princeton University Press, 1957.
——. *Creation and Recreation*. Toronto: University of Toronto Press, 1980.
——. *The Critical Path: An Essay on the Social Context of Literary Criticism*. Bloomington: Indiana University Press, 1971.
——. *The Educated Imagination*. Bloomington: Indiana University Press, 1964.
——. *Fables of Identity: Studies in Poetic Mythology*. New York: Harcourt, Brace & World, 1963.
——. *Fearful Symmetry: A Study of William Blake*. Princeton: Princeton University Press, 1947.
——. *The Great Code: The Bible and Literature*. New York: Harcourt Brace Jovanovich, 1982.
——. "Literature and Myth." In James Ernest Thorpe, ed., *Relations of Literary Study*. New York: Modern Language Association of America, 1967.
——. "Literature as a Critique of Pure Reason." Unpublished lecture, September 1982.
——. *The Modern Century*. Toronto: Oxford University Press, 1967.
——. *Spiritus Mundi: Essays on Literature, Myth, and Society*. Bloomington: Indiana University Press, 1976.

——. *The Stubborn Structure: Essays on Criticism and Society*. Ithaca: Cornell University Press, 1970.

——. *The Well-Tempered Critic*. Bloomington: Indiana University Press, 1963.

Goodheart, Eugene. *The Failure of Criticism*. Cambridge: Harvard University Press, 1978.

Goody, John Rankine, and Ian Watt. "The Consequences of Literacy." *Comparative Studies in Society and History*, 5 (1963). Repr. in John Rankine Goody, ed., *Literacy in Traditional Societies*. Cambridge: Cambridge University Press, 1968.

Jakobson, Roman. "Grammatical Parallelism and Its Russian Facet." In *Selected Writings*, III. The Hague: Mouton, 1981, pp. 98–135. First published in *Language* 42 (1966).

——. "Linguistics and Poetics." In *Selected Writings*, III, pp. 18–51. First published in Thomas A. Sebeok, *Style in Language*. New York, 1960.

——. "Nachwort." In *Form und Sinn: Sprachwissenschaftliche Betrachtungen*. Munich: W. Fink, 1974.

——. *Novejšaja russkaja poèzija*. Prague, 1921. Repr. in *Selected Writings*, V, 1979. (Partial Fr. trans.: "La nouvelle poésie russe." In *Questions de poétique*. Paris: Editions du Seuil, 1973.)

——. "What Is Poetry?" In *Selected Writings*, III, pp. 740–750. (Trans. of "Co je poesie?" *Volné směry* 30 (1933–1934.)

Jakubinskij, L. "O poètičeskom glossemosochetanii." In *Poètika*. Petrograd, 1919.

——. "O zvukakh stikhotvornogo jazyka." In *Sborniki po teorii poèticheskogo jazyka* 1. St. Petersburg, 1916.

Jolles, André. *Einfache Formen*. Halle: Max Niemeyer, 1930.

Kruszewski, N. *Ocherk nauki o jazyke*. Kazan, 1883.

Lanson, G. *Essais de méthode, de critique et d'histoire littéraire*. Paris: Hachette, 1965.

Maurice Blanchot. *Critique*, 229 (June 1966), special issue.

Medvedev, Pavel Nikolaevich/Bakhtin, Mikhail. *The Formal Method in Literary Scholarship: A Critical Introduction to Sociological Poetics*. Trans. Albert J. Wehrle. Baltimore: Johns Hopkins University Press, 1977. (*Formal'nyj metod v literaturovedenii*. Leningrad, 1928.)

Moritz, Karl Philipp. *Schriften zur Ästhetik und Poetik*. Tübingen: Max Niemeyer Verlag, 1962.

Prétexte: Roland Barthes. Actes du Colloque de Cerisy, 1977. Paris: Union Générale d'Editions, coll. "10/18," 1978.

Rousseau, Jean-Jacques. "Ebauches des Confessions," in *Oeuvres complètes*, vol. I. Paris: Gallimard, coll. "La Pléiade," 1959, repr. 1976, pp. 1148–1164.

Said, Edward. *The World, the Text, the Critic*. Cambridge: Harvard University Press, 1983.

Sartre, Jean-Paul. *Baudelaire*. Trans. Martin Turnell. Norfolk, Conn.: New Directions, 1950. (*Baudelaire*. Paris: Gallimard, 1947; repr. 1976.)
——. *The Family Idiot: Gustave F!aubert*. Trans. Carol Cosman. Chicago: University of Chicago Press, 1981. (*L'Idiot de la famille*. Paris: Gallimard, vols. I–II, 1971; vol. III, 1972.)
——. *Literary Essays*. Trans. Annette Michelson. New York: Philosophical Library, 1957. (*Situations I*. Paris: Gallimard, 1947.)
——. "On *The Idiot of the Family*." In *Michel Contat and Michel Rybalka*, eds., *Sartre in the Seventies: Interviews and Essays*. Trans. Paul Auster and Lydia Davis. London: André Deutsch, 1978, pp. 109–32. ("Un entretien avec Jean-Paul Sartre." *Le Monde*, 14 May 1971.)
——. *Saint Genet, Actor and Martyr*. Trans. Bernard Frechtman. New York: George Braziller, 1963. (*Saint Genet*. Paris: Gallimard, 1952.)
——. *What Is Literature?* Trans. Bernard Frechtman. Gloucester, Mass.: Peter Smith, 1978. (*Qu'est-ce que la littérature?* Paris: Gallimard, 1948, repr. 1969.)
——. *The Words*. Trans. Bernard Frechtman. New York: George Braziller, 1964. (*Les Mots*. Paris: Gallimard, 1963).
Schelling, Friedrich Wilhelm Joseph von. *Philosophie der Kunst, Sämmtliche Werke*, vol. V. Stuttgart and Augsburg: J. Cotta, 1859.
Schlegel, August Wilhelm. *Die Kunstlehr*. (*Vorlesungen über schöne Literatur und Kunst*, vol. 1.) Stuttgart: W. Kohlhammer, 1963.
Schlegel, Friedrich. *Lucinde and the Fragments*. Trans. Peter Firchow. Minneapolis: University of Minnesota Press, 1971. ("Fragmenten." In *Kritische Friedrich Schlegel Ausgabe*, vol. 11. Munich and Vienna: Paderborn, 1960.)
Scholes, Robert. *Textual Power: Literary Theory and the Teaching of English*. New Haven: Yale University Press, 1985.
Shklovskij, Viktor Borisovich. "Art as Technique." In L. T. Lemon and M. J. Reis, eds., *Russian Formalist Criticism: Four Essays*. Lincoln: University of Nebraska Press, 1965. ("Iskusstvo kak priëm." In *Teorija prozy*. Moscow, 1929.)
——. "The Connection between Devices of *Syuzhet* Construction and General Stylistic Devices." In S. Bann and J. E. Bowlt, eds., *Russian Formalism*. Edinburgh: Scottish Academic Press, 1973. ("Svjaz priëmov sjuzhetoslozhenija s obshchimi priëmami stilja." In *Teorija prozy*. Moscow, 1929.)
——. "O poèzii i zaumnon jazyke." In *Sborniki po teorii poèticheskogo jazyka* 1. St. Petersburg, 1916.
——. "Potebnja." In *Poètika*. Petrograd, 1919.
——. "The Resurrection of the Word." In S. Bann and J. E. Bowlt, eds., *Russian Formalism*. Edinburgh: Scottish Academic Press, 1973. ("Voskreshenie slova," 1914. In W.-D. Stempel, ed., *Texte der russischen Formalisten*, vol. II. Munich, 1972.)

——. *Third Factory.* Trans. Richard Sheldon. Ann Arbor: Ardis, 1977. (*Tretja fabrika.* Moscow, 1926.)

Spinoza, Benedictus de. *A Theologico-Political Treatise & A Political Treatise.* New York: Dover, 1951. (*Tractatus theologico-politicus.* Hamburg: Künraht, 1670.)

Strauss, Leo. *Natural Right and History.* Chicago: University of Chicago Press, 1953.

——. *Persecution and the Art of Writing.* Westport, Conn.: Greenwood Press, 1973.

Todorov, Tzvetan. *The Conquest of America.* Trans. Richard Howard. New York: Harper & Row, 1984. (*La Conquête de l'Amérique.* Paris: Editions du Seuil, 1982.)

——. *The Fantastic: A Structural Approach to a Literary Genre.* Trans. Richard Howard. Ithaca: Cornell University Press, 1975. (*Introduction à la littérature fantastique.* Paris: Editions du Seuil, 1970.)

——. *Introduction to Poetics.* Trans. Richard Howard. Minneapolis: University of Minnesota Press, 1981. (*Poétique.* Paris: Editions du Seuil, 1973.)

——. *Mikhail Bakhtin, The Dialogical Principle.* Trans. Wlad Godzich. Minneapolis: University of Minnesota Press, 1984. (*Mikhaïl Bakhtine, le principe dialogique.* Paris: Editions du Seuil, 1981.)

——. *Symbolism and Interpretation.* Trans. Catherine Porter. Ithaca: Cornell University Press, 1982. (*Symbolisme et interprétation.* Paris: Editions du Seuil, 1978.)

——. *Theories of the Symbol.* Trans. Catherine Porter. Ithaca: Cornell University Press, 1982. (*Théories du symbole.* Paris: Editions du Seuil, 1977.)

Tomashevski, Boris Viktorovich. "Thematics." In L. T. Lemon and M. J. Reis, eds., *Russian Formalist Criticism: Four Essays.* Lincoln: University of Nebraska Press, 1965. (*Teorija literatury. Poètika.* Moscow, 1927.)

Tynianov, Juri. "Literaturnyj fakt." In *Arkhaisty i novatory.* Leningrad, 1929. (Fr. trans. "Le fait littéraire." *Manteia* 9–10 [1970].)

——. "On Literary Evolution." In Ladislav Matejka and Krystyna Pomorska, eds., *Readings in Russian Poetics: Formalist and Structuralist Views.* Ann Arbor: Michigan Slavic Publications, 1978. Pp. 66–78. ("O literaturnoj èvoljucii." In *Arkhaisty i novatory.* Leningrad, 1929.)

Voloshinov, Valentin/Bakhtin, Mikhail. *Freudianism: A Marxist Critique.* Trans. I. R. Titunik. New York: Academic Press, 1973. (*Frejdizm.* Moscow-Leningrad, 1927.)

——. *Marxism and the Philosophy of Language.* Trans. L. Matejka and I. R. Titunik. New York and London: Seminar Press, 1973. (*Marksizm i filosofija jazyka.* Leningrad, 1929.)

Watt, Ian. *Conrad in the Nineteenth Century.* Berkeley: University of California Press, 1979.

——. "The First Paragraph of *The Ambassadors.*" *Essays in Criticism,* 10 (1960), 250–274.

———. "Flat-footed and Fly-blown. The Realities of Realism." Unpublished lecture, March 1978.

———. "Literature and Society." In Robert N. Wilson, ed., *The Arts in Society*. Englewood Cliffs, N.J.: Prentice-Hall, 1964, pp. 299–314.

———. "On Not Attempting to Be a Piano." *Profession 78*. New York, 1978.

———. *The Rise of the Novel: Studies in Defoe, Richardson and Fielding*. London: Chatto & Windus, 1957.

———. "Serious Reflections on *The Rise of the Novel*." *Novel*, 1 (1968), 205–218.

———. "Story and Idea in Conrad's *The Shadow-Line*." *The Critical Quarterly* 2 (1960); and in Mark Schorer, ed., *Modern British Fiction*. New York: Oxford University Press, 1961. Pp. 133–148.

INDEX

Index

Marx, Karl, 103
Mauriac, François, 76–77
Medvedev, Pavel N., 72–73
Meyerhold, Vsevolod, 37
Michelet, Jules, 143–44
Miller, J. Hillis, 186
Milton, John, 89, 95, 139
Mitterrand, François, 175
Montaigne, Michel de, 58, 66, 136
Montesquieu, Charles de Secondat,
    Baron de, 42, 87, 110, 130, 136, 182
Moritz, Karl Philipp, 5, 17, 45
Mukarovský, Jan, 18
Müller, Gunter, 177

Nietzsche, Friedrich Wilhelm, 61, 64
Novalis (Friedrich von Hardenberg), 5,
    8, 18–19, 31, 42, 45

Orwell, George, 100

Pascal, Blaise, 124
Pasternak, Boris, 157
Péguy, Charles, 175
Pfeiffer, Jean, 55
Philonenko, Alexis, 184
Pirandello, Luigi, 186
Plato, 118, 176, 184
Ponge, Francis, 120–21
Poulet, Georges, 55, 161, 173
Propp, Vladimir, 24
Proust, Marcel, 57, 63
Pushkin, Alexander Sergeyevich, 26, 78

Quintilian, Marcus Fabius Quintilianus,
    167

Rabelais, François, 71, 83
Racine, Jean, 127–28, 130–31, 136
Reformatskii, Aleksandr
    Aleksandrovich, 24
Richard, Jean-Pierre, 173
Richards, I. A., 116, 120, 177
Richardson, Samuel, 106, 116
Rilke, Rainer Maria, 57
Rousseau, Jean-Jacques, 58–59, 85, 102,
    122, 136, 143–44, 151–52, 160n., 184

Sade, Donatien Alphonse François,
    Marquis de, 61, 64, 112, 160

Said, Edward, 184
Sartre, Jean-Paul, 44–55, 57, 59, 62–63,
    76–77, 81, 85, 88, 98, 102, 119, 160n.,
    164–66
Schaeffer, Jean-Marie, 174
Schelling, Friedrich Wilhelm Joseph
    von, 9, 17, 20, 73
Schiller, Johann Christoph Friedrich
    von, 31
Schlegel, August Wilhelm, 8, 17–19, 45
Schlegel, Karl Wilhelm Friedrich von, 5,
    8, 31–32
Schleiermacher, Friedrich Ernst Daniel,
    107
Scholes, Robert, 182, 184–88, 190
Shakespeare, William, 89, 117–18
Shelley, Percy Bysshe, 42, 95
Shklovskij, Viktor, 12–15, 18–21,
    23–24, 26, 37–38, 42
Solzhenitsyn, Alexander, 168
Sophocles, 117
Spinoza, Benedict de, 6–7, 63–64, 87,
    94, 162, 174
Spitzer, Leo, 177
Stalin, Joseph, 188
Stanislawski, Konstantin, 37
Starobinski, Jean, 55, 173, 180
Stendhal (Marie Henri Beyle), 166, 173
Strauss, Leo, 173

Thomas, D. M., 168
Tolstoy, Leo, 41, 117
Tomashevskij, Boris, 23–24
Tretiakov, Sergei Mikhailovich, 37–38
Trotsky, Leon, 188
Turgenev, Ivan Sergeevich, 119
Tynjanov, Juri, 15, 18, 24, 26–28, 124

Valéry, Paul, 45, 57, 95, 175
Vico, Giovanni Battista, 89
Vinogradov, Viktor, 24
Voloshinov, Valentin, 75
Voltaire, François Marie Arouet de, 152

Watt, Ian, 106–121, 166, 180
Weber, Max, 93

Yeats, William Butler, 117

Zhirmunski, Viktor, 17, 24
Zinoviev, Grigori, 188

203